STAR WARS

LAST FLIGHT OF
THE HARBINGER

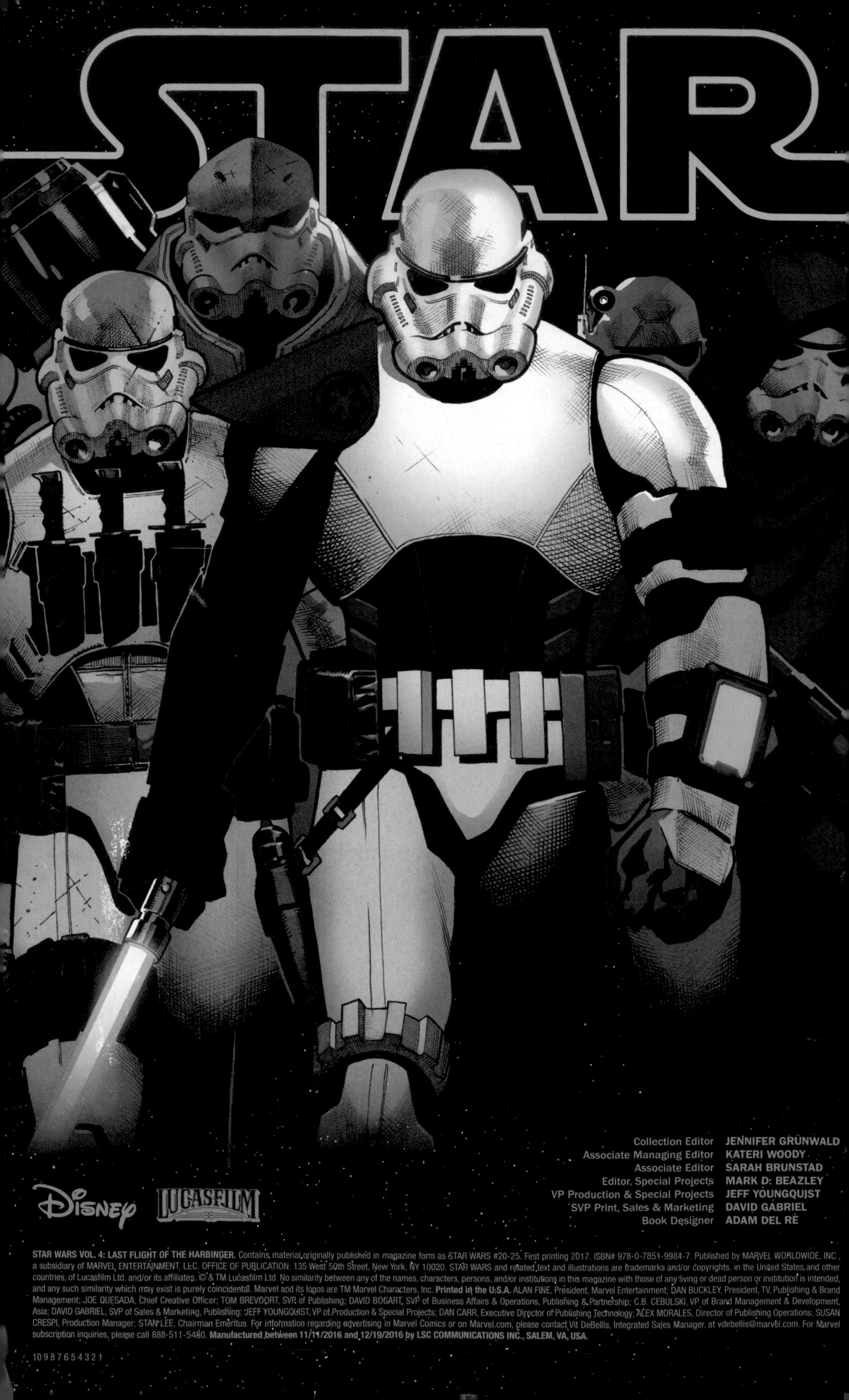
STAR

Collection Editor JENNIFER GRÜNWALD
Associate Managing Editor KATERI WOODY
Associate Editor SARAH BRUNSTAD
Editor, Special Projects MARK D. BEAZLEY
VP Production & Special Projects JEFF YOUNGQUIST
SVP Print, Sales & Marketing DAVID GABRIEL
Book Designer ADAM DEL RE

STAR WARS VOL. 4: LAST FLIGHT OF THE HARBINGER. Contains material originally published in magazine form as STAR WARS #20-25. First printing 2017. ISBN# 978-0-7851-9984-7. Published by MARVEL WORLDWIDE, INC., a subsidiary of MARVEL ENTERTAINMENT, LLC. OFFICE OF PUBLICATION: 135 West 50th Street, New York, NY 10020. **Printed in the U.S.A.** ALAN FINE, President, Marvel Entertainment; DAN BUCKLEY, President, TV, Publishing & Brand Management; JOE QUESADA, Chief Creative Officer; TOM BREVOORT, SVP of Publishing; DAVID BOGART, SVP of Business Affairs & Operations, Publishing & Partnership; C.B. CEBULSKI, VP of Brand Management & Development, Asia; DAVID GABRIEL, SVP of Sales & Marketing, Publishing; JEFF YOUNGQUIST, VP of Production & Special Projects; DAN CARR, Executive Director of Publishing Technology; ALEX MORALES, Director of Publishing Operations; SUSAN CRESPI, Production Manager; STAN LEE, Chairman Emeritus. For information regarding advertising in Marvel Comics or on Marvel.com, please contact Vit DeBellis, Integrated Sales Manager, at vdebellis@marvel.com. For Marvel subscription inquiries, please call 888-511-5480. **Manufactured between 11/11/2016 and 12/19/2016 by LSC COMMUNICATIONS INC., SALEM, VA, USA.**

10 9 8 7 6 5 4 3 2 1

WARS

LAST FLIGHT OF THE HARBINGER

ISSUE #20

Artist/Cover	MIKE MAYHEW
Letterer	VC's CHRIS ELIOPOULOS

ISSUES #21-25

Artist	JORGE MOLINA
Inker, #24	SCOTT HANNA
Color Artist	MATT MILLA
Letterers	VC's CHRIS ELIOPOULOS (#21, #23) &
	JOE CARAMAGNA (#22, #24-25)
Cover Art	DAVID AJA (#21),
	MIKE DEODATO & FRANK MARTIN (#22) AND
	MIKE DEODATO & RAIN BEREDO (#23-25)

"DROID DILEMMA"

Writer/Artist/Letterer	CHRIS ELIOPOULOS
Color Artist	JORDIE BELLAIRE

Assistant Editor	HEATHER ANTOS
Editor	JORDAN D. WHITE
Executive Editor	C.B. CEBULSKI

Editor in Chief	AXEL ALONSO
Chief Creative Officer	JOE QUESADA
Publisher	DAN BUCKLEY

For Lucasfilm:

Senior Editor	FRANK PARISI
Creative Director	MICHAEL SIGLAIN
Lucasfilm Story Group	RAYNE ROBERTS, PABLO HIDALGO,

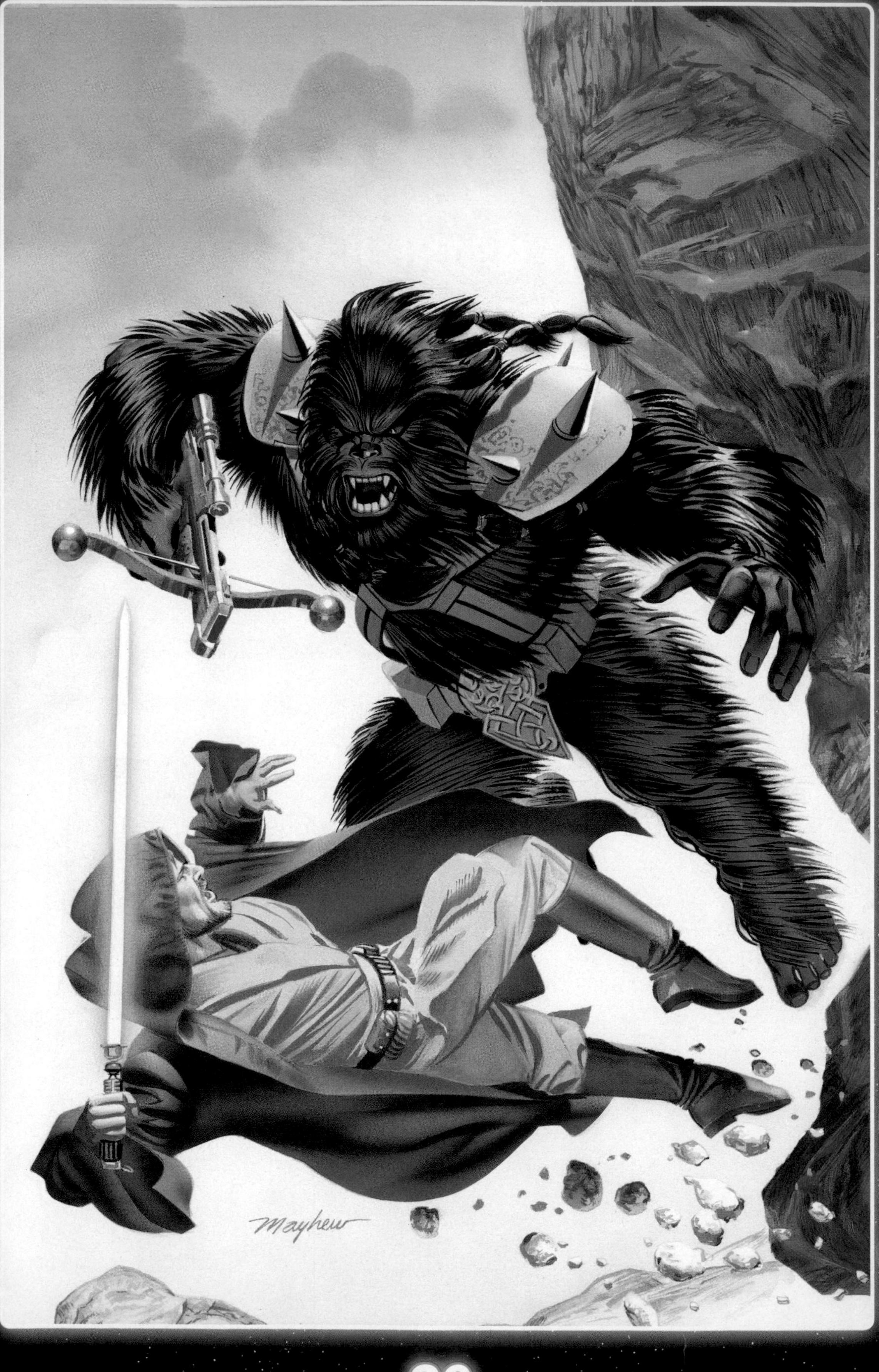
mayhew

FROM THE JOURNALS OF

OLD BEN KENOBI

WHILE SEARCHING FOR ANSWERS IN HIS

QUEST TO BECOME A JEDI,

LUKE SKYWALKER HAS UNCOVERED A

JOURNAL WRITTEN BY JEDI MASTER

BI-WAN KENOBI. THE JOURNAL DETAILS

KENOBI'S ADVENTURES WHILE WATCHING

OVER YOUNG LUKE ON TATOOINE,

INCLUDING WHEN JABBA THE HUTT

HIRED THE WOOKIEE BLACK KRRSANTAN TO HUNT

OBI-WAN DOWN FOR DEFEATING HIS THUGS

DURING THE GREAT DROUGHT.

WHAT FOLLOWS IS AN EXCERPT

FROM THAT JOURNAL.

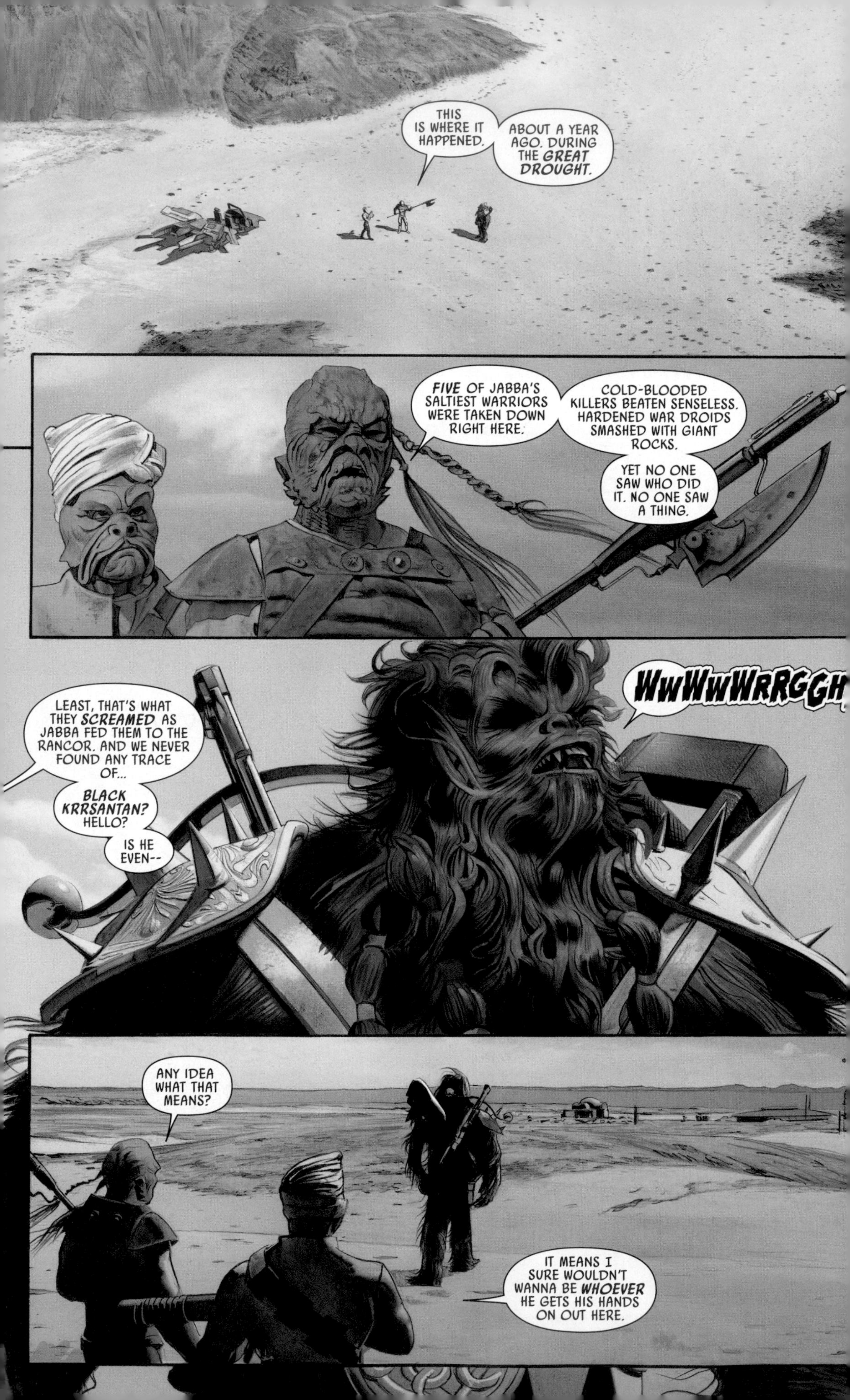
THIS IS WHERE IT HAPPENED.
ABOUT A YEAR AGO. DURING THE GREAT DROUGHT.
FIVE OF JABBA'S SALTIEST WARRIORS WERE TAKEN DOWN RIGHT HERE.
COLD-BLOODED KILLERS BEATEN SENSELESS. HARDENED WAR DROIDS SMASHED WITH GIANT ROCKS.
YET NO ONE SAW WHO DID IT. NO ONE SAW A THING.
LEAST, THAT'S WHAT THEY SCREAMED AS JABBA FED THEM TO THE RANCOR. AND WE NEVER FOUND ANY TRACE OF...
BLACK KRRSANTAN? HELLO?
IS HE EVEN--
WWWWWRRGGH
ANY IDEA WHAT THAT MEANS?
IT MEANS I SURE WOULDN'T WANNA BE WHOEVER HE GETS HIS HANDS ON OUT HERE.

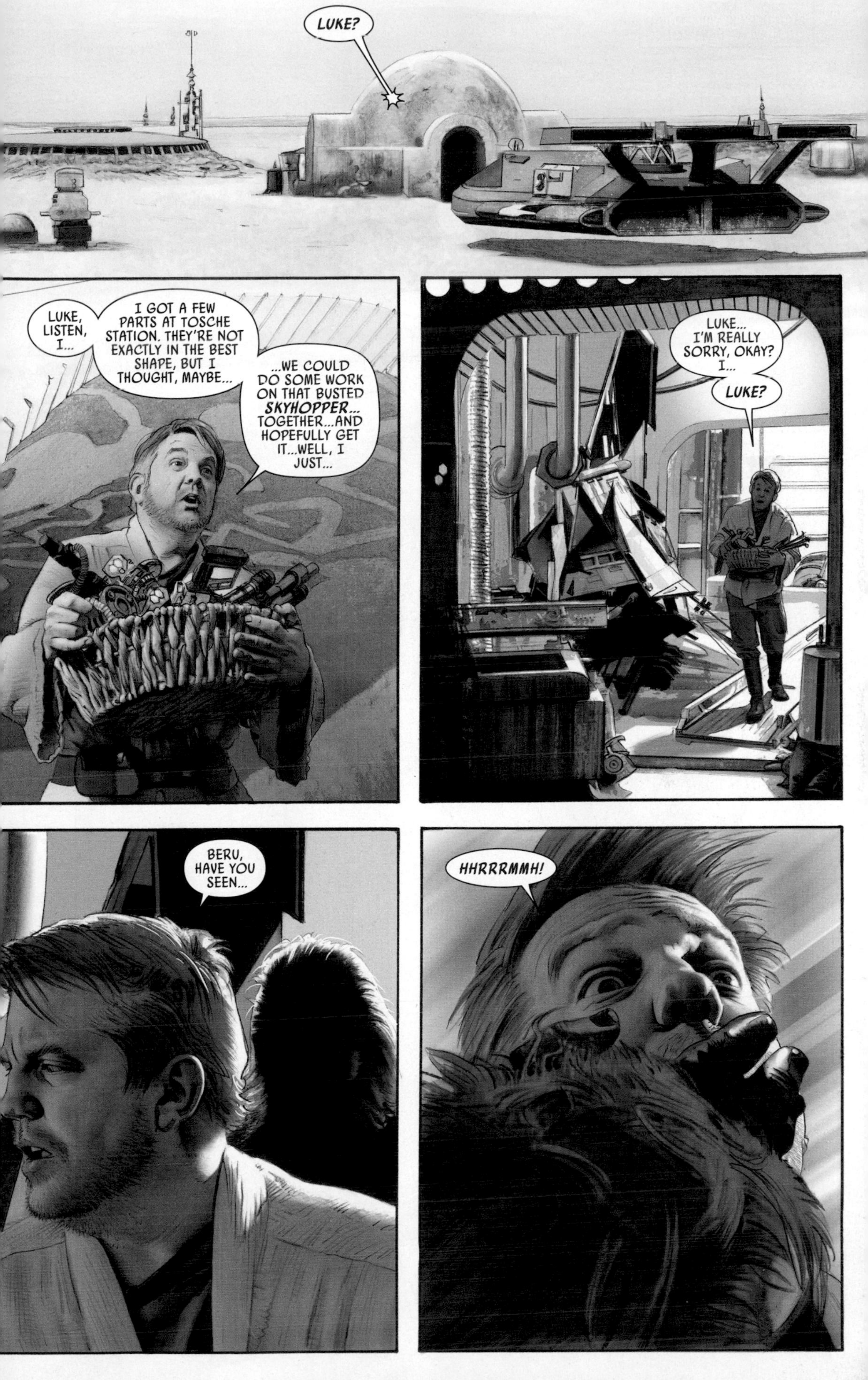
LUKE?
LUKE, LISTEN, I...
I GOT A FEW PARTS AT TOSCHE STATION. THEY'RE NOT EXACTLY IN THE BEST SHAPE, BUT I THOUGHT, MAYBE...
...WE COULD DO SOME WORK ON THAT BUSTED SKYHOPPER... TOGETHER...AND HOPEFULLY GET IT...WELL, I JUST...
LUKE... I'M REALLY SORRY, OKAY? I...
LUKE?
BERU, HAVE YOU SEEN...
HHRRRMMH!

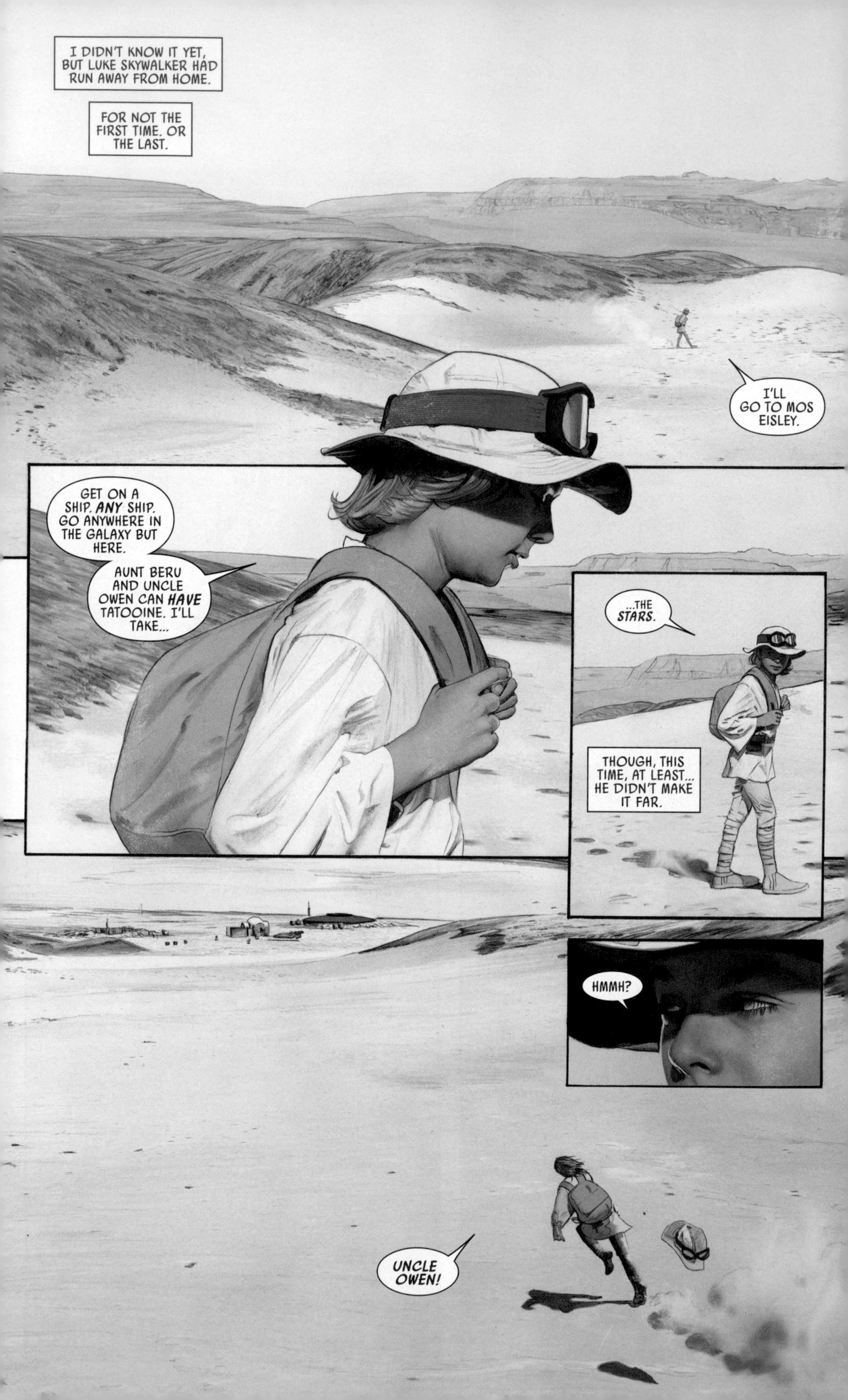
I DIDN'T KNOW IT YET, BUT LUKE SKYWALKER HAD RUN AWAY FROM HOME.
FOR NOT THE FIRST TIME. OR THE LAST.
I'LL GO TO MOS EISLEY.
GET ON A SHIP. ANY SHIP. GO ANYWHERE IN THE GALAXY BUT HERE.
AUNT BERU AND UNCLE OWEN CAN HAVE TATOOINE. I'LL TAKE...
...THE STARS.
THOUGH, THIS TIME, AT LEAST... HE DIDN'T MAKE IT FAR.
HMMH?
UNCLE OWEN!

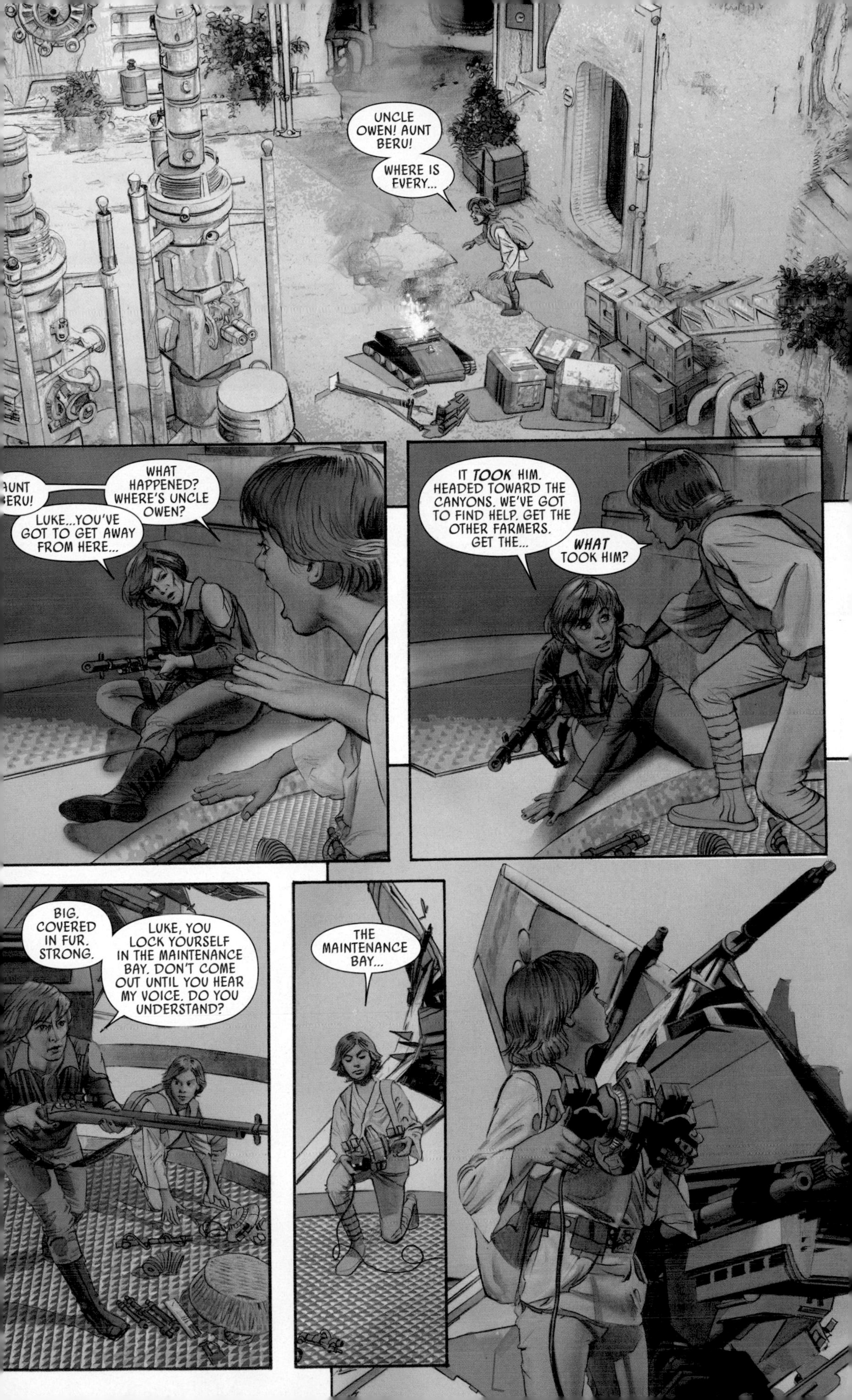
UNCLE OWEN! AUNT BERU!
WHERE IS EVERY...
AUNT BERU!
WHAT HAPPENED? WHERE'S UNCLE OWEN?
LUKE...YOU'VE GOT TO GET AWAY FROM HERE...
IT *TOOK* HIM. HEADED TOWARD THE CANYONS. WE'VE GOT TO FIND HELP. GET THE OTHER FARMERS. GET THE...
WHAT TOOK HIM?
BIG. COVERED IN FUR. STRONG.
LUKE, YOU LOCK YOURSELF IN THE MAINTENANCE BAY. DON'T COME OUT UNTIL YOU HEAR MY VOICE. DO YOU UNDERSTAND?
THE MAINTENANCE BAY...

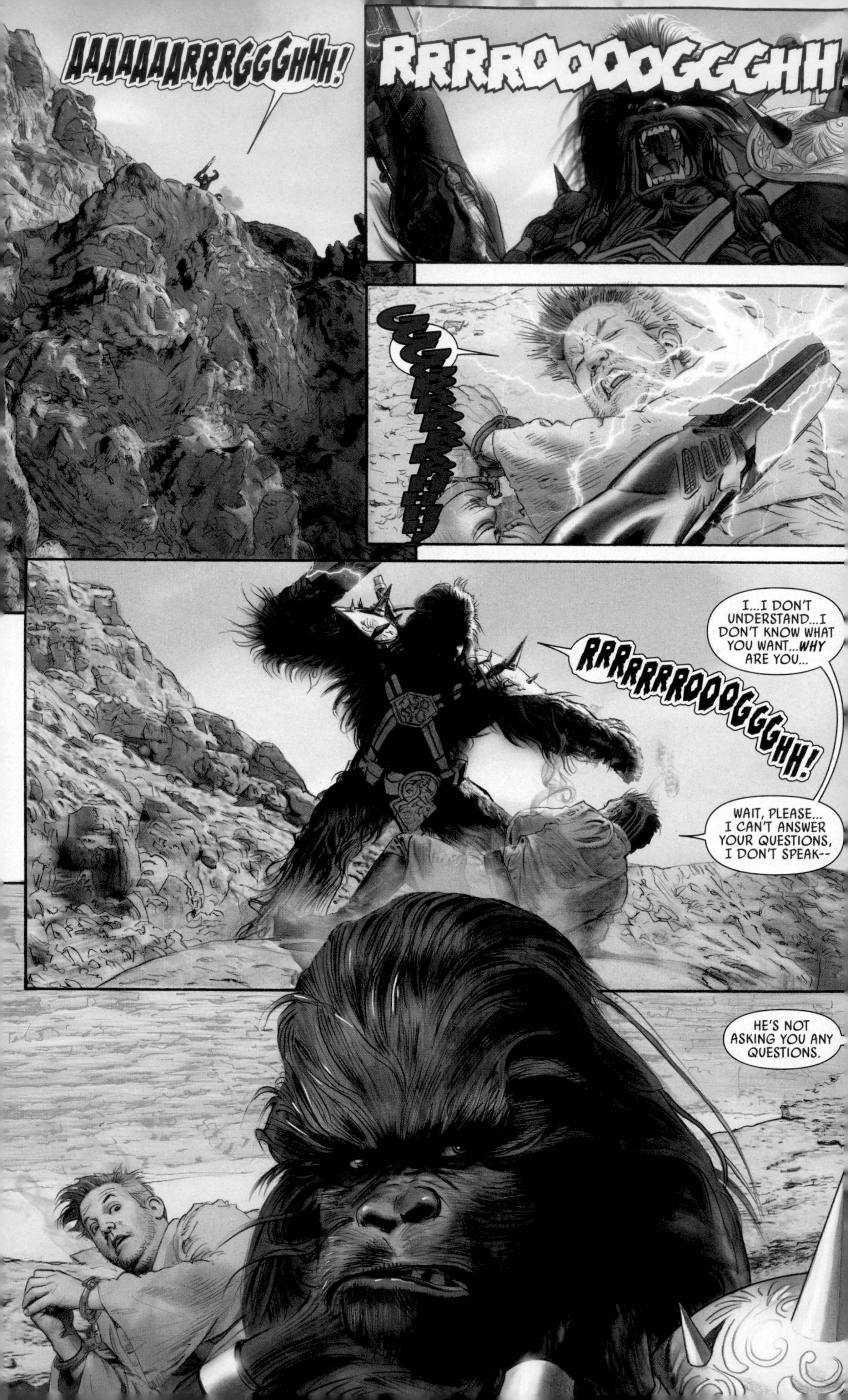
AAAAAAARRRGGGHHH!
RRRROOOOGGGHH!
GGGGRRRRHHHH
RRRRRRROOOGGGHH!
I...I DON'T UNDERSTAND...I DON'T KNOW WHAT YOU WANT...**WHY** ARE YOU...
WAIT, PLEASE... I CAN'T ANSWER YOUR QUESTIONS, I DON'T SPEAK--
HE'S NOT ASKING YOU ANY QUESTIONS.

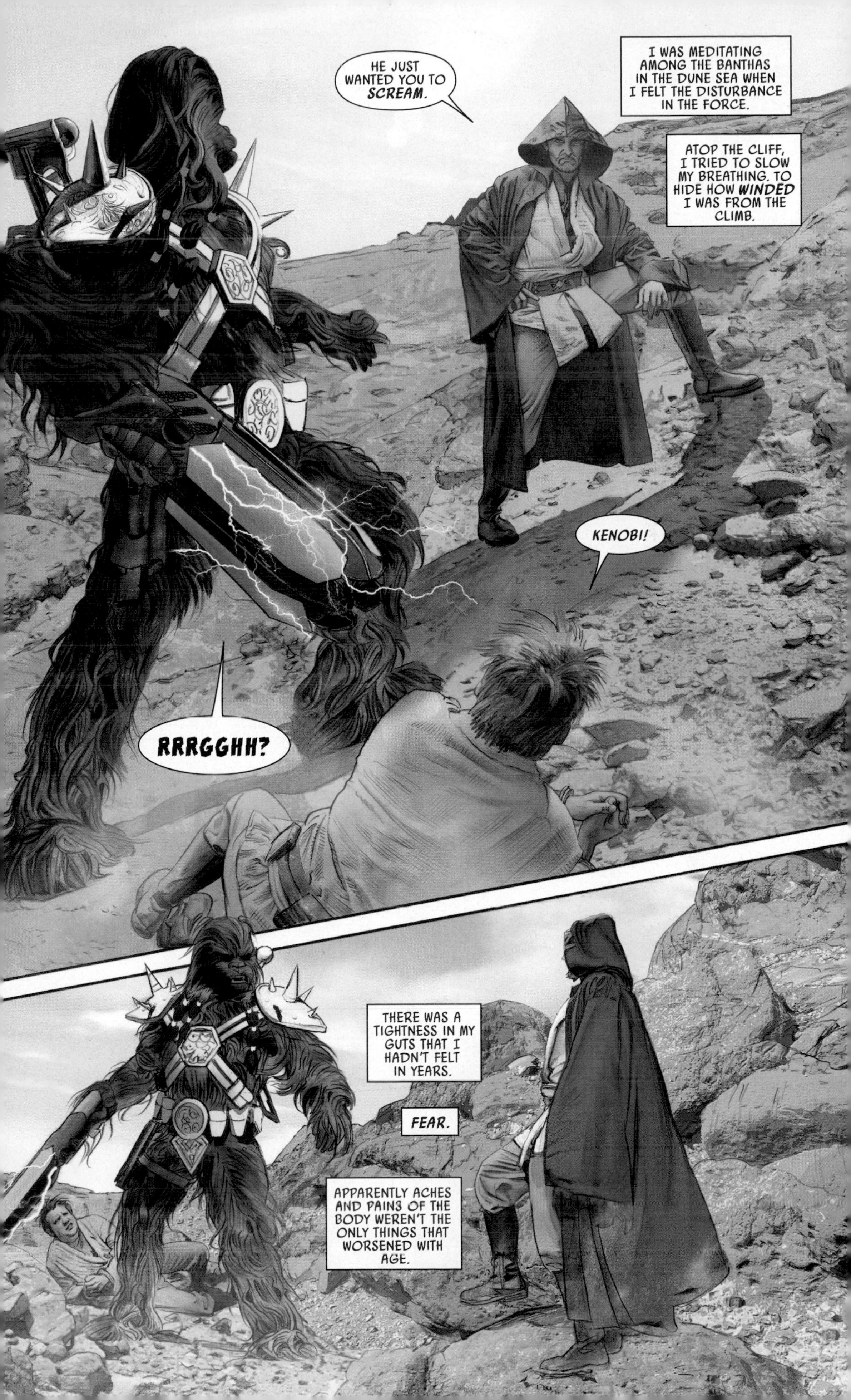
I WAS MEDITATING AMONG THE BANTHAS IN THE DUNE SEA WHEN I FELT THE DISTURBANCE IN THE FORCE.
HE JUST WANTED YOU TO SCREAM.
ATOP THE CLIFF, I TRIED TO SLOW MY BREATHING. TO HIDE HOW WINDED I WAS FROM THE CLIMB.
KENOBI!
RRRGGHH?
THERE WAS A TIGHTNESS IN MY GUTS THAT I HADN'T FELT IN YEARS.
FEAR.
APPARENTLY ACHES AND PAINS OF THE BODY WEREN'T THE ONLY THINGS THAT WORSENED WITH AGE.

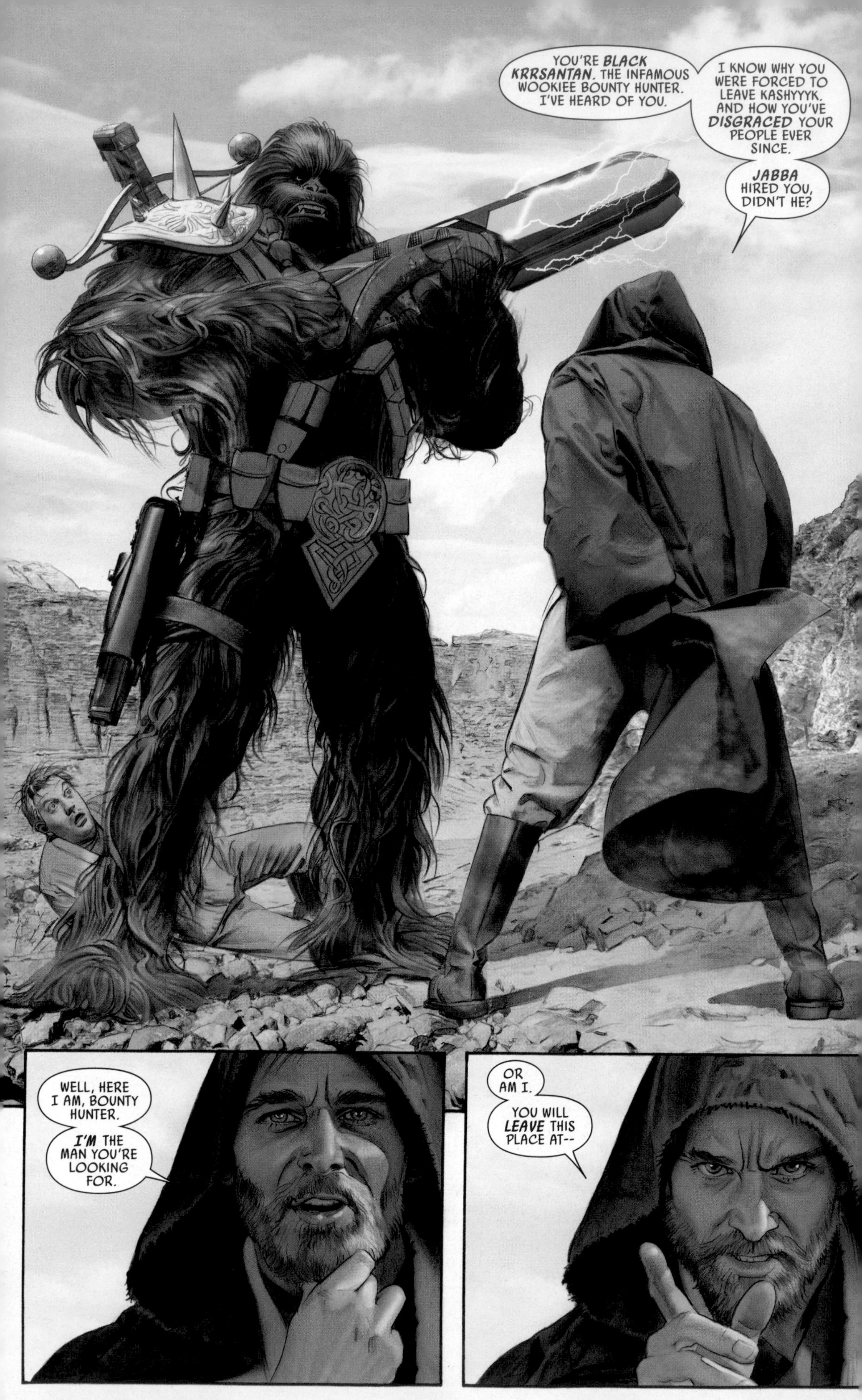
YOU'RE BLACK KRRSANTAN. THE INFAMOUS WOOKIEE BOUNTY HUNTER. I'VE HEARD OF YOU.
I KNOW WHY YOU WERE FORCED TO LEAVE KASHYYYK. AND HOW YOU'VE DISGRACED YOUR PEOPLE EVER SINCE.
JABBA HIRED YOU, DIDN'T HE?
WELL, HERE I AM, BOUNTY HUNTER.
I'M THE MAN YOU'RE LOOKING FOR.
OR AM I.
YOU WILL LEAVE THIS PLACE AT--

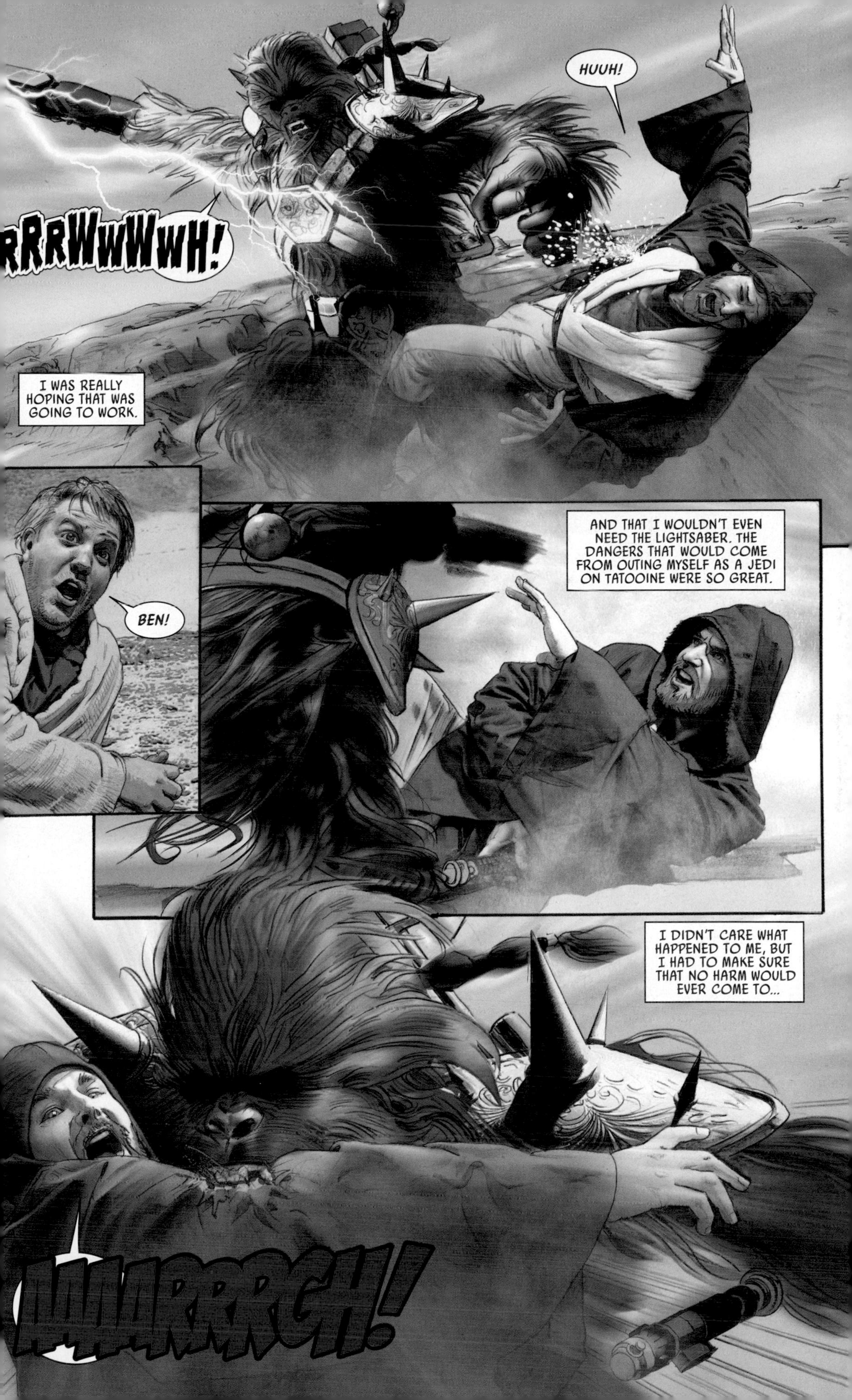
HUUH!
RRRWWWWH!
I WAS REALLY HOPING THAT WAS GOING TO WORK.
BEN!
AND THAT I WOULDN'T EVEN NEED THE LIGHTSABER. THE DANGERS THAT WOULD COME FROM OUTING MYSELF AS A JEDI ON TATOOINE WERE SO GREAT.
I DIDN'T CARE WHAT HAPPENED TO ME, BUT I HAD TO MAKE SURE THAT NO HARM WOULD EVER COME TO...
AWWRRRCH!

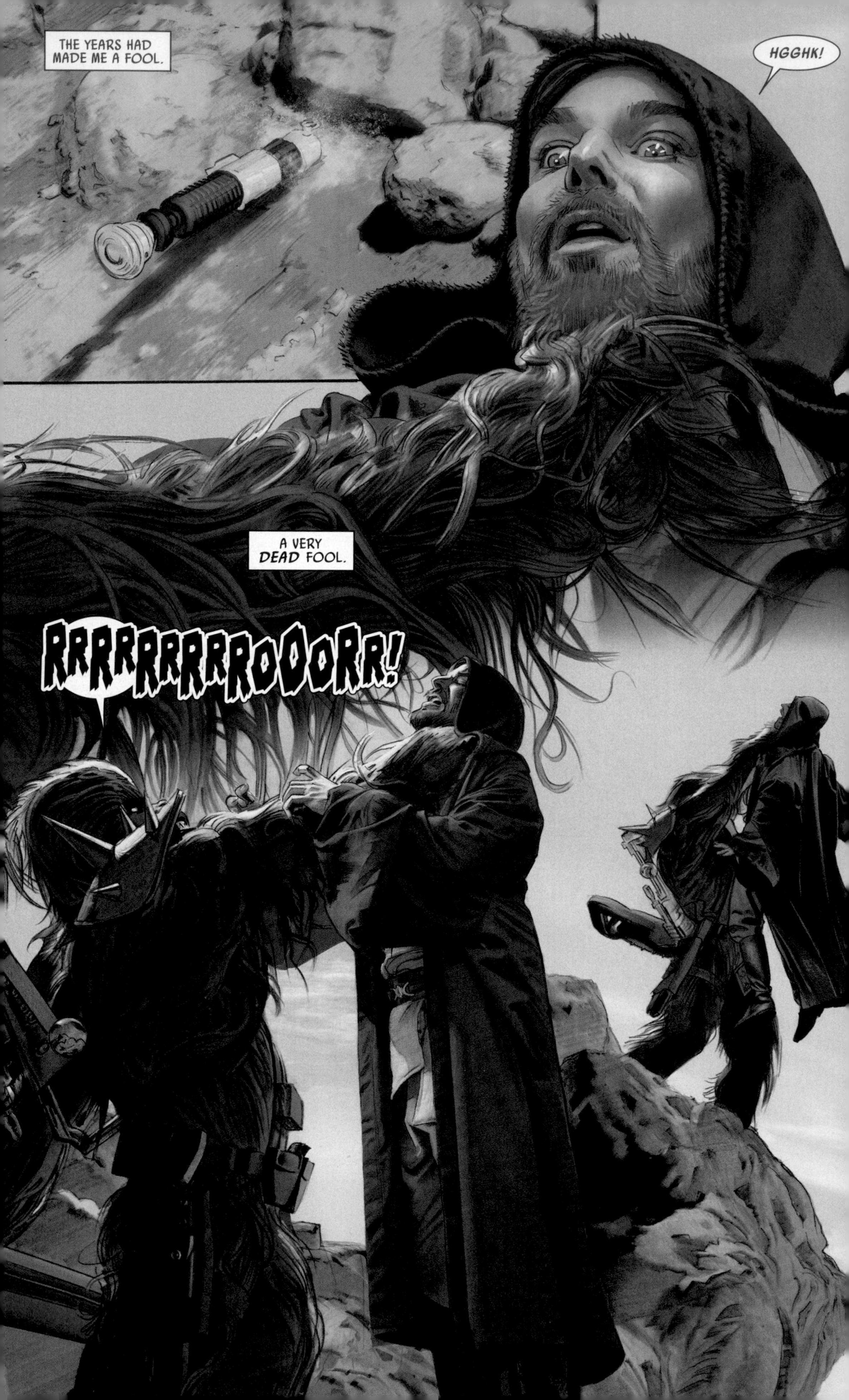
THE YEARS HAD MADE ME A FOOL.
HGGHK!
A VERY DEAD FOOL.
RRRRRRRRROOORR!

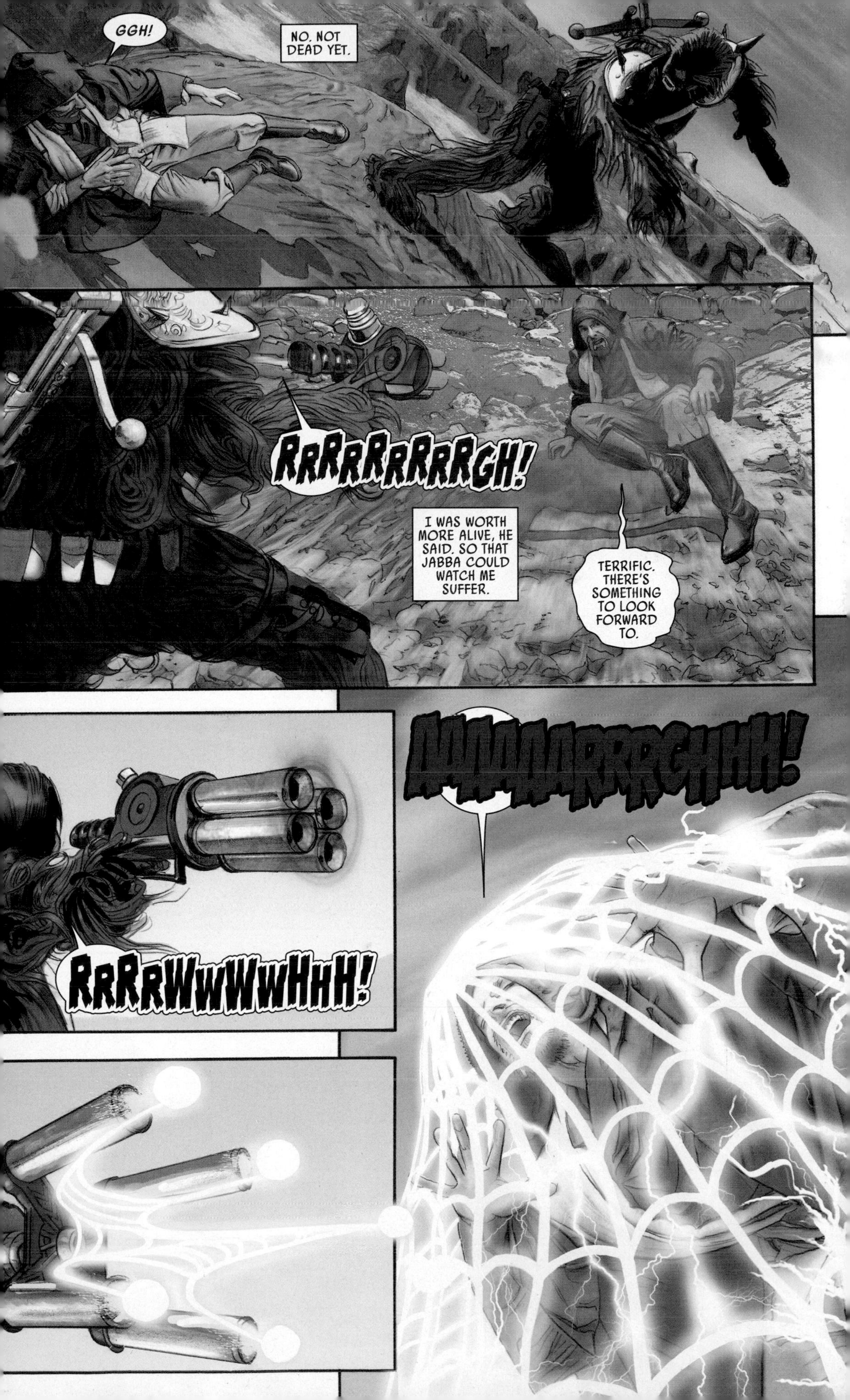
GGH!
NO. NOT DEAD YET.
RRRRRRRRRRGH!
I WAS WORTH MORE ALIVE, HE SAID. SO THAT JABBA COULD WATCH ME SUFFER.
TERRIFIC. THERE'S SOMETHING TO LOOK FORWARD TO.
RRRRWWWWWHHH!
AAAAAARRRRGHHH!

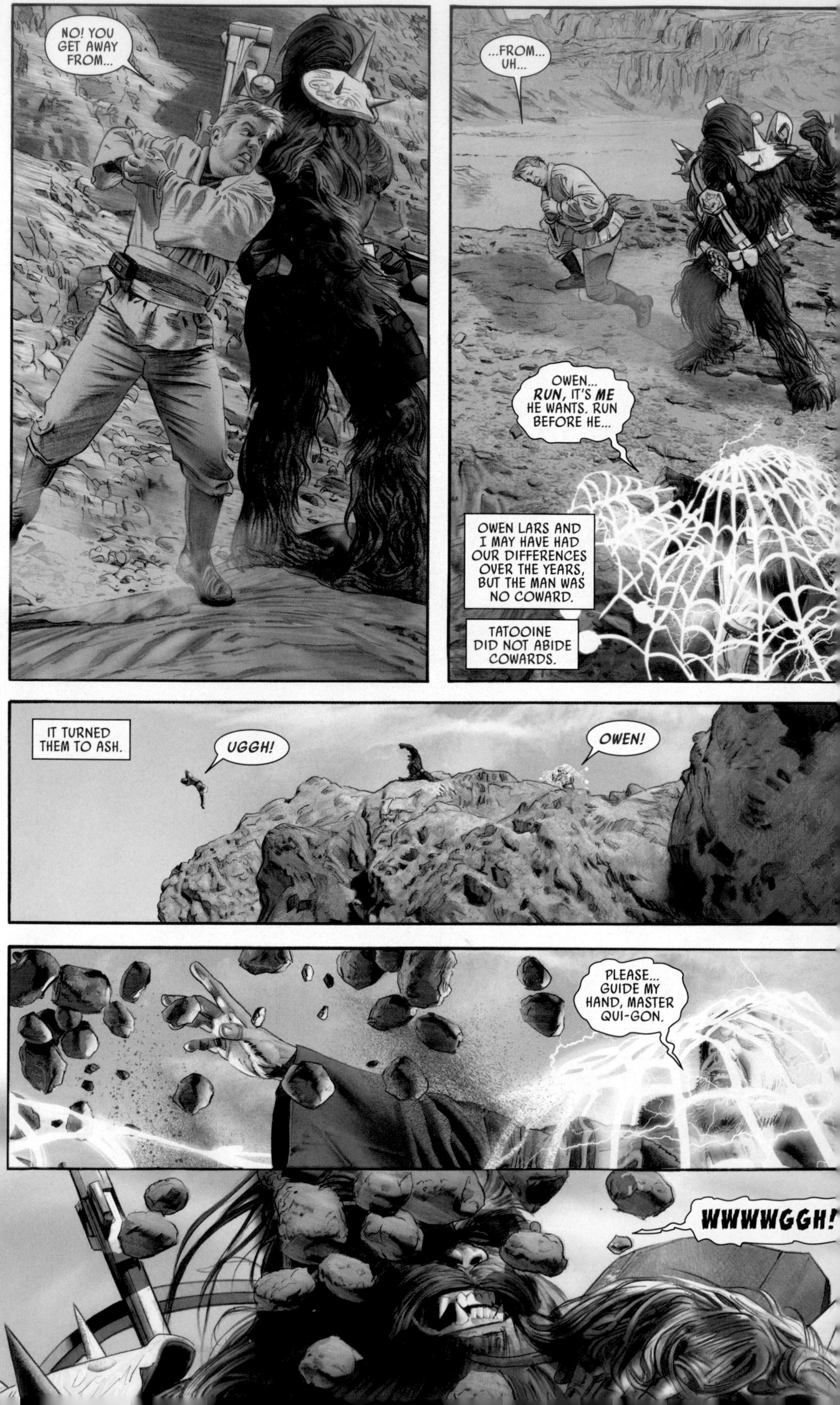
NO! YOU GET AWAY FROM...
...FROM... UH...
OWEN... RUN, IT'S ME HE WANTS. RUN BEFORE HE...
OWEN LARS AND I MAY HAVE HAD OUR DIFFERENCES OVER THE YEARS, BUT THE MAN WAS NO COWARD.
TATOOINE DID NOT ABIDE COWARDS.
IT TURNED THEM TO ASH.
UGGH!
OWEN!
PLEASE... GUIDE MY HAND, MASTER QUI-GON.
WWWWGGH!

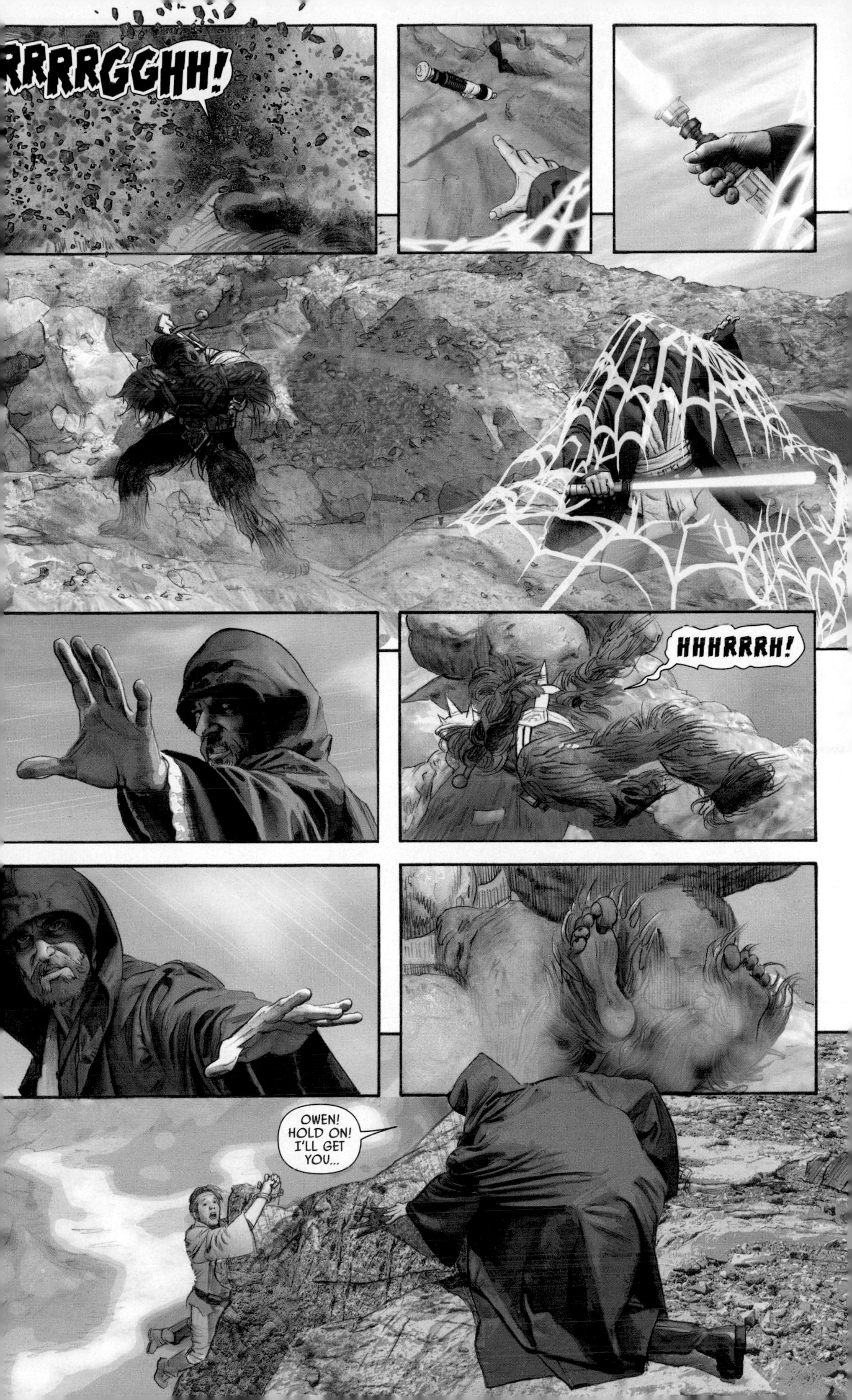
RRRRGGHH!
HHHRRRH!
OWEN! HOLD ON! I'LL GET YOU...

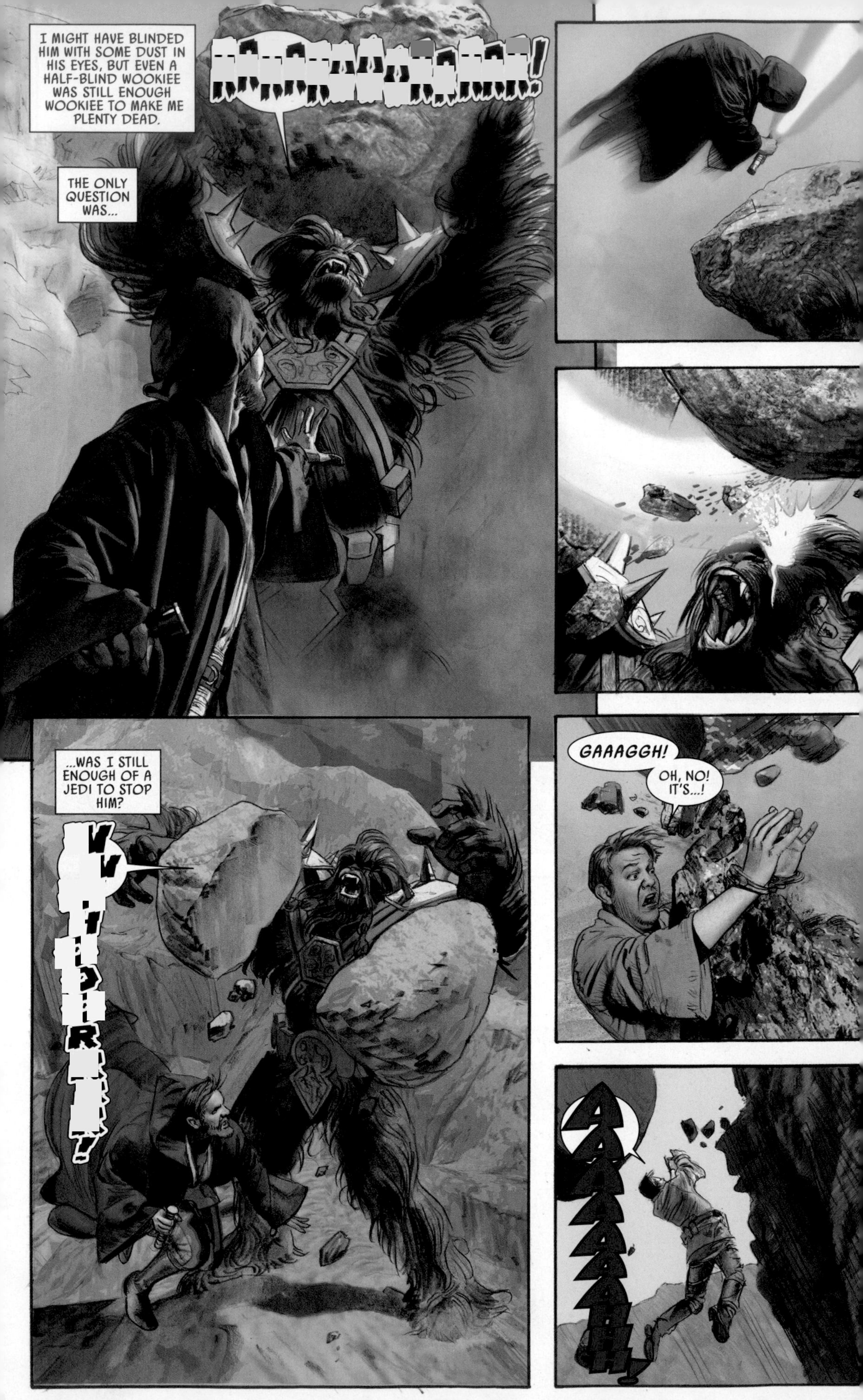
I MIGHT HAVE BLINDED HIM WITH SOME DUST IN HIS EYES, BUT EVEN A HALF-BLIND WOOKIEE WAS STILL ENOUGH WOOKIEE TO MAKE ME PLENTY DEAD.
THE ONLY QUESTION WAS...
...WAS I STILL ENOUGH OF A JEDI TO STOP HIM?
GAAAGGH!
OH, NO! IT'S...!

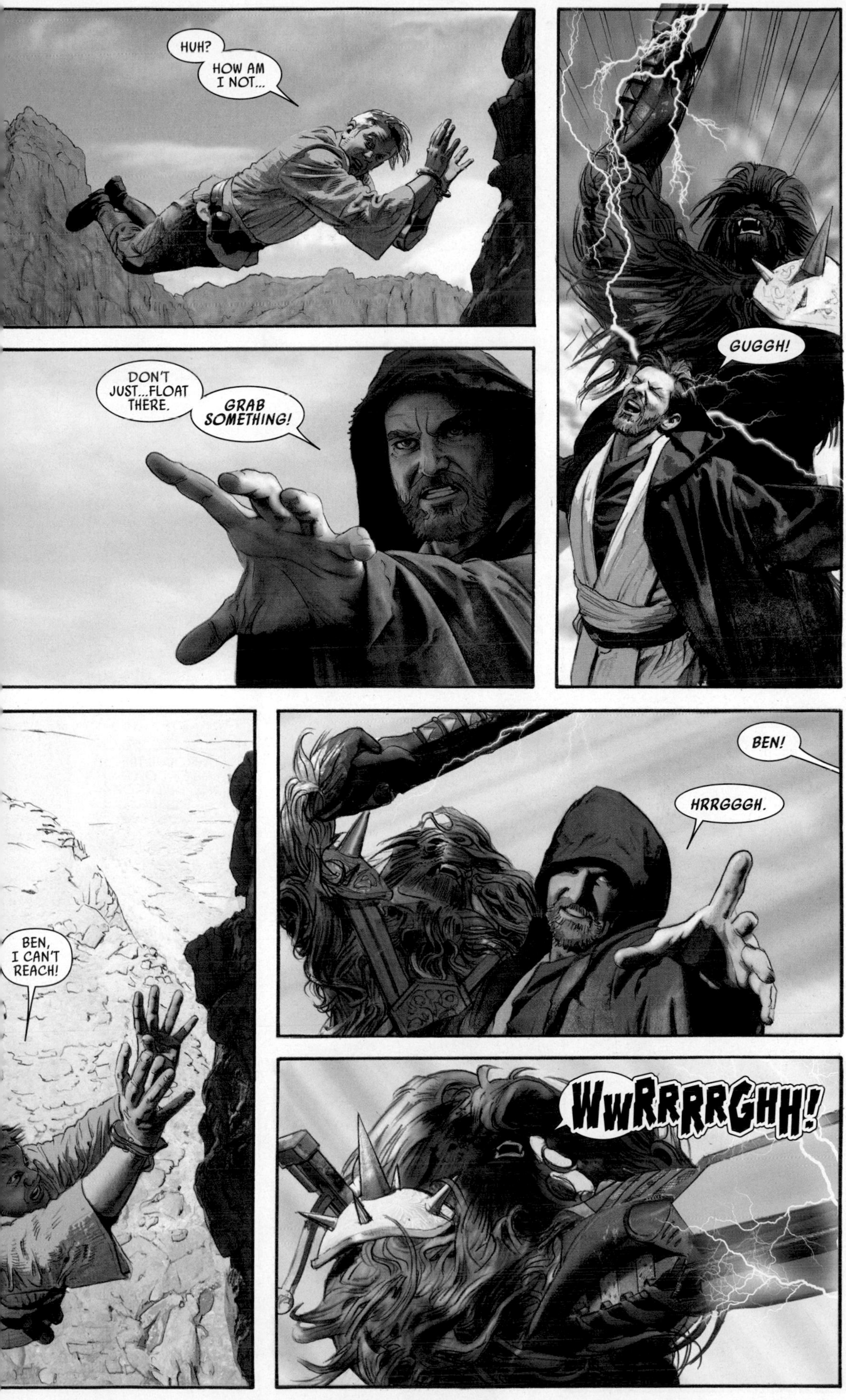
HUH?
HOW AM I NOT...
DON'T JUST...FLOAT THERE.
GRAB SOMETHING!
GUGGH!
BEN, I CAN'T REACH!
BEN!
HRRGGGH.
WWRRRRRGHH!

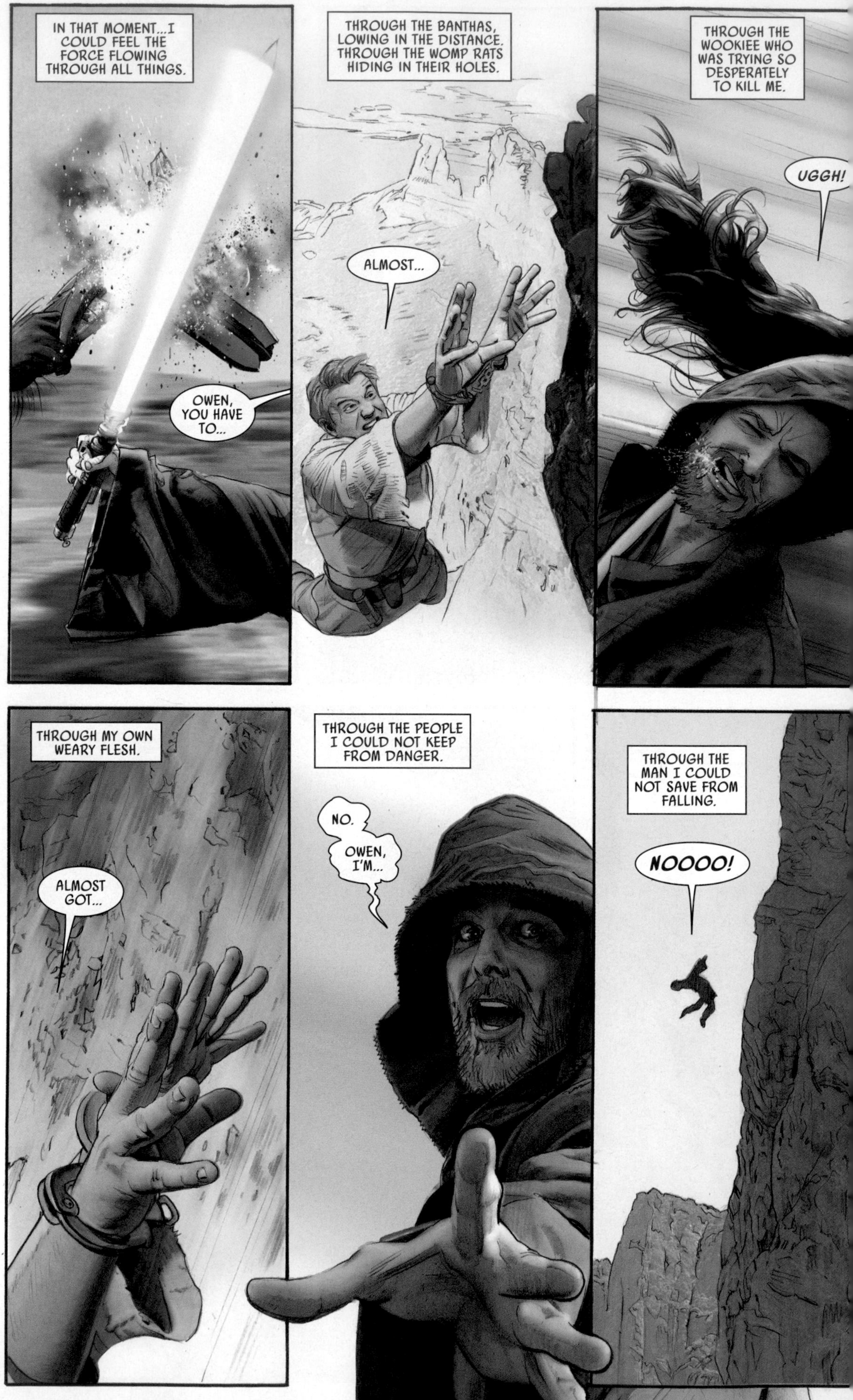
IN THAT MOMENT...I COULD FEEL THE FORCE FLOWING THROUGH ALL THINGS.
OWEN, YOU HAVE TO...
THROUGH THE BANTHAS, LOWING IN THE DISTANCE. THROUGH THE WOMP RATS HIDING IN THEIR HOLES.
ALMOST...
THROUGH THE WOOKIEE WHO WAS TRYING SO DESPERATELY TO KILL ME.
UGGH!
THROUGH MY OWN WEARY FLESH.
ALMOST GOT...
THROUGH THE PEOPLE I COULD NOT KEEP FROM DANGER.
NO.
OWEN, I'M...
THROUGH THE MAN I COULD NOT SAVE FROM FALLING.
NOOOO!

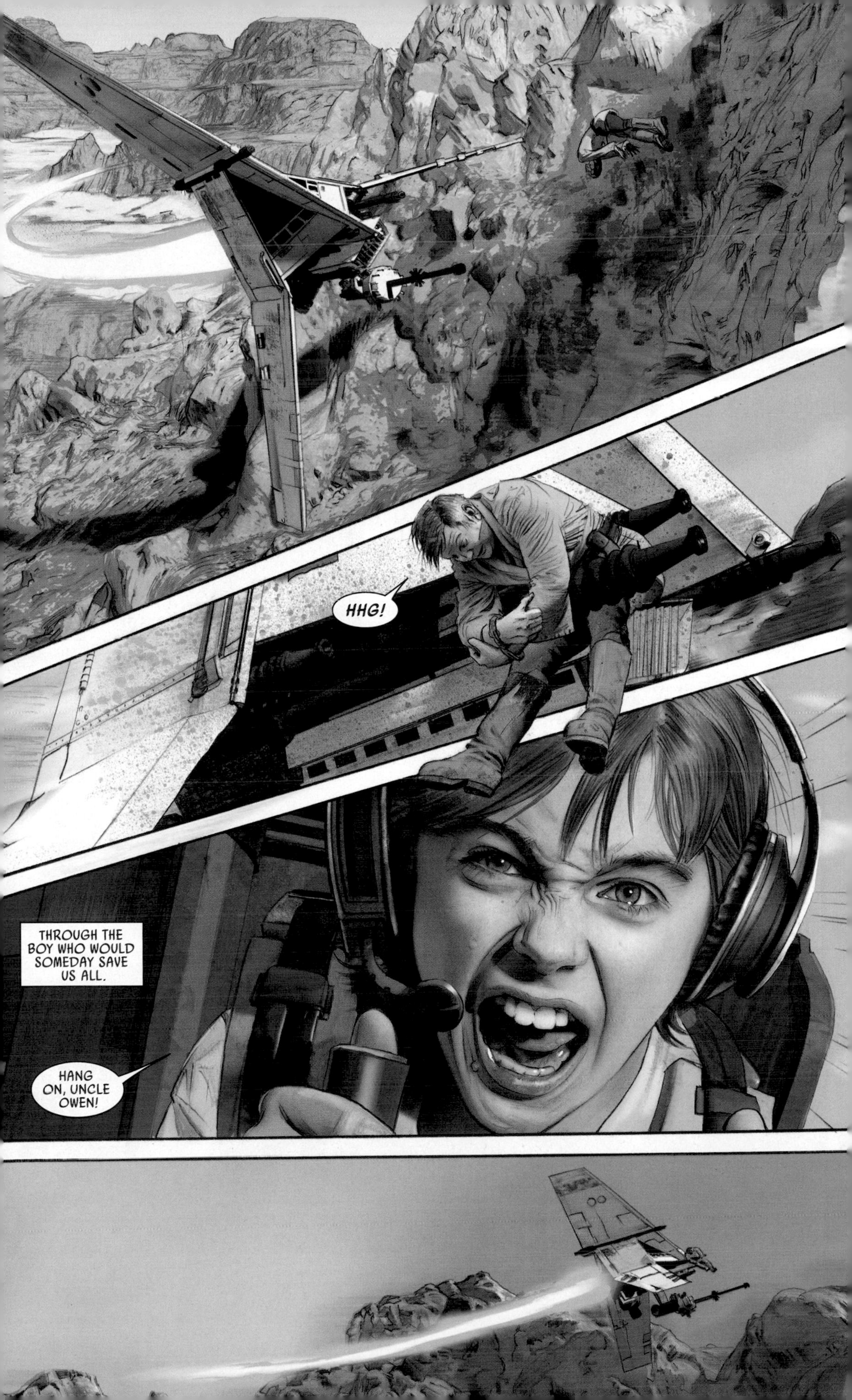
HHG!
THROUGH THE BOY WHO WOULD SOMEDAY SAVE US ALL.
HANG ON, UNCLE OWEN!

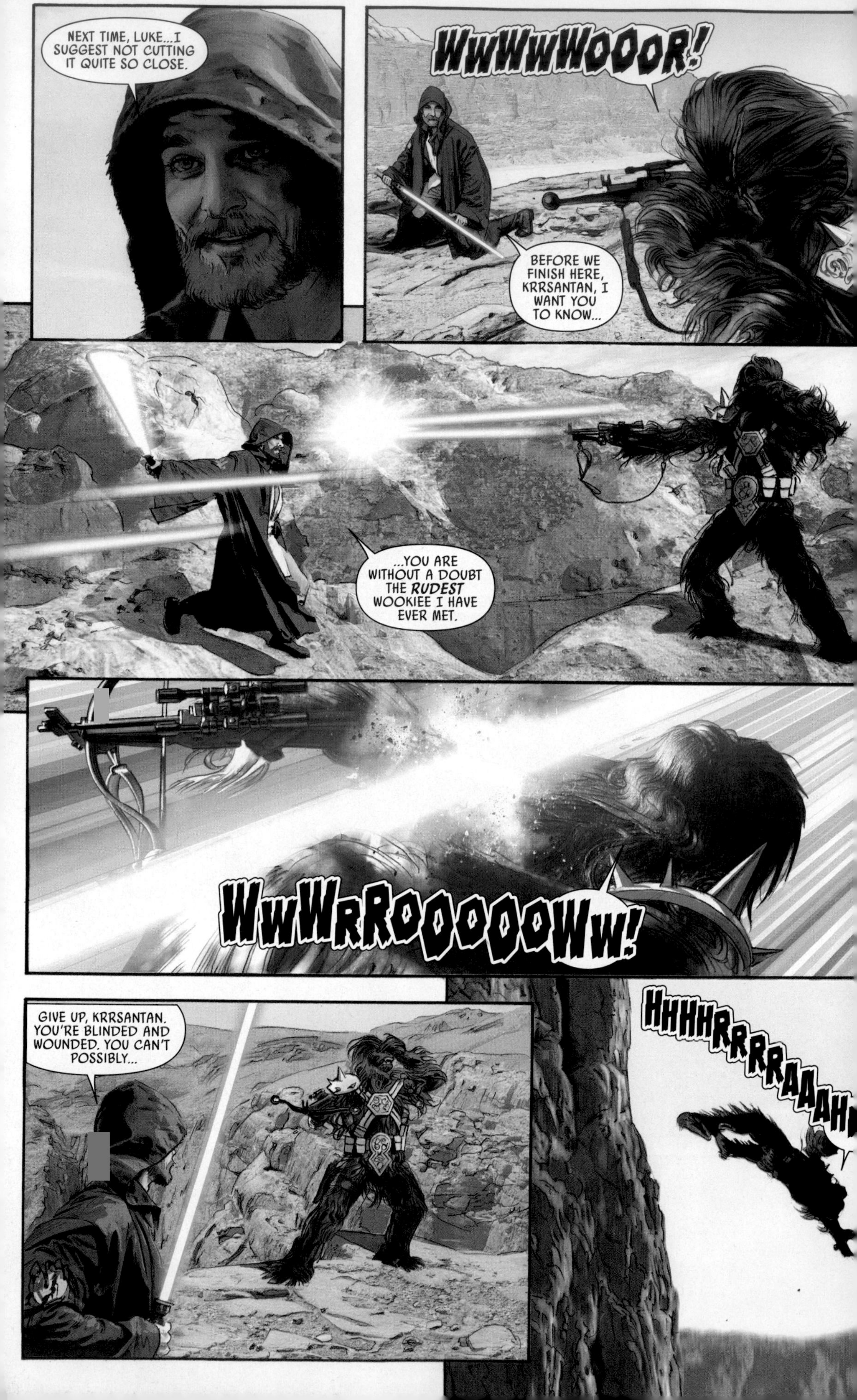
NEXT TIME, LUKE...I SUGGEST NOT CUTTING IT QUITE SO CLOSE.
WWWWWOOOR!
BEFORE WE FINISH HERE, KRRSANTAN, I WANT YOU TO KNOW...
...YOU ARE WITHOUT A DOUBT THE RUDEST WOOKIEE I HAVE EVER MET.
WWWRROOOOOWW!
GIVE UP, KRRSANTAN. YOU'RE BLINDED AND WOUNDED. YOU CAN'T POSSIBLY...
HHHHRRRRRAAAAH

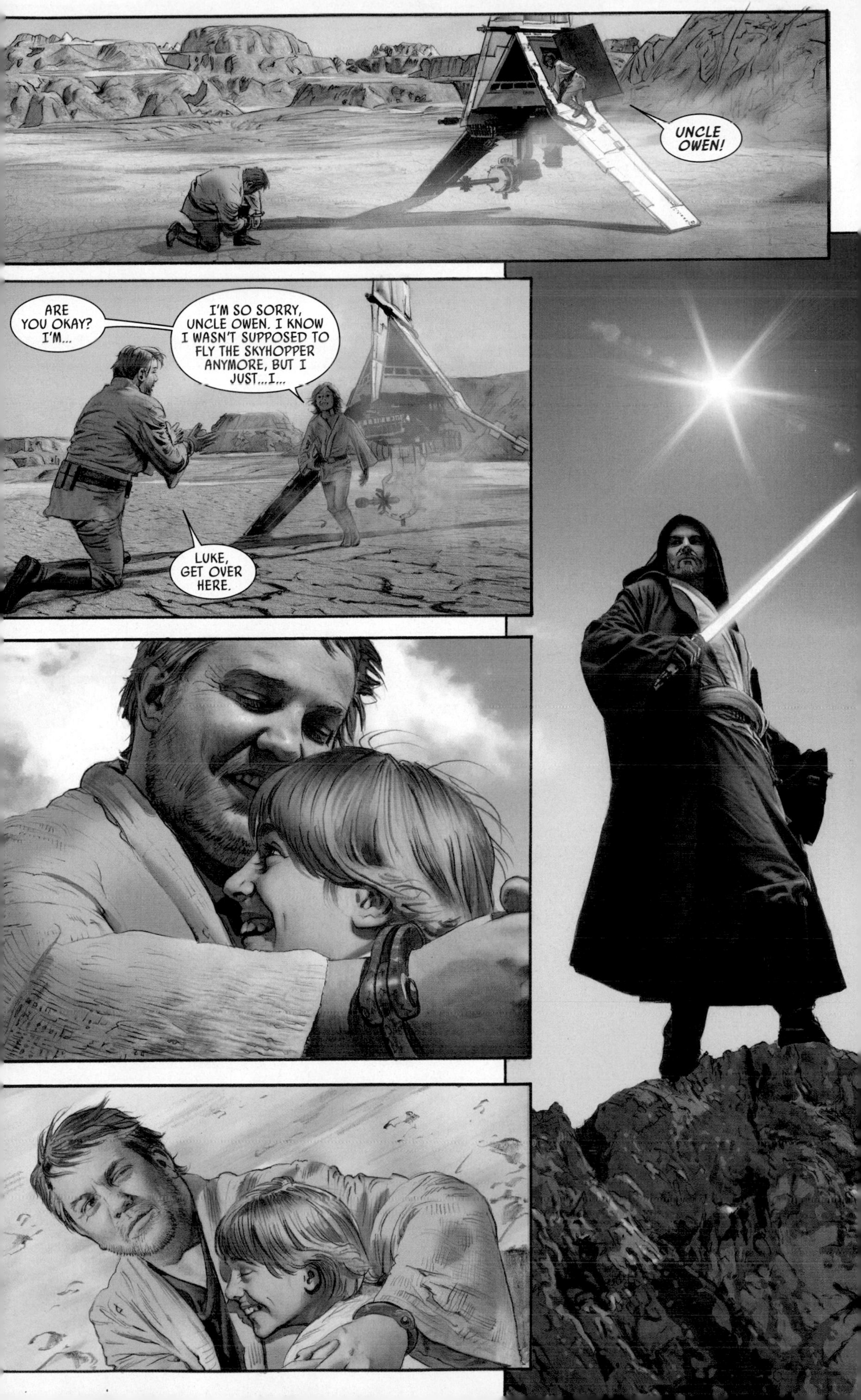
UNCLE OWEN!
ARE YOU OKAY? I'M...
I'M SO SORRY, UNCLE OWEN. I KNOW I WASN'T SUPPOSED TO FLY THE SKYHOPPER ANYMORE, BUT I JUST...I...
LUKE, GET OVER HERE.

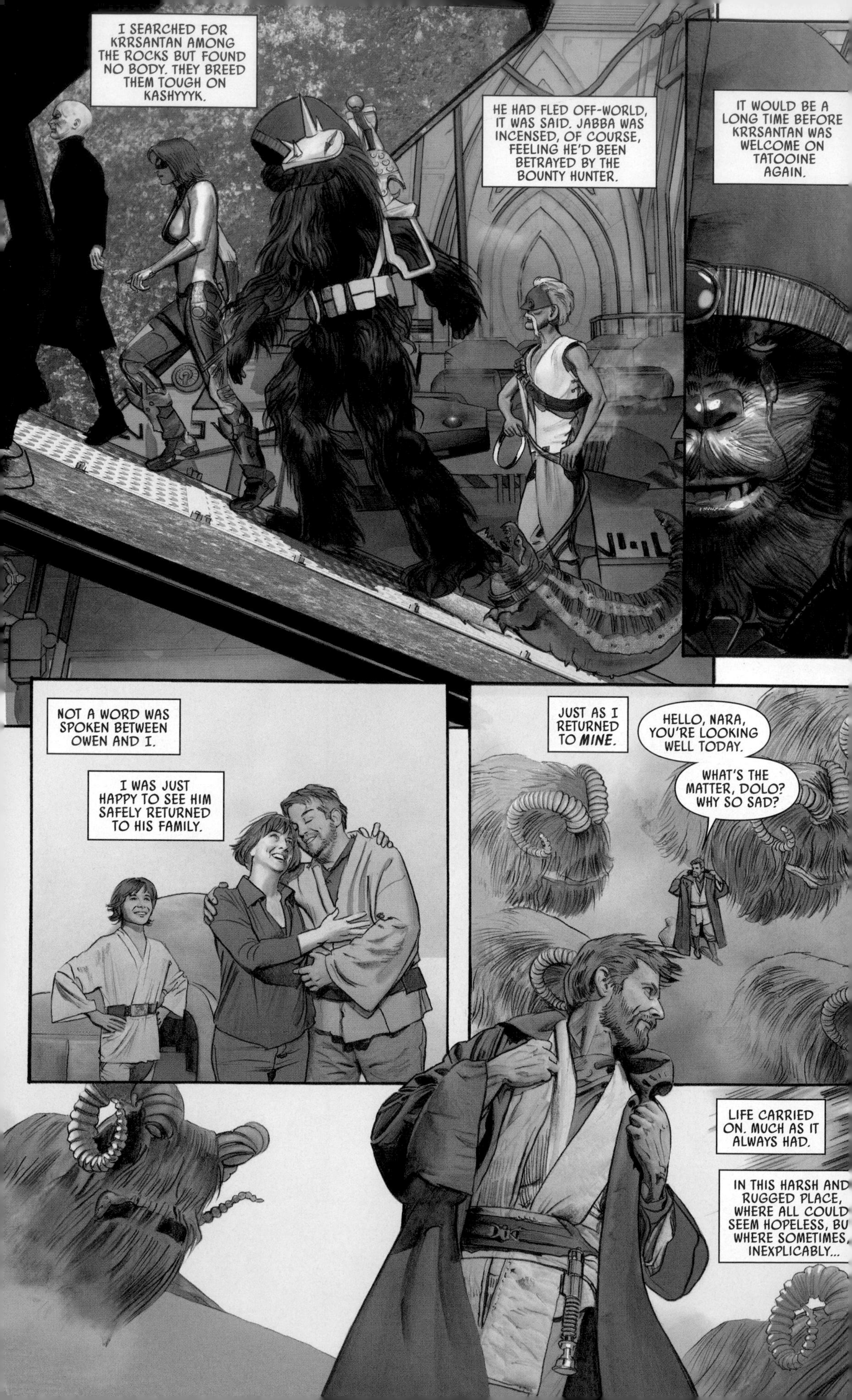
I SEARCHED FOR KRRSANTAN AMONG THE ROCKS BUT FOUND NO BODY. THEY BREED THEM TOUGH ON KASHYYYK.
HE HAD FLED OFF-WORLD, IT WAS SAID. JABBA WAS INCENSED, OF COURSE, FEELING HE'D BEEN BETRAYED BY THE BOUNTY HUNTER.
IT WOULD BE A LONG TIME BEFORE KRRSANTAN WAS WELCOME ON TATOOINE AGAIN.
NOT A WORD WAS SPOKEN BETWEEN OWEN AND I.
I WAS JUST HAPPY TO SEE HIM SAFELY RETURNED TO HIS FAMILY.
JUST AS I RETURNED TO *MINE.*
HELLO, NARA, YOU'RE LOOKING WELL TODAY.
WHAT'S THE MATTER, DOLO? WHY SO SAD?
LIFE CARRIED ON. MUCH AS IT ALWAYS HAD.
IN THIS HARSH AND RUGGED PLACE, WHERE ALL COULD SEEM HOPELESS, BU WHERE SOMETIMES, INEXPLICABLY...

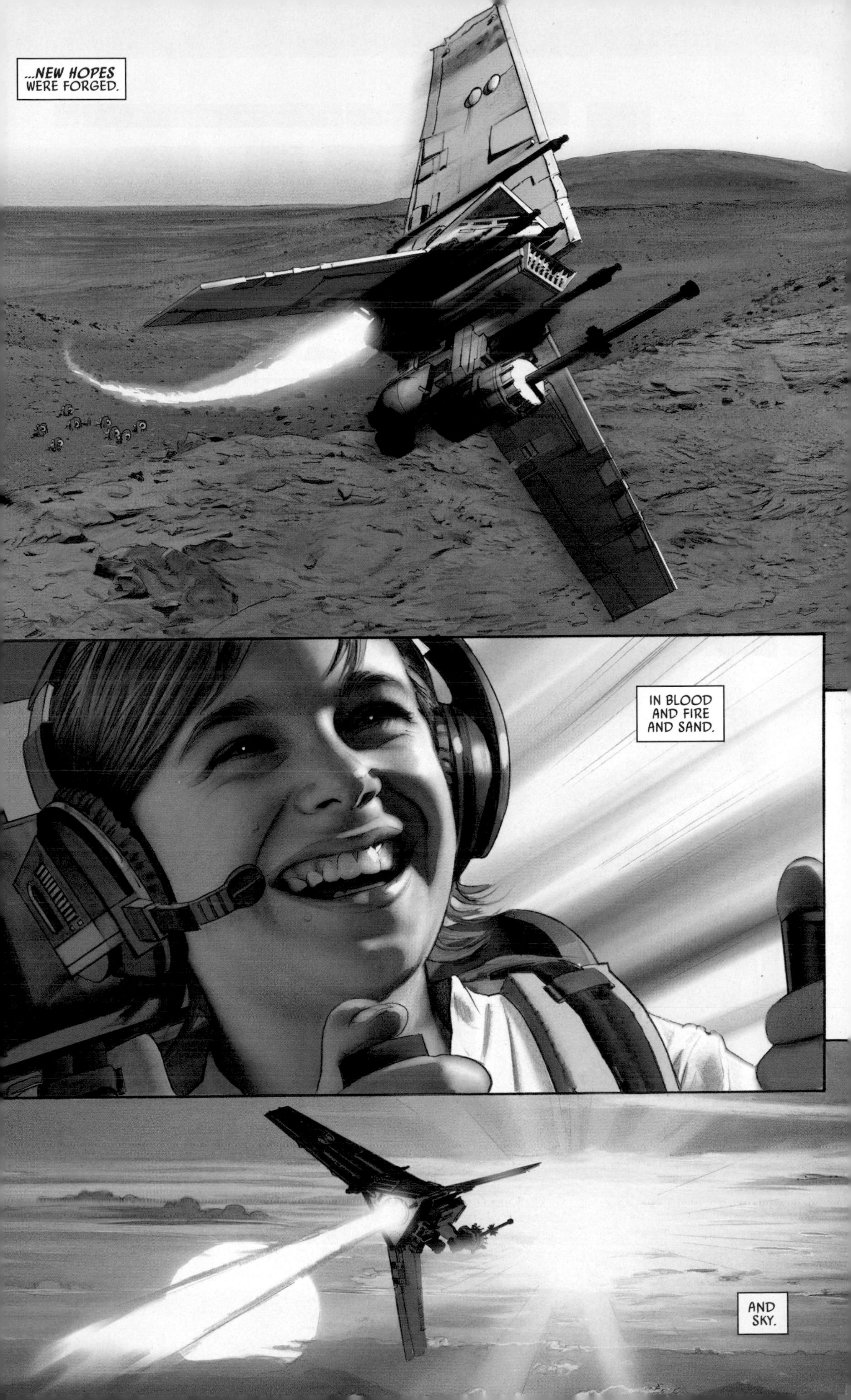
...NEW HOPES WERE FORGED.
IN BLOOD AND FIRE AND SAND.
AND SKY.

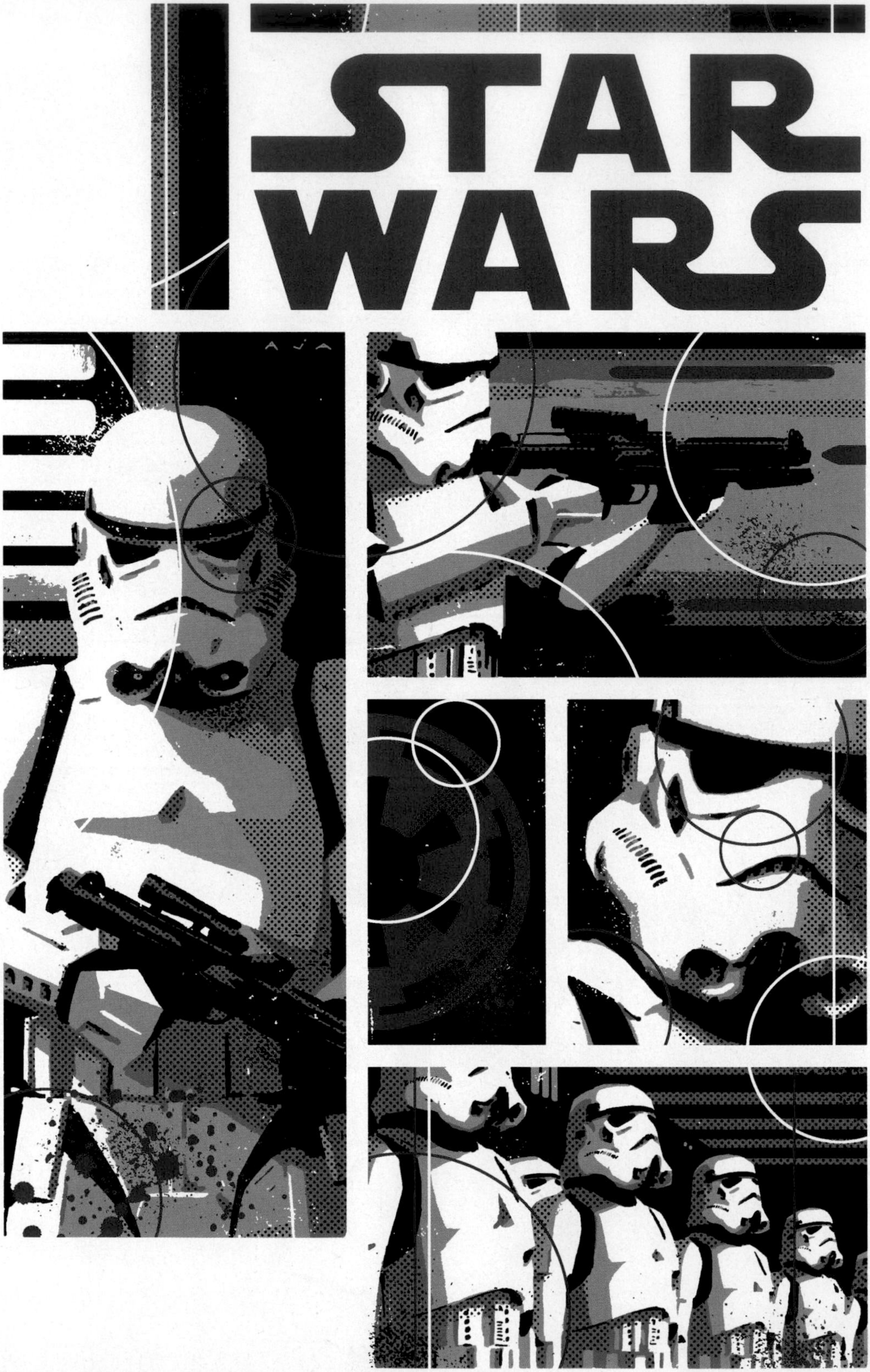
STAR WARS

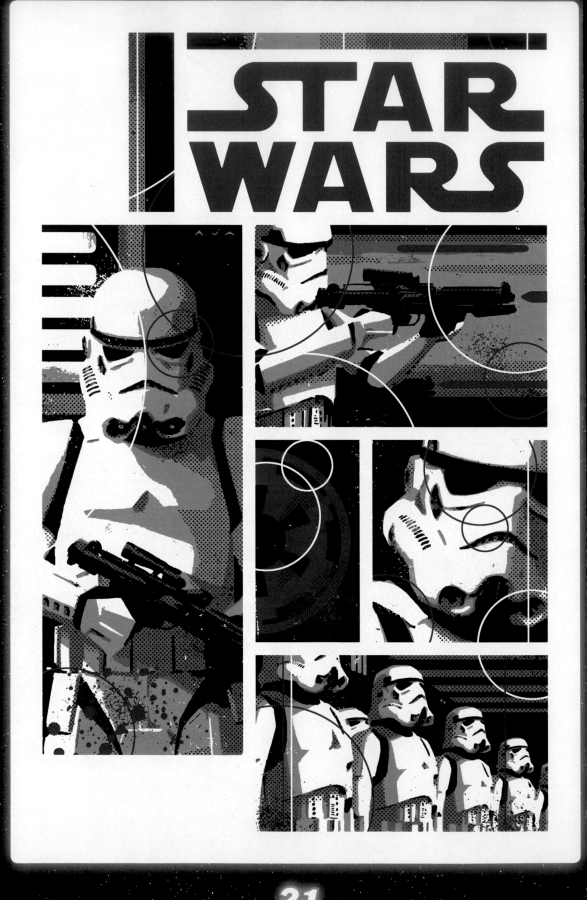

Book V

THE LAST FLIGHT OF THE HARBINGER

It is a crucial time for the Empire. Rebel forces are proliferating across the galaxy, and their elimination is imperative for Imperial reign.

For a mission this vital, the right team is essential – an elite group of stormtroopers, hand-picked for their skills, loyalty to the Empire, and complete dedication to destroying the Rebellion.

Leading this team is the ruthless Sergeant Kreel – former undercover Imperial spy known as the Gamemaster and warden on the infamous smuggler's moon Nar Shaddaa – a man who answers directly to Darth Vader. Rebel pilot Luke Skywalker has evaded Sergeant Kreel's attacks once before, but he, and the rest of the Rebellion, have not seen the last of the Empire's wrath....

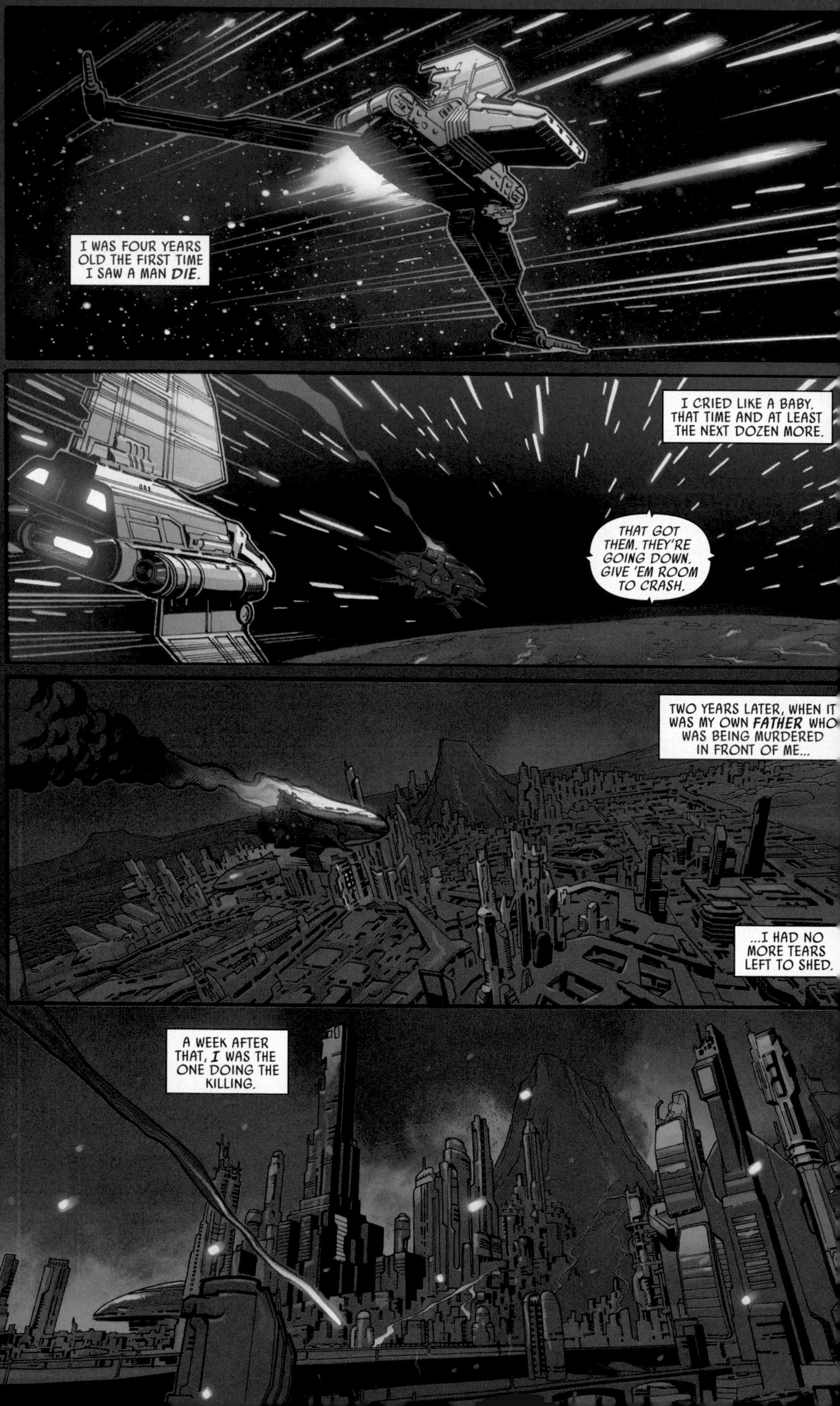

I WAS FOUR YEARS OLD THE FIRST TIME I SAW A MAN DIE.
I CRIED LIKE A BABY. THAT TIME AND AT LEAST THE NEXT DOZEN MORE.
THAT GOT THEM. THEY'RE GOING DOWN. GIVE 'EM ROOM TO CRASH.
TWO YEARS LATER, WHEN IT WAS MY OWN FATHER WHO WAS BEING MURDERED IN FRONT OF ME...
...I HAD NO MORE TEARS LEFT TO SHED.
A WEEK AFTER THAT, I WAS THE ONE DOING THE KILLING.

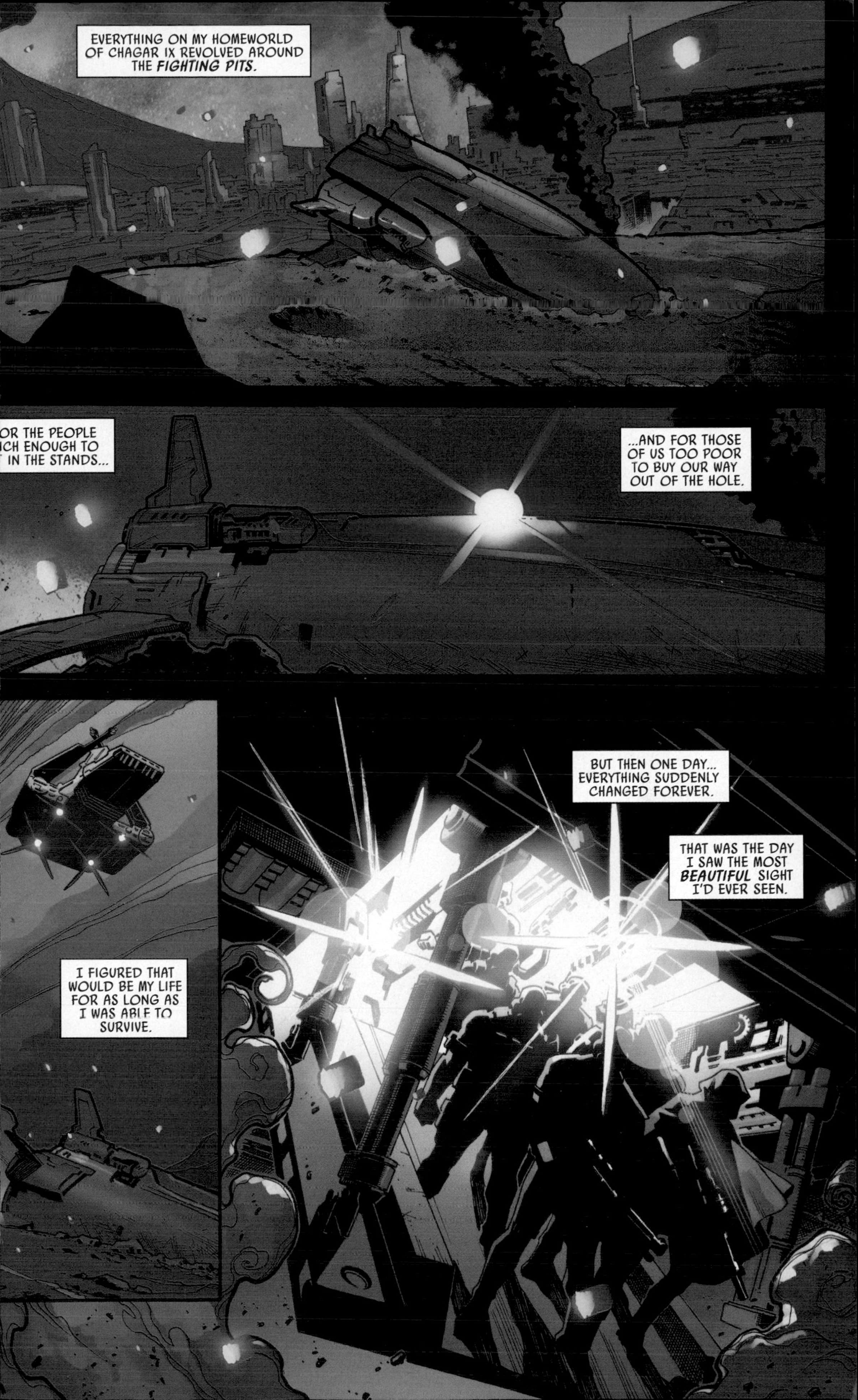
EVERYTHING ON MY HOMEWORLD OF CHAGAR IX REVOLVED AROUND THE FIGHTING PITS.
OR THE PEOPLE ICH ENOUGH TO T IN THE STANDS...
...AND FOR THOSE OF US TOO POOR TO BUY OUR WAY OUT OF THE HOLE.
I FIGURED THAT WOULD BE MY LIFE FOR AS LONG AS I WAS ABLE TO SURVIVE.
BUT THEN ONE DAY... EVERYTHING SUDDENLY CHANGED FOREVER.
THAT WAS THE DAY I SAW THE MOST BEAUTIFUL SIGHT I'D EVER SEEN.

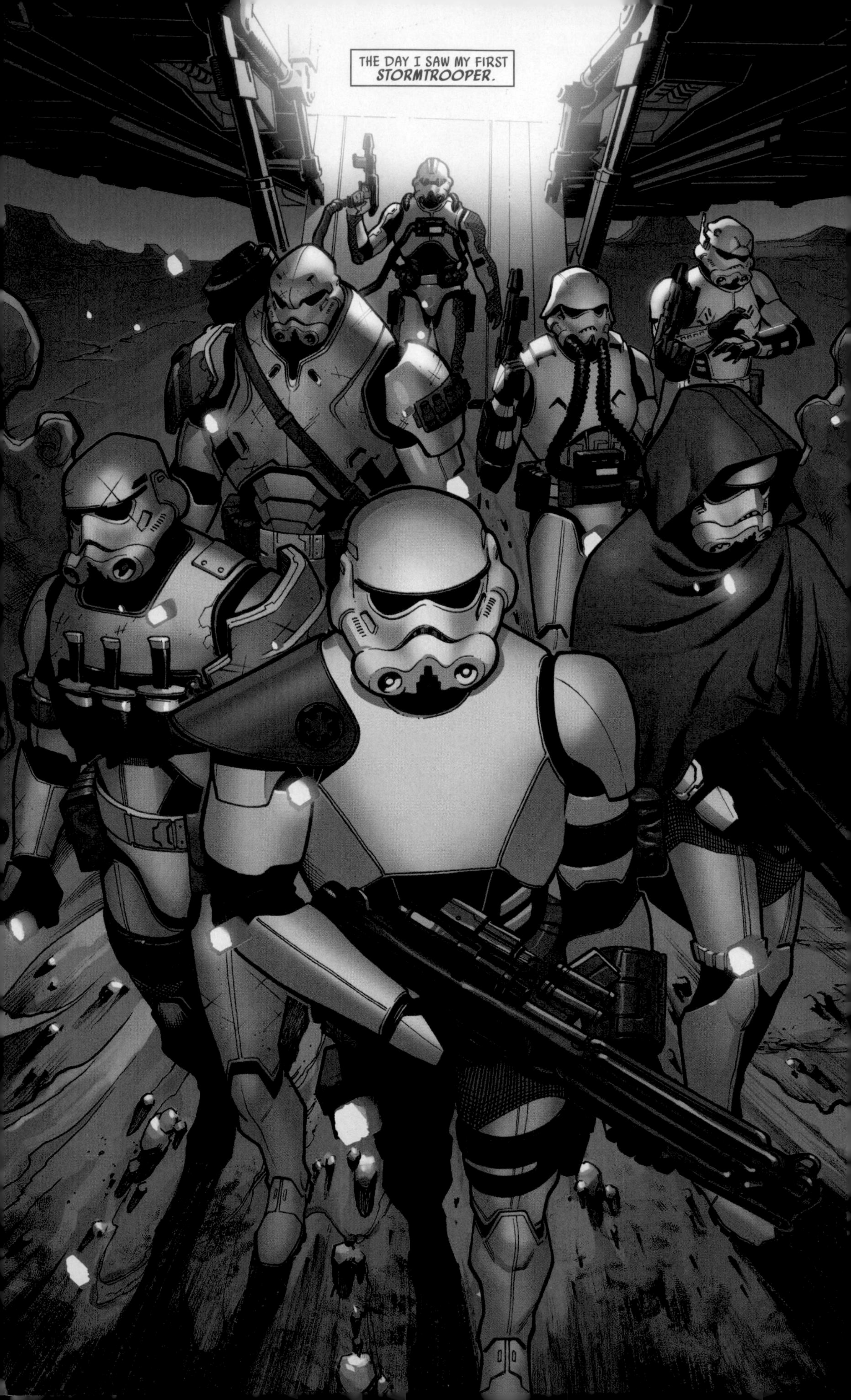
THE DAY I SAW MY FIRST STORMTROOPER.

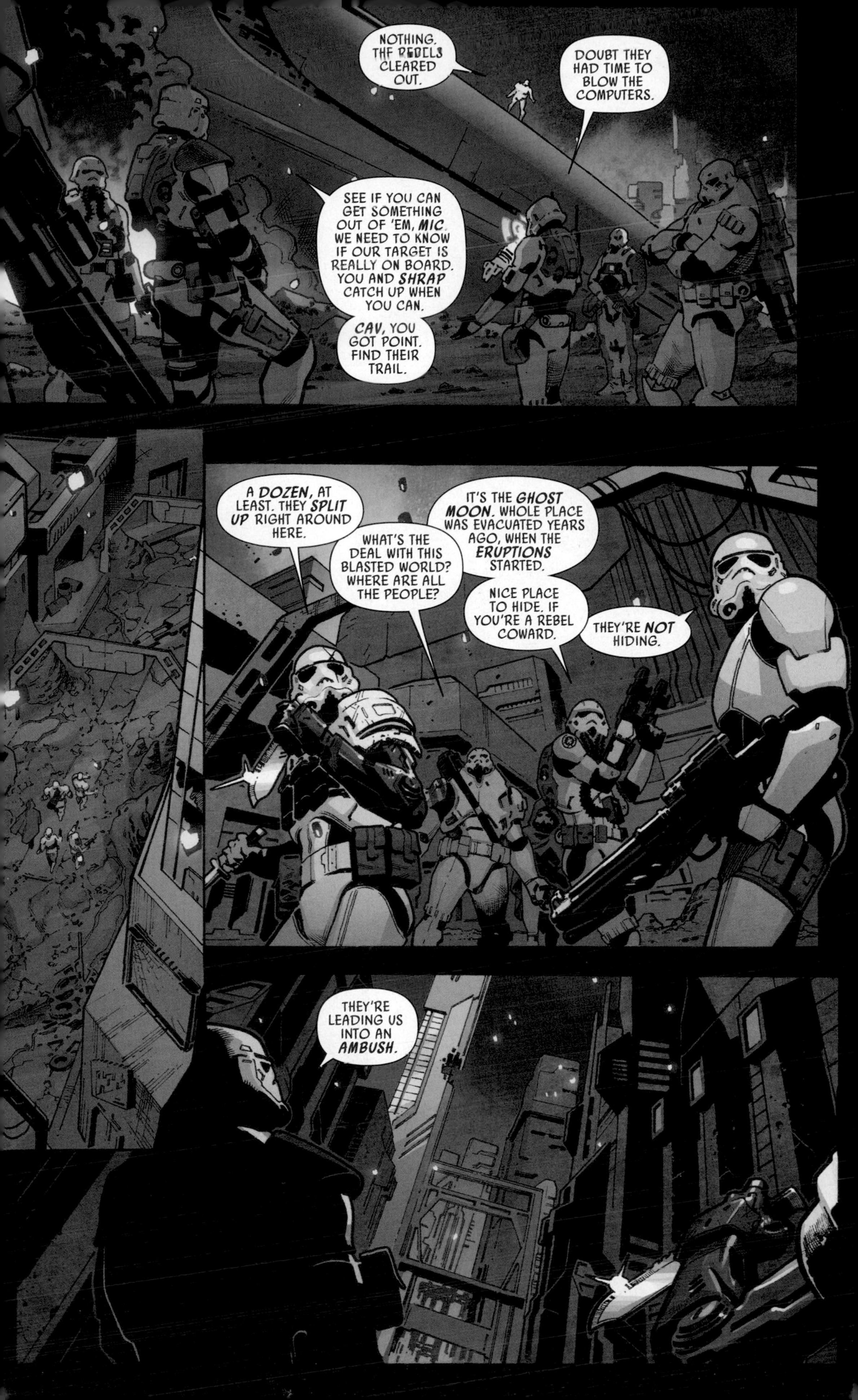
NOTHING. THE REBELS CLEARED OUT.
DOUBT THEY HAD TIME TO BLOW THE COMPUTERS.
SEE IF YOU CAN GET SOMETHING OUT OF 'EM, MIC. WE NEED TO KNOW IF OUR TARGET IS REALLY ON BOARD. YOU AND SHRAP CATCH UP WHEN YOU CAN.
CAV, YOU GOT POINT. FIND THEIR TRAIL.
A DOZEN, AT LEAST. THEY SPLIT UP RIGHT AROUND HERE.
WHAT'S THE DEAL WITH THIS BLASTED WORLD? WHERE ARE ALL THE PEOPLE?
IT'S THE GHOST MOON. WHOLE PLACE WAS EVACUATED YEARS AGO, WHEN THE ERUPTIONS STARTED.
NICE PLACE TO HIDE. IF YOU'RE A REBEL COWARD.
THEY'RE NOT HIDING.
THEY'RE LEADING US INTO AN AMBUSH.

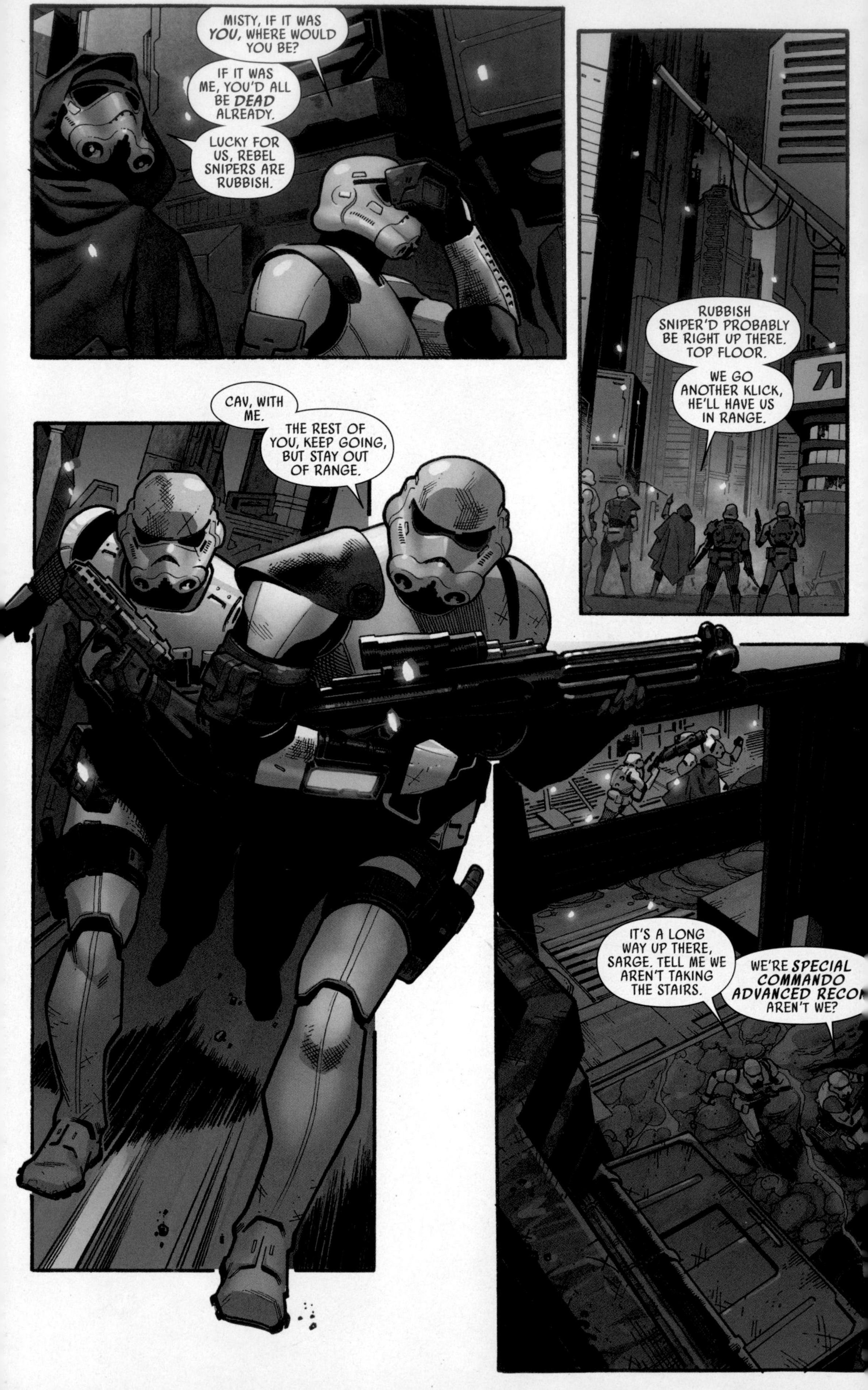

MISTY, IF IT WAS *YOU,* WHERE WOULD YOU BE?
IF IT WAS ME, YOU'D ALL BE *DEAD* ALREADY.
LUCKY FOR US, REBEL SNIPERS ARE RUBBISH.
RUBBISH SNIPER'D PROBABLY BE RIGHT UP THERE. TOP FLOOR.
WE GO ANOTHER KLICK, HE'LL HAVE US IN RANGE.
CAV, WITH ME.
THE REST OF YOU, KEEP GOING, BUT STAY OUT OF RANGE.
IT'S A LONG WAY UP THERE, SARGE. TELL ME WE AREN'T TAKING THE STAIRS.
WE'RE *SPECIAL COMMANDO ADVANCED RECO*
AREN'T WE?

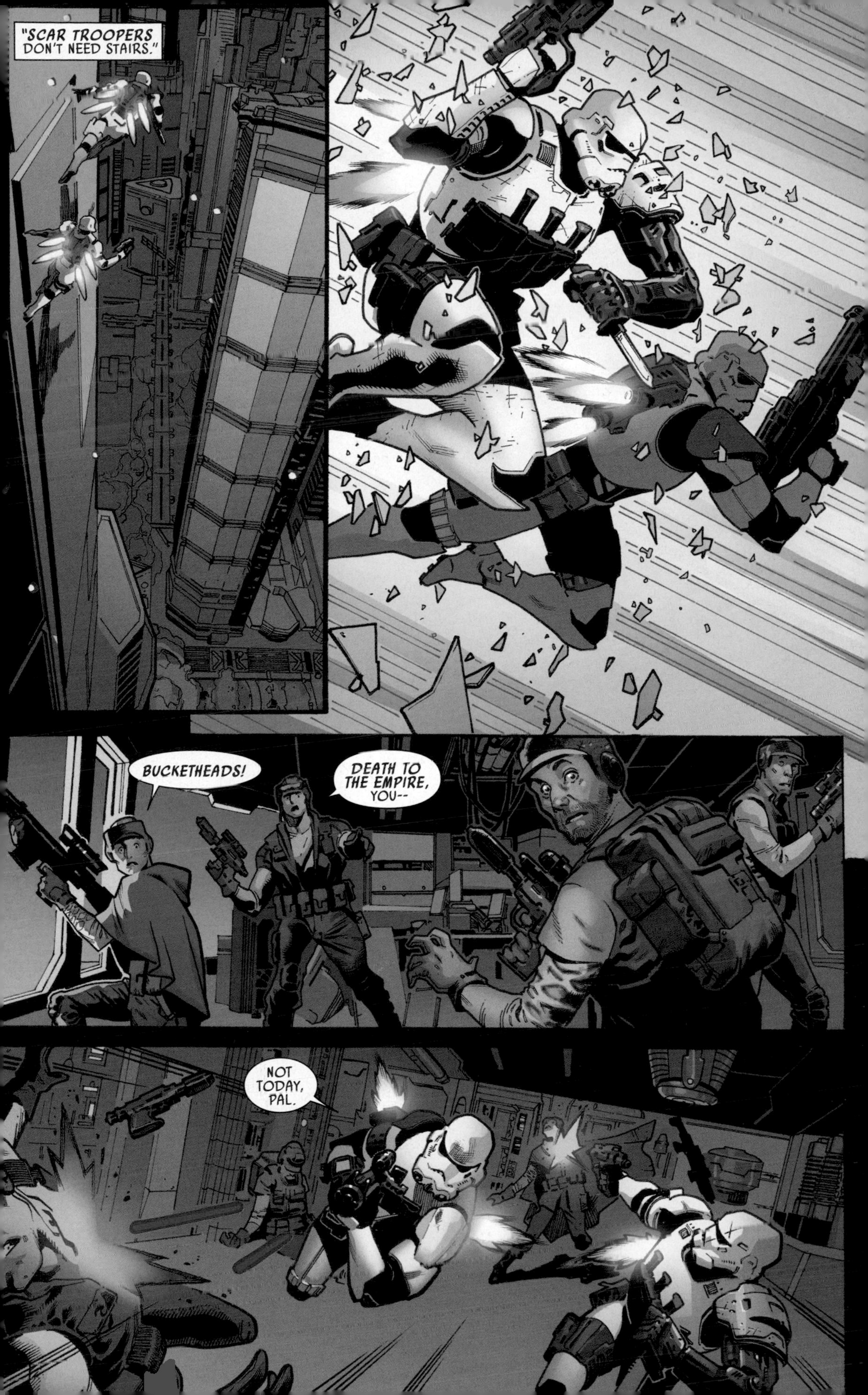
"SCAR TROOPERS DON'T NEED STAIRS."
BUCKETHEADS!
DEATH TO THE EMPIRE, YOU--
NOT TODAY, PAL.

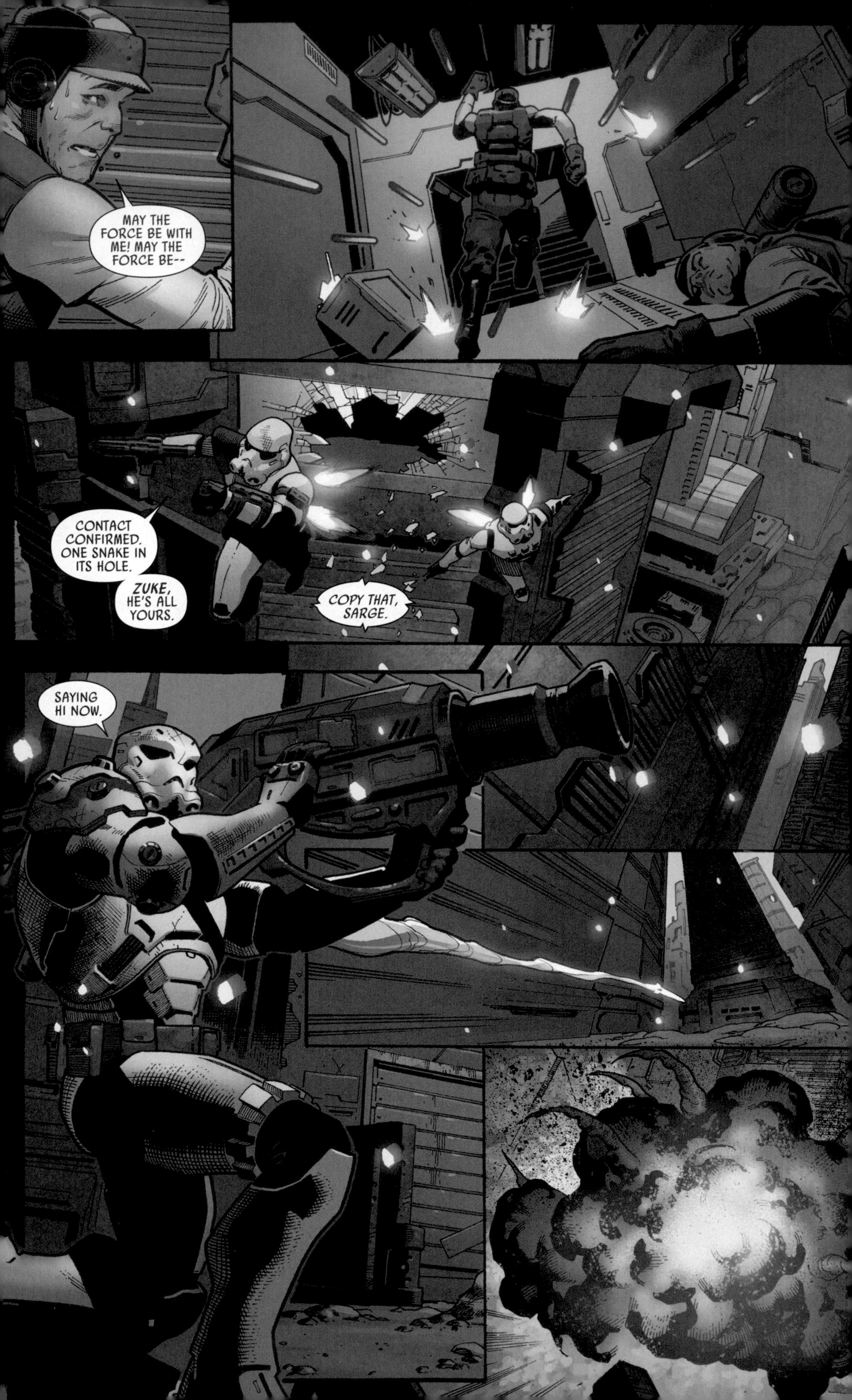

MAY THE FORCE BE WITH ME! MAY THE FORCE BE--
CONTACT CONFIRMED. ONE SNAKE IN ITS HOLE.
ZUKE, HE'S ALL YOURS.
COPY THAT, SARGE.
SAYING HI NOW.

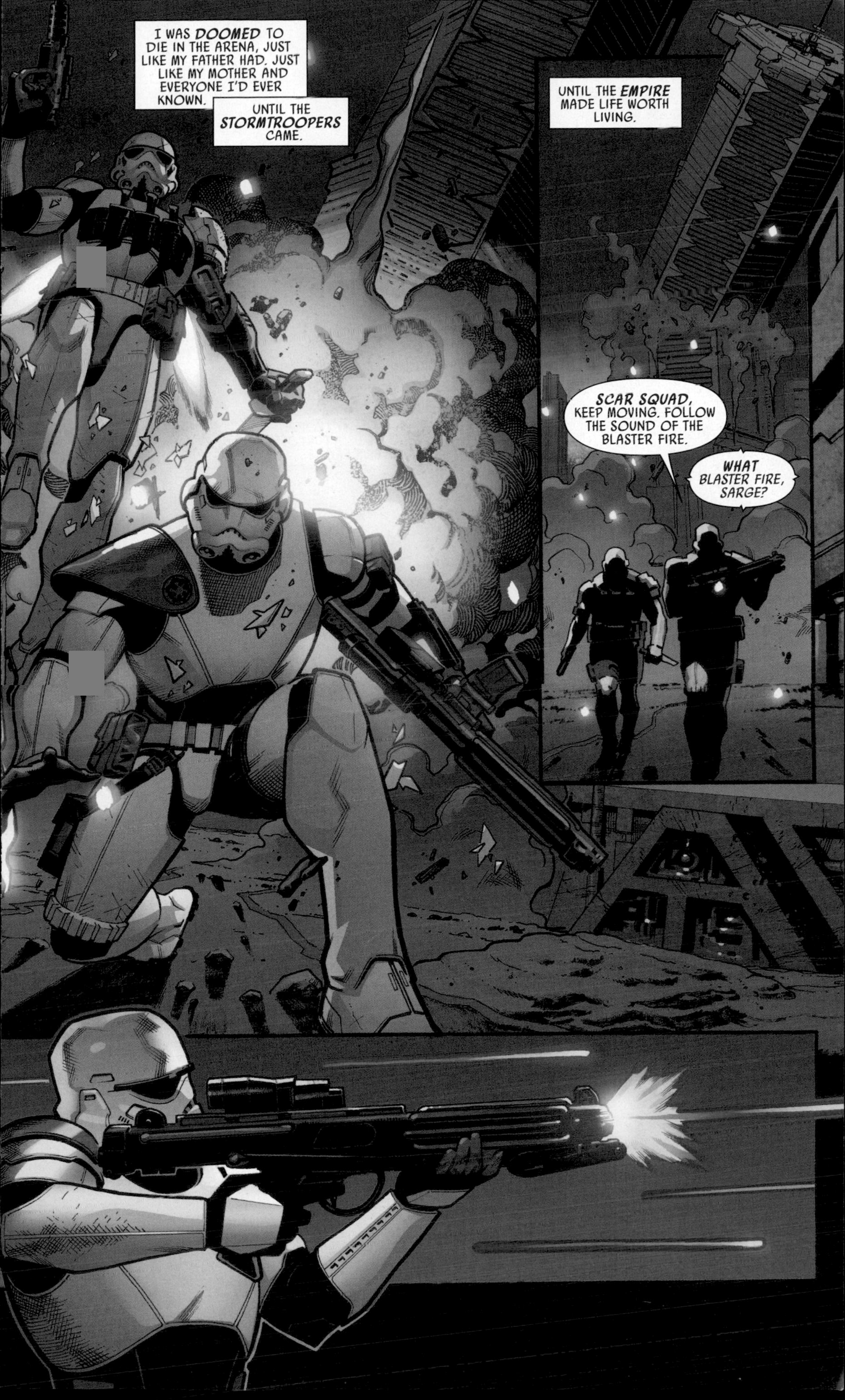
I WAS DOOMED TO DIE IN THE ARENA, JUST LIKE MY FATHER HAD. JUST LIKE MY MOTHER AND EVERYONE I'D EVER KNOWN.
UNTIL THE STORMTROOPERS CAME.
UNTIL THE EMPIRE MADE LIFE WORTH LIVING.
SCAR SQUAD, KEEP MOVING. FOLLOW THE SOUND OF THE BLASTER FIRE.
WHAT BLASTER FIRE, SARGE?

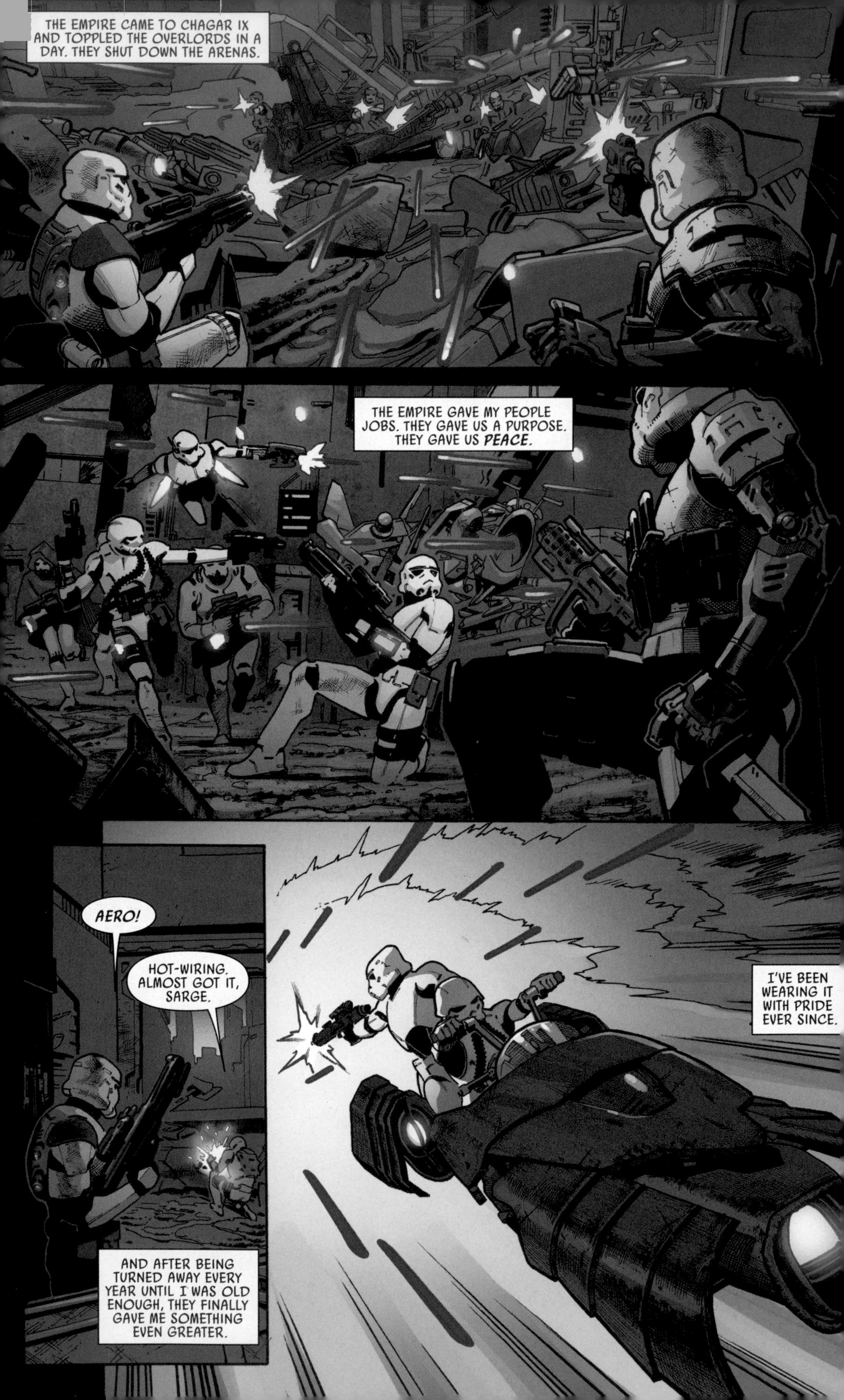
THE EMPIRE CAME TO CHAGAR IX AND TOPPLED THE OVERLORDS IN A DAY. THEY SHUT DOWN THE ARENAS.
THE EMPIRE GAVE MY PEOPLE JOBS. THEY GAVE US A PURPOSE. THEY GAVE US PEACE.
AERO!
HOT-WIRING. ALMOST GOT IT, SARGE.
AND AFTER BEING TURNED AWAY EVERY YEAR UNTIL I WAS OLD ENOUGH, THEY FINALLY GAVE ME SOMETHING EVEN GREATER.
I'VE BEEN WEARING IT WITH PRIDE EVER SINCE.

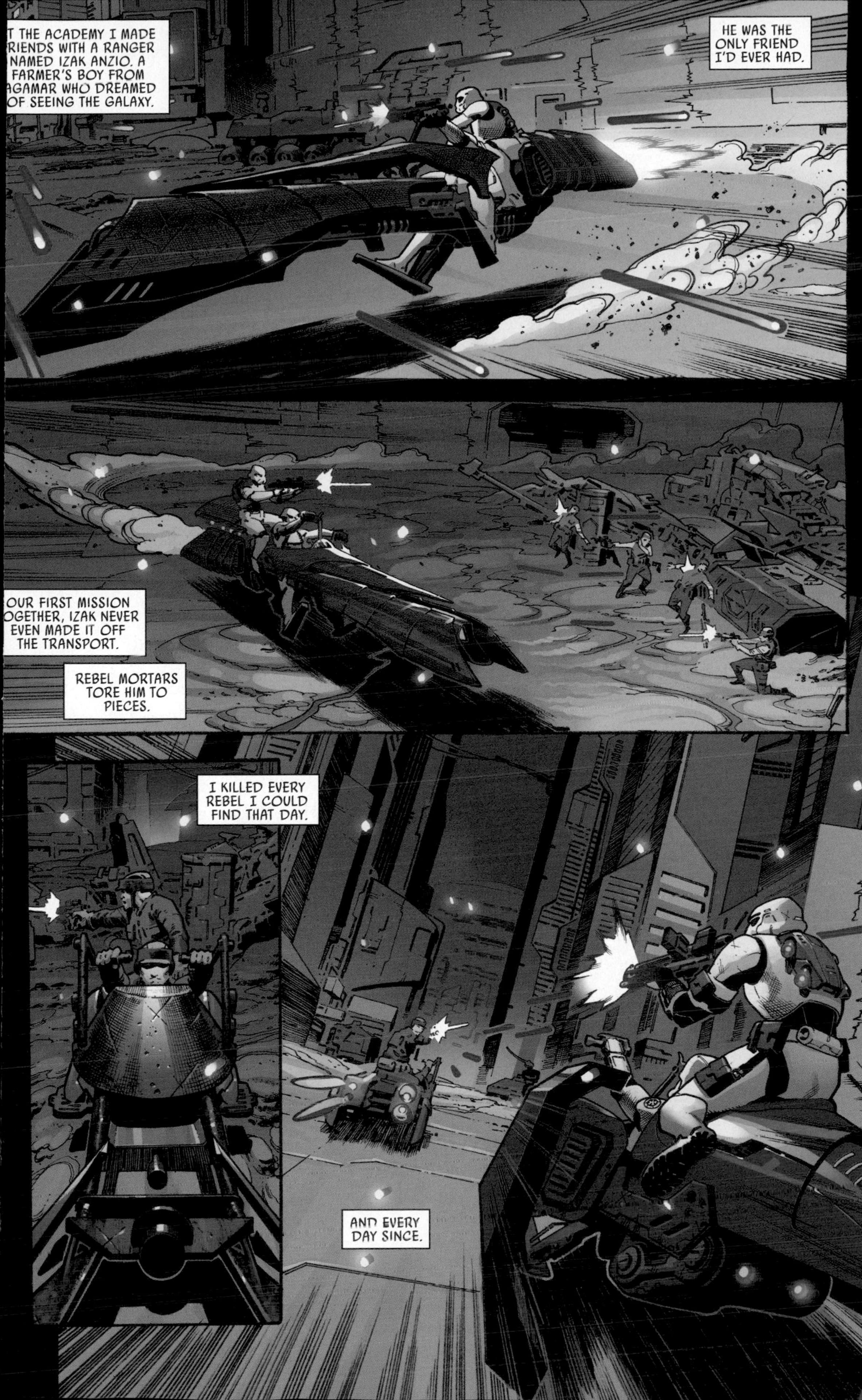
T THE ACADEMY I MADE RIENDS WITH A RANGER NAMED IZAK ANZIO. A FARMER'S BOY FROM AGAMAR WHO DREAMED OF SEEING THE GALAXY.
HE WAS THE ONLY FRIEND I'D EVER HAD.
OUR FIRST MISSION OGETHER, IZAK NEVER EVEN MADE IT OFF THE TRANSPORT.
REBEL MORTARS TORE HIM TO PIECES.
I KILLED EVERY REBEL I COULD FIND THAT DAY.
AND EVERY DAY SINCE.

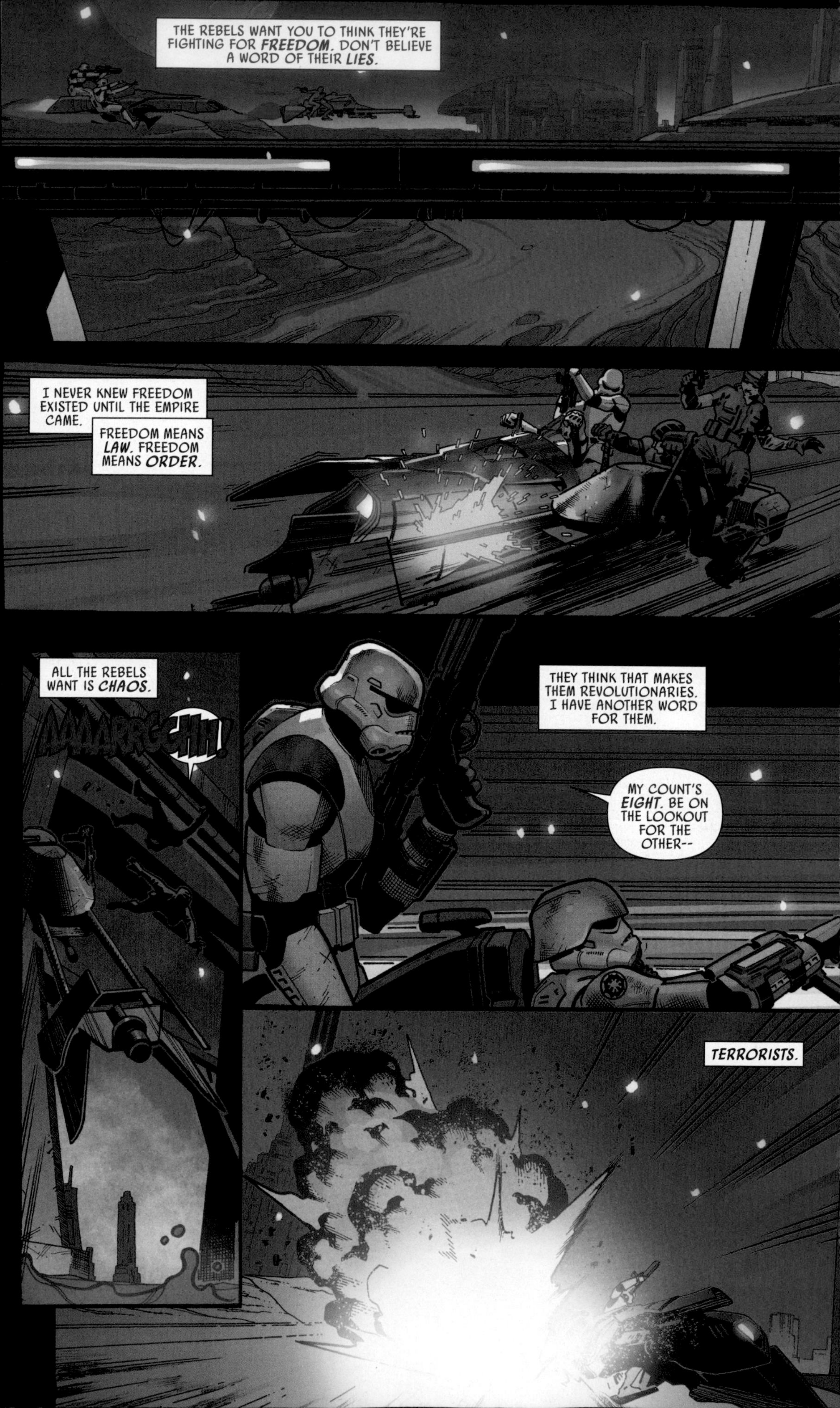

THE REBELS WANT YOU TO THINK THEY'RE FIGHTING FOR FREEDOM. DON'T BELIEVE A WORD OF THEIR LIES.
I NEVER KNEW FREEDOM EXISTED UNTIL THE EMPIRE CAME.
FREEDOM MEANS LAW. FREEDOM MEANS ORDER.
ALL THE REBELS WANT IS CHAOS.
AAAARRGGHH!
THEY THINK THAT MAKES THEM REVOLUTIONARIES. I HAVE ANOTHER WORD FOR THEM.
MY COUNT'S EIGHT. BE ON THE LOOKOUT FOR THE OTHER--
TERRORISTS.

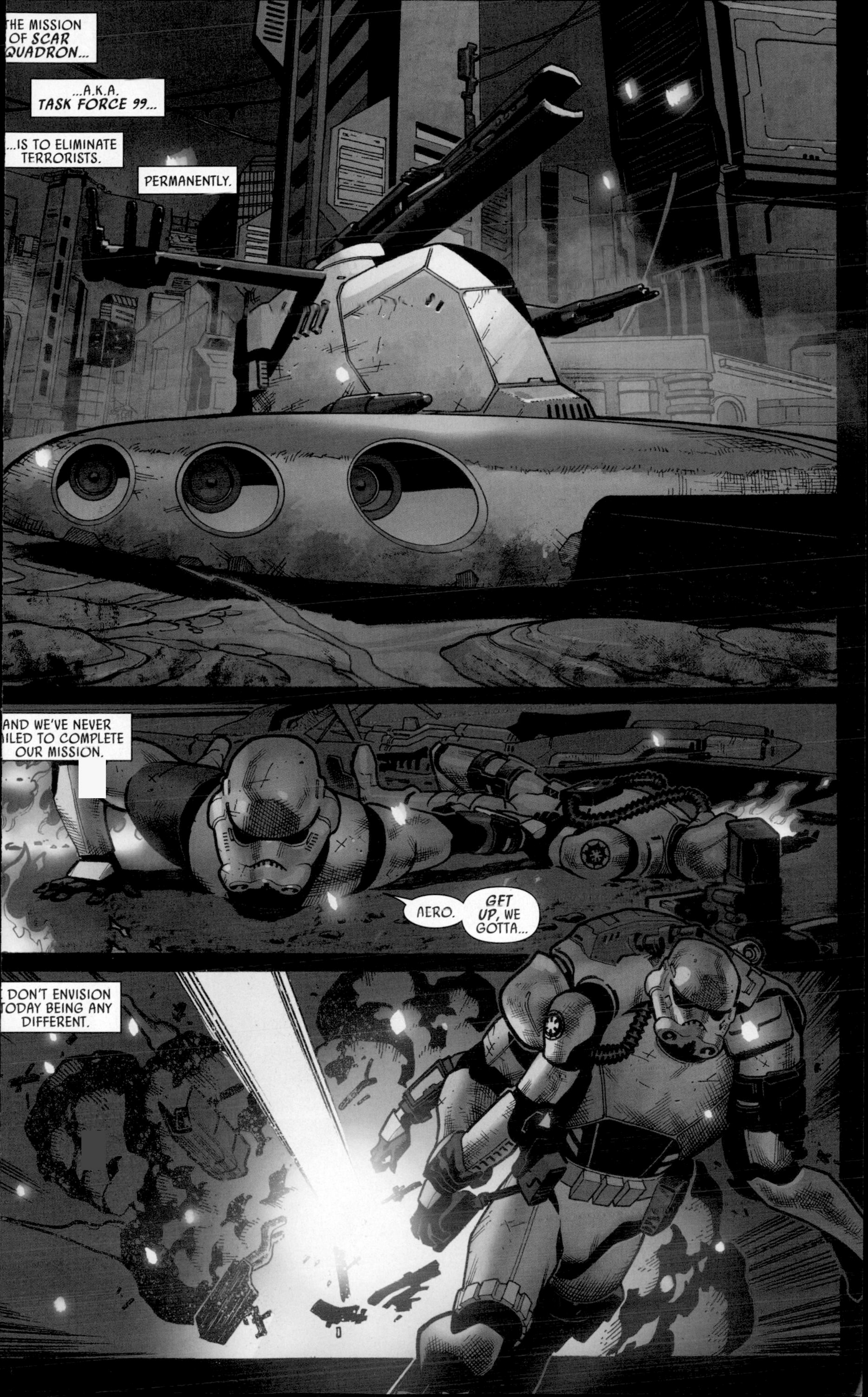
THE MISSION OF SCAR QUADRON...
...A.K.A. TASK FORCE 99...
...IS TO ELIMINATE TERRORISTS.
PERMANENTLY.
AND WE'VE NEVER ILED TO COMPLETE OUR MISSION.
AERO.
GET UP, WE GOTTA...
I DON'T ENVISION TODAY BEING ANY DIFFERENT.

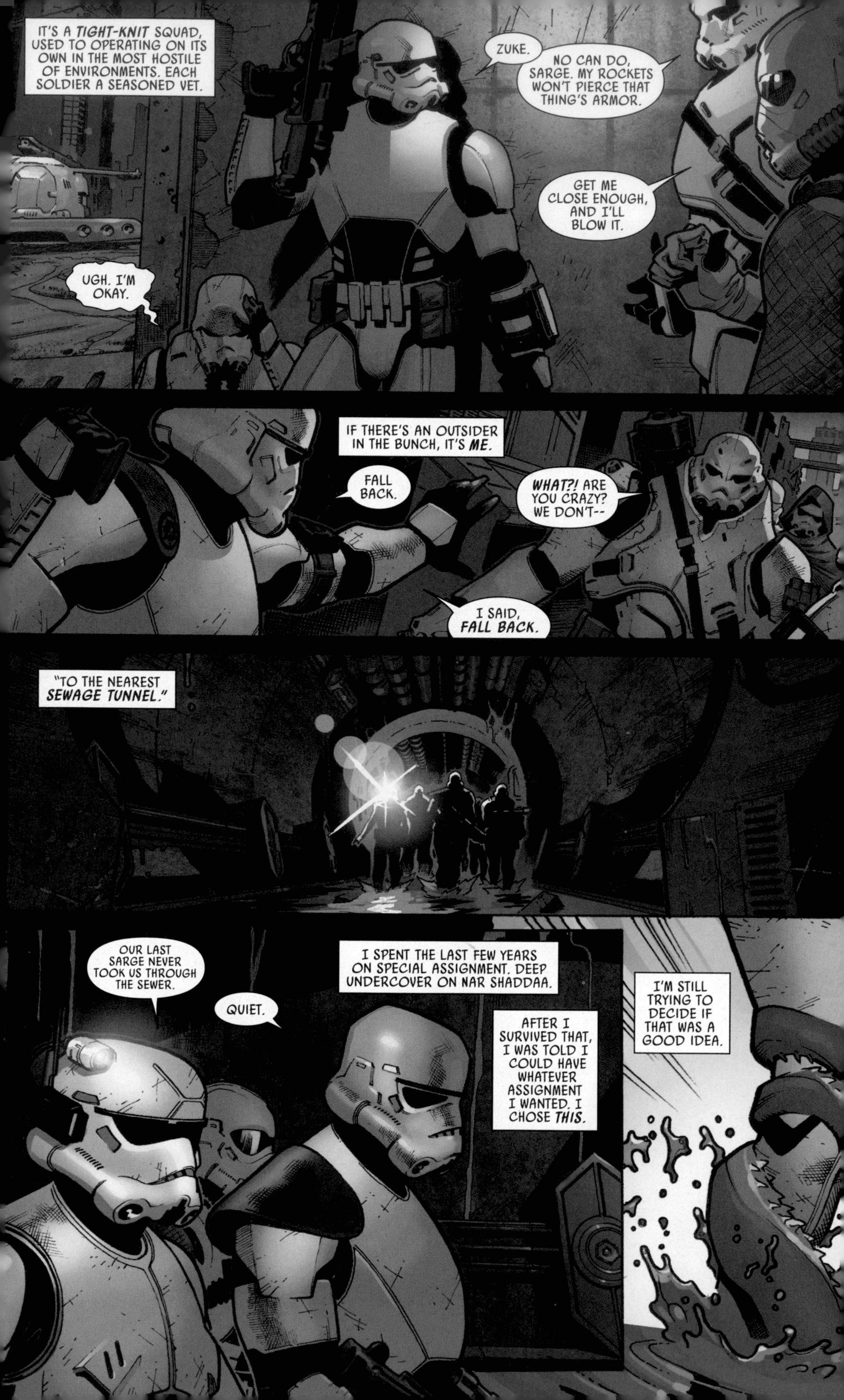
IT'S A TIGHT-KNIT SQUAD, USED TO OPERATING ON ITS OWN IN THE MOST HOSTILE OF ENVIRONMENTS. EACH SOLDIER A SEASONED VET.
ZUKE.
NO CAN DO, SARGE. MY ROCKETS WON'T PIERCE THAT THING'S ARMOR.
GET ME CLOSE ENOUGH, AND I'LL BLOW IT.
UGH. I'M OKAY.
IF THERE'S AN OUTSIDER IN THE BUNCH, IT'S ME.
FALL BACK.
WHAT?! ARE YOU CRAZY? WE DON'T--
I SAID, FALL BACK.
"TO THE NEAREST SEWAGE TUNNEL."
OUR LAST SARGE NEVER TOOK US THROUGH THE SEWER.
QUIET.
I SPENT THE LAST FEW YEARS ON SPECIAL ASSIGNMENT. DEEP UNDERCOVER ON NAR SHADDAA.
AFTER I SURVIVED THAT, I WAS TOLD I COULD HAVE WHATEVER ASSIGNMENT I WANTED. I CHOSE THIS.
I'M STILL TRYING TO DECIDE IF THAT WAS A GOOD IDEA.

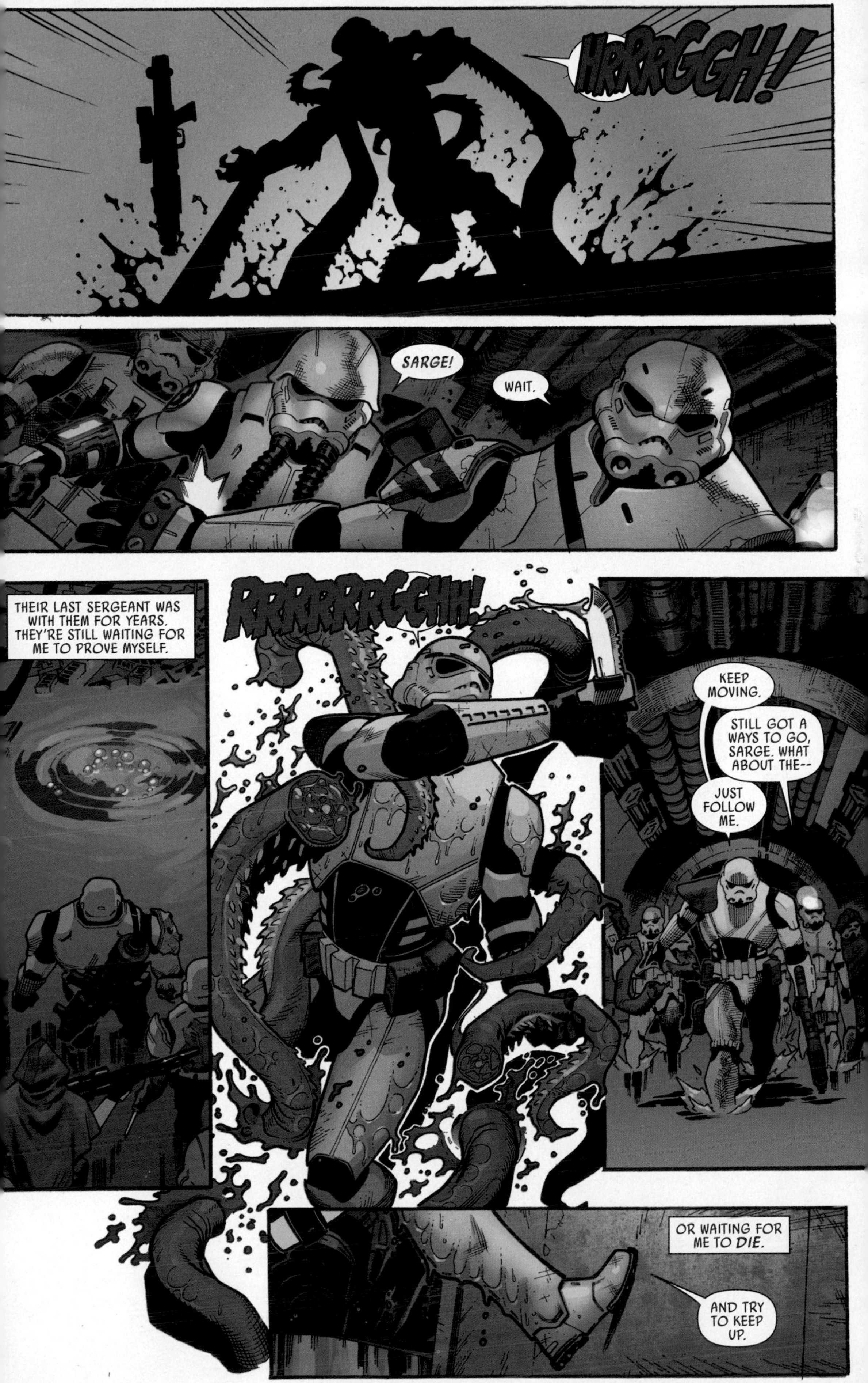
HRRRGGH!
SARGE!
WAIT.
THEIR LAST SERGEANT WAS WITH THEM FOR YEARS. THEY'RE STILL WAITING FOR ME TO PROVE MYSELF.
RRRRRRRGGHH!
KEEP MOVING.
STILL GOT A WAYS TO GO, SARGE. WHAT ABOUT THE--
JUST FOLLOW ME.
OR WAITING FOR ME TO *DIE*.
AND TRY TO KEEP UP.

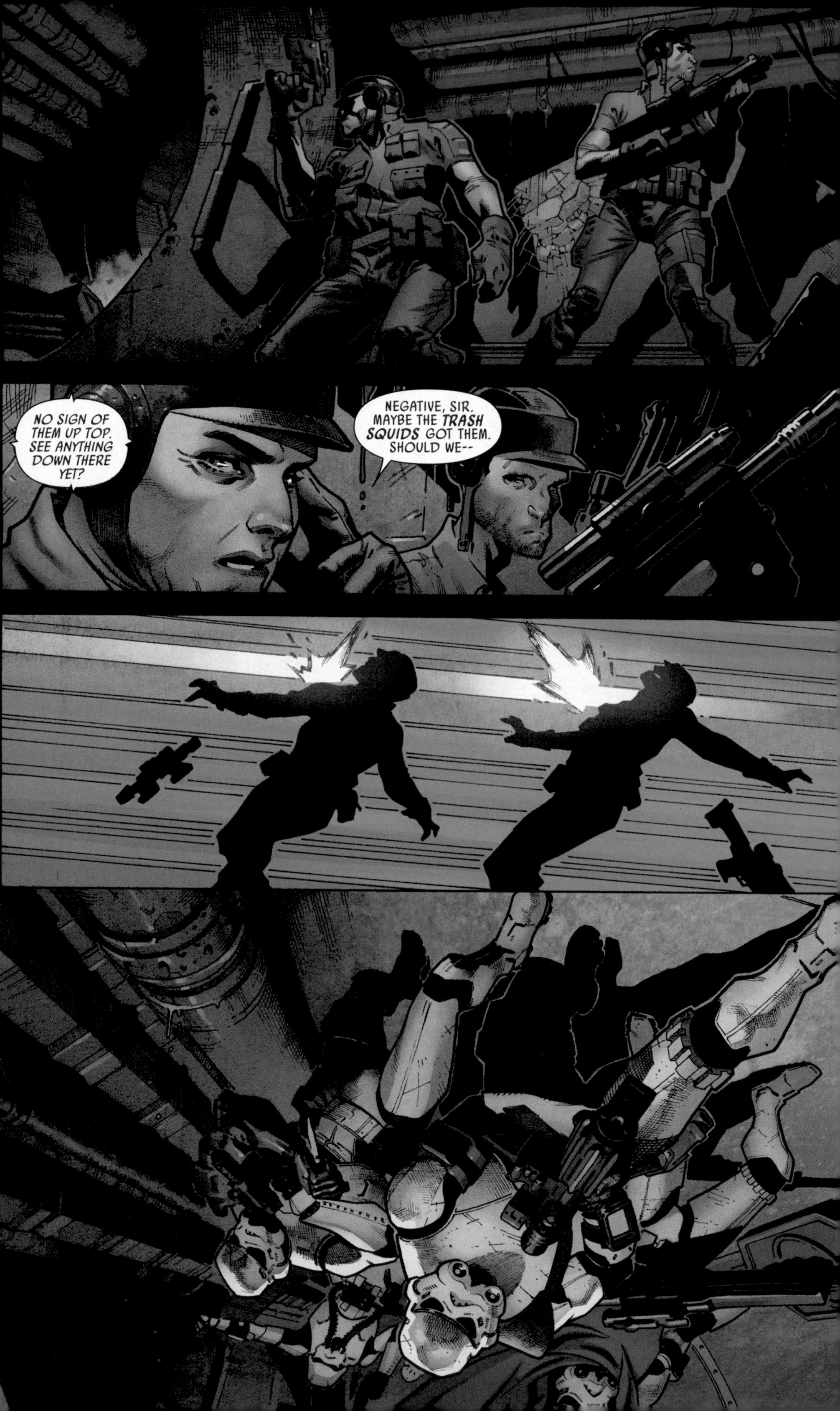
NO SIGN OF THEM UP TOP. SEE ANYTHING DOWN THERE YET?
NEGATIVE, SIR. MAYBE THE TRASH SQUIDS GOT THEM. SHOULD WE--

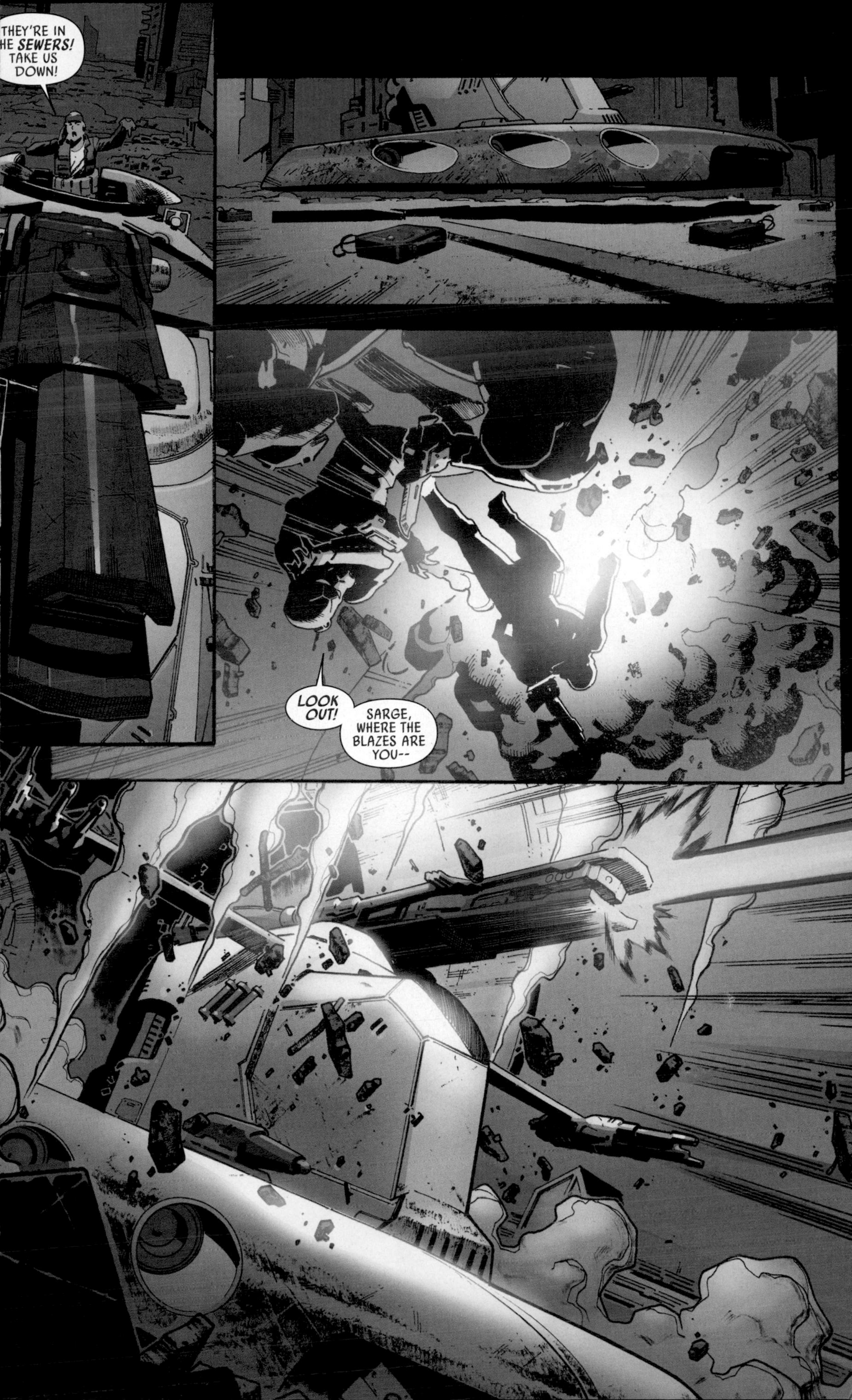
THEY'RE IN THE SEWERS! TAKE US DOWN!
LOOK OUT!
SARGE, WHERE THE BLAZES ARE YOU--

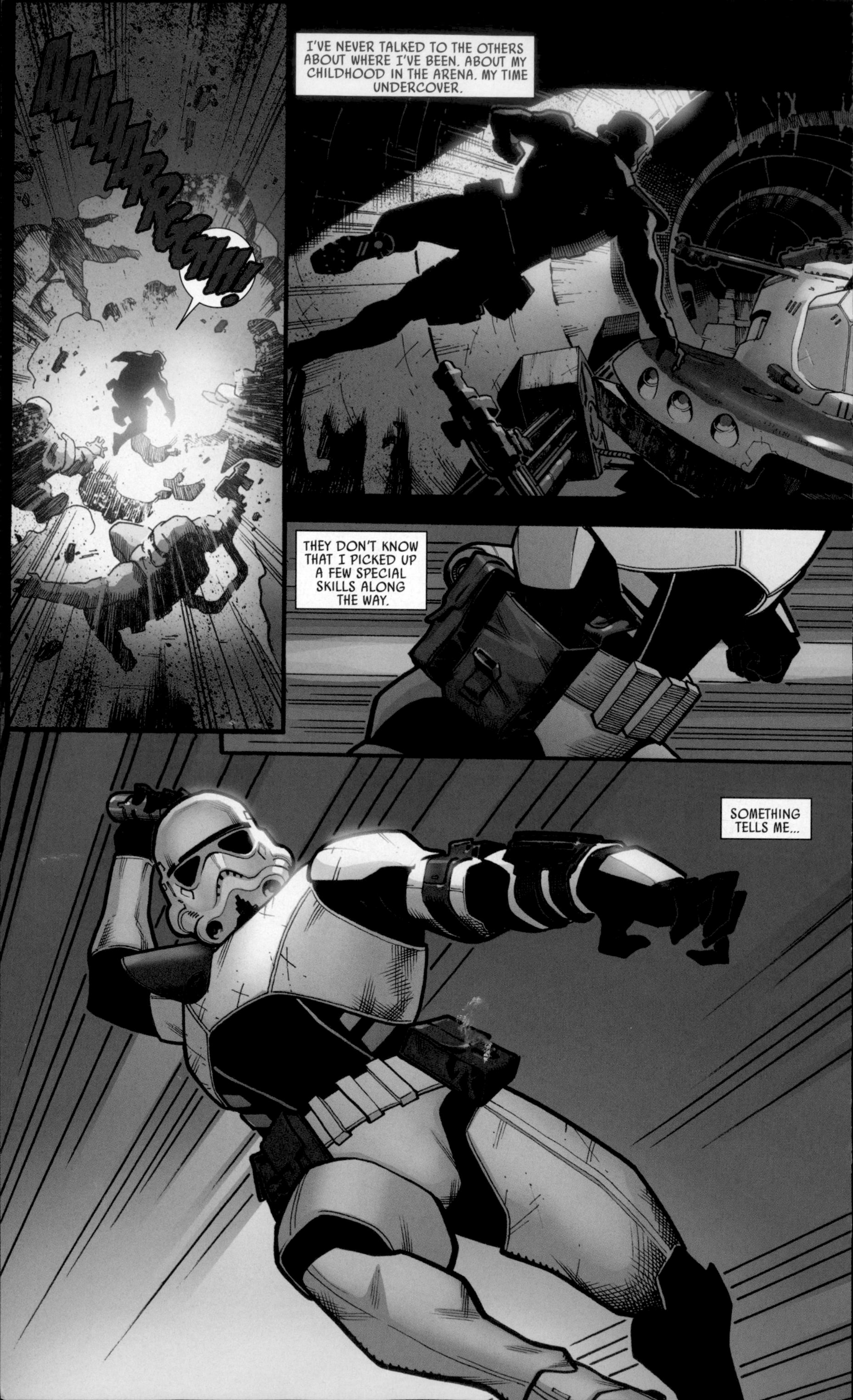
AAAAHHRRGGHH!
I'VE NEVER TALKED TO THE OTHERS ABOUT WHERE I'VE BEEN. ABOUT MY CHILDHOOD IN THE ARENA. MY TIME UNDERCOVER.
THEY DON'T KNOW THAT I PICKED UP A FEW SPECIAL SKILLS ALONG THE WAY.
SOMETHING TELLS ME...

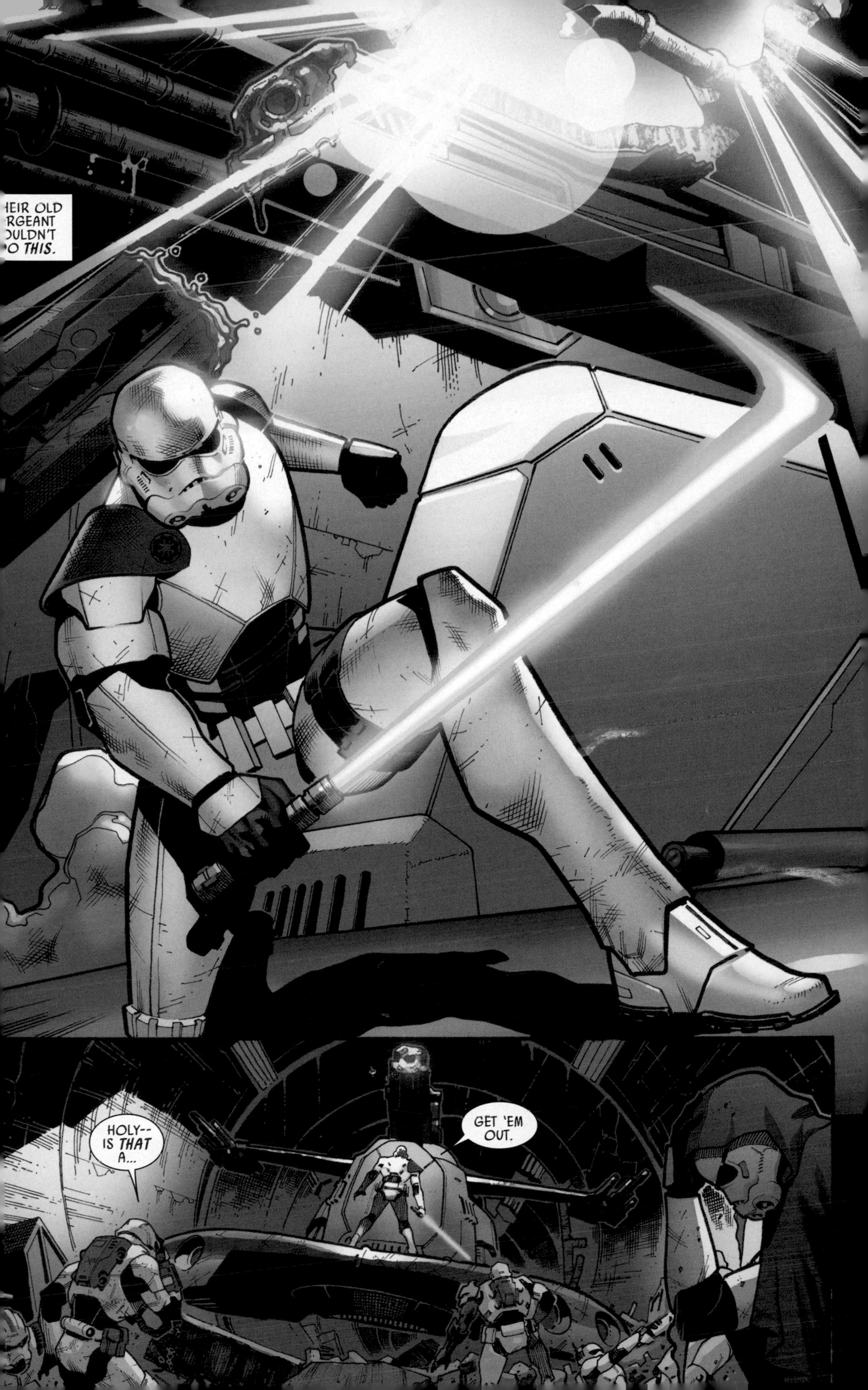
HEIR OLD
RGEANT
OULDN'T
O THIS.
HOLY-- IS THAT A...
GET 'EM OUT.

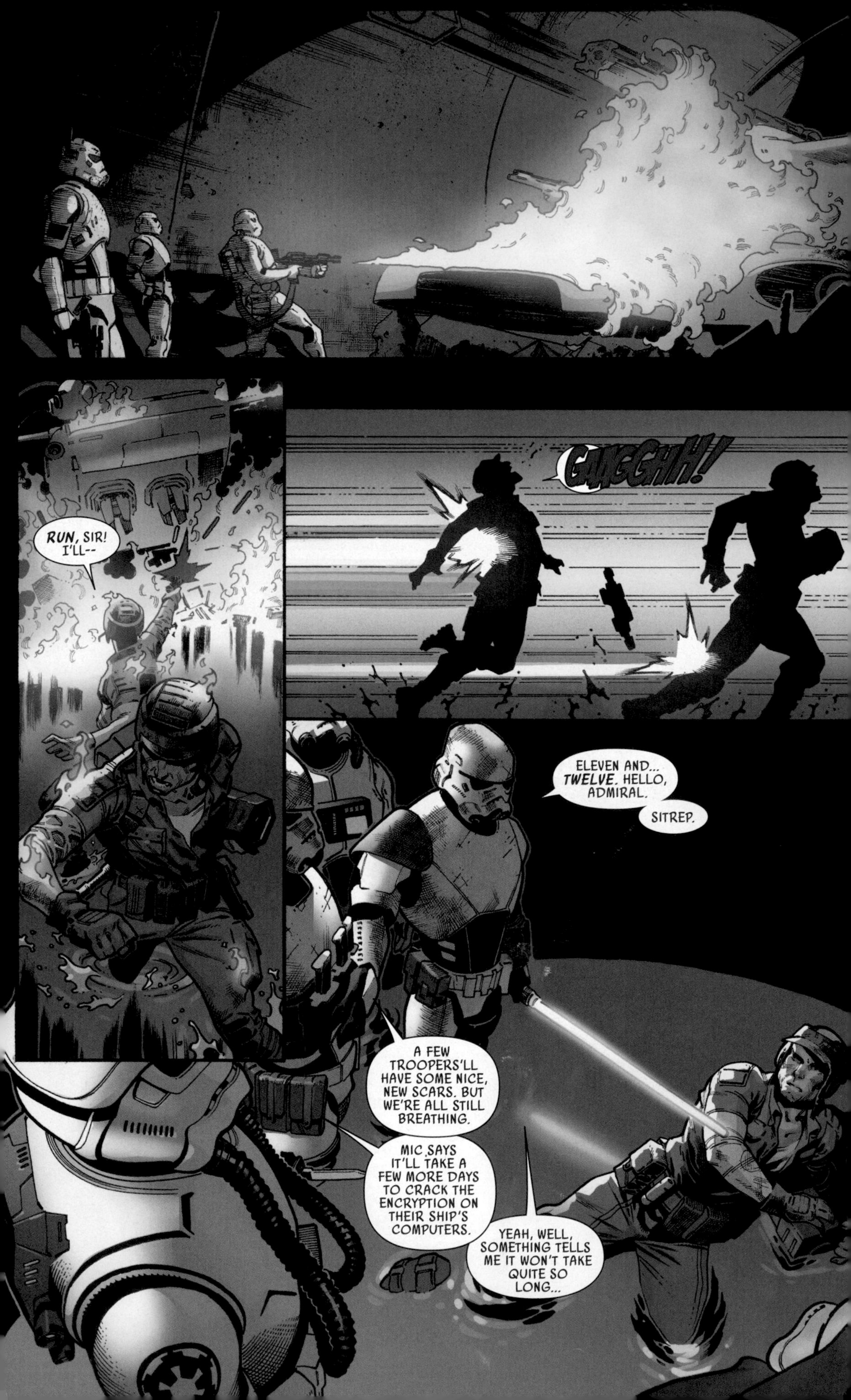
RUN, SIR! I'LL--
GUUGGHH!
ELEVEN AND... TWELVE. HELLO, ADMIRAL.
SITREP.
A FEW TROOPERS'LL HAVE SOME NICE, NEW SCARS. BUT WE'RE ALL STILL BREATHING.
MIC SAYS IT'LL TAKE A FEW MORE DAYS TO CRACK THE ENCRYPTION ON THEIR SHIP'S COMPUTERS.
YEAH, WELL, SOMETHING TELLS ME IT WON'T TAKE QUITE SO LONG...

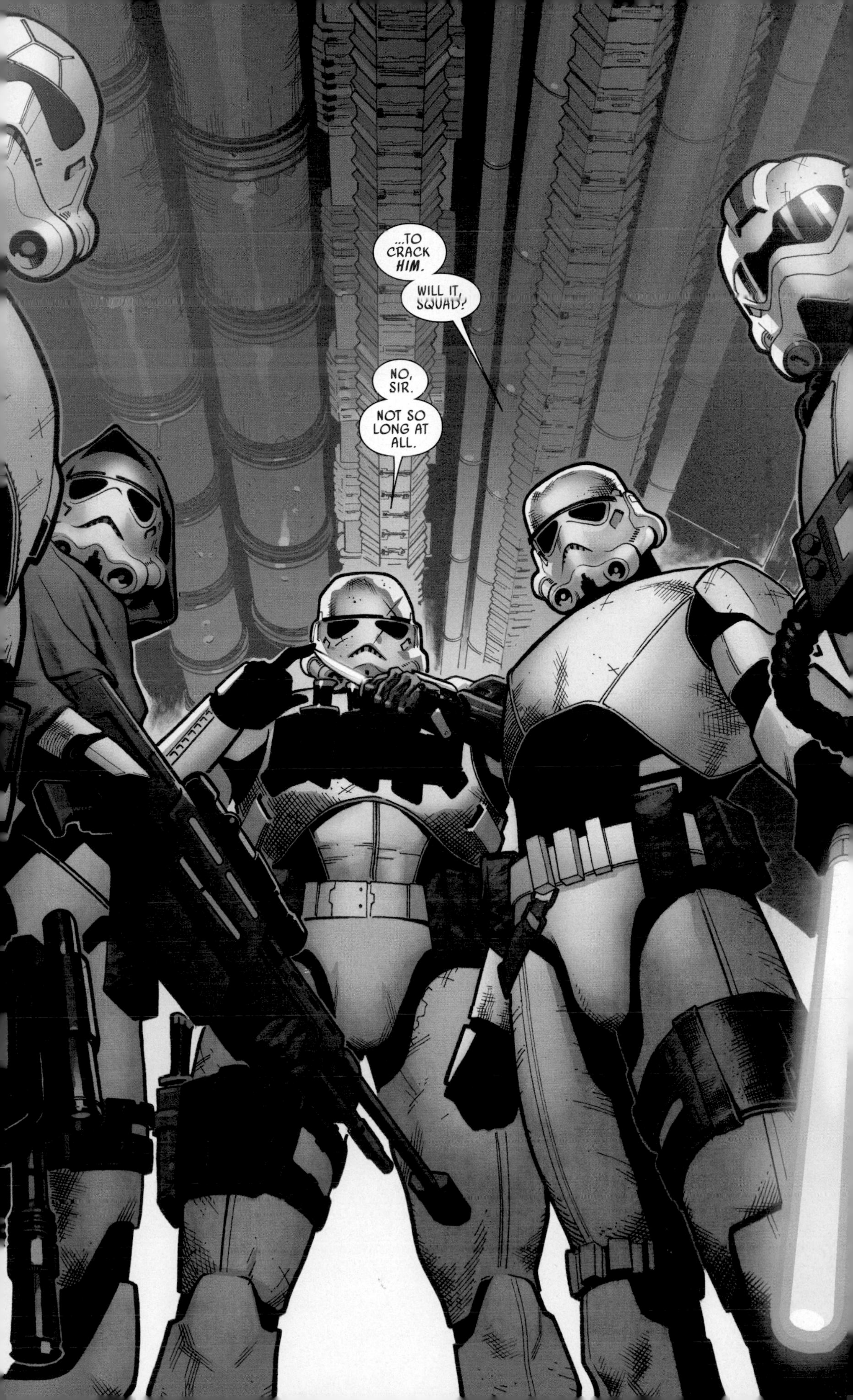
...TO CRACK HIM.
WILL IT, SQUAD?
NO, SIR.
NOT SO LONG AT ALL.

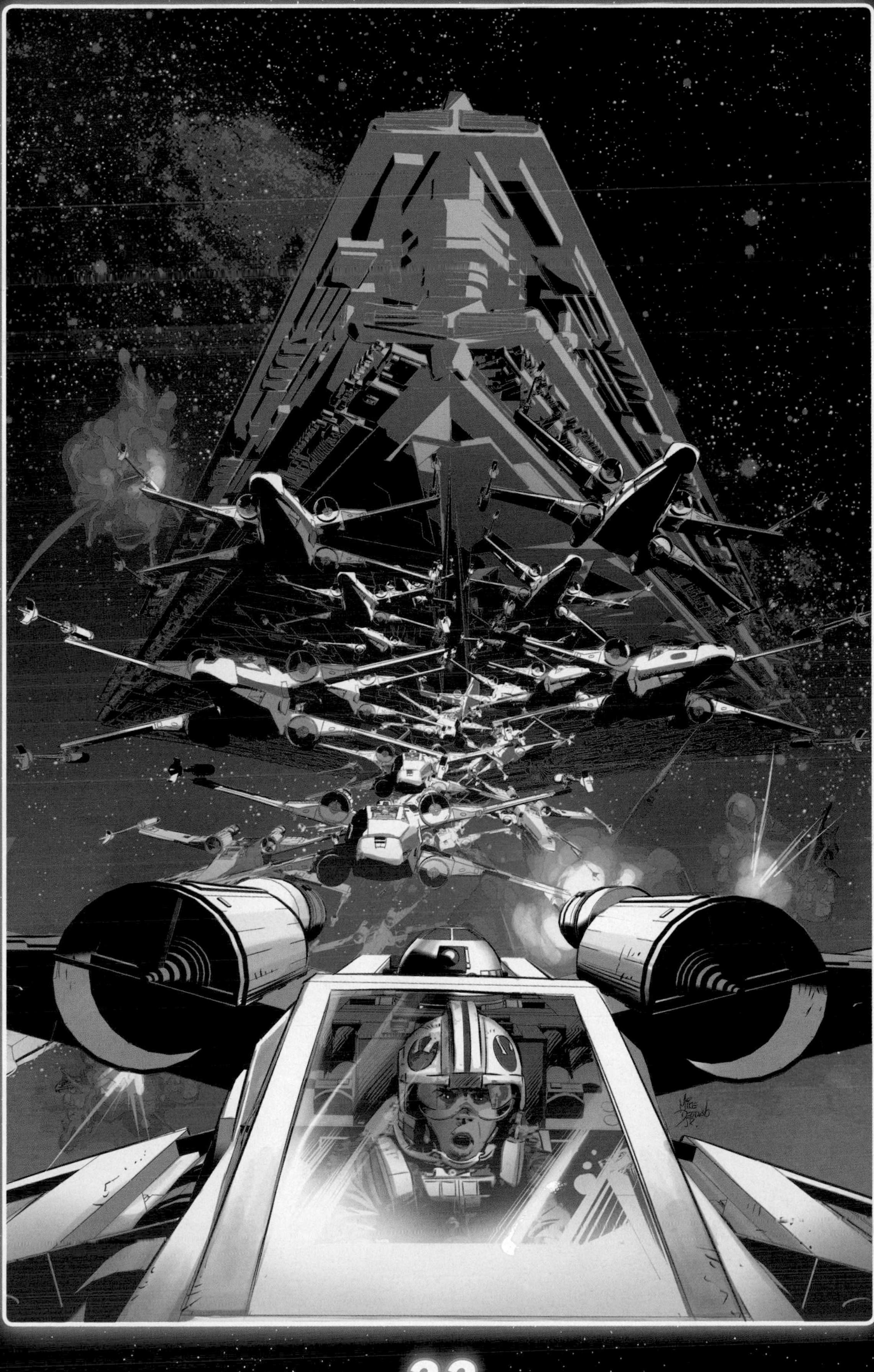

22

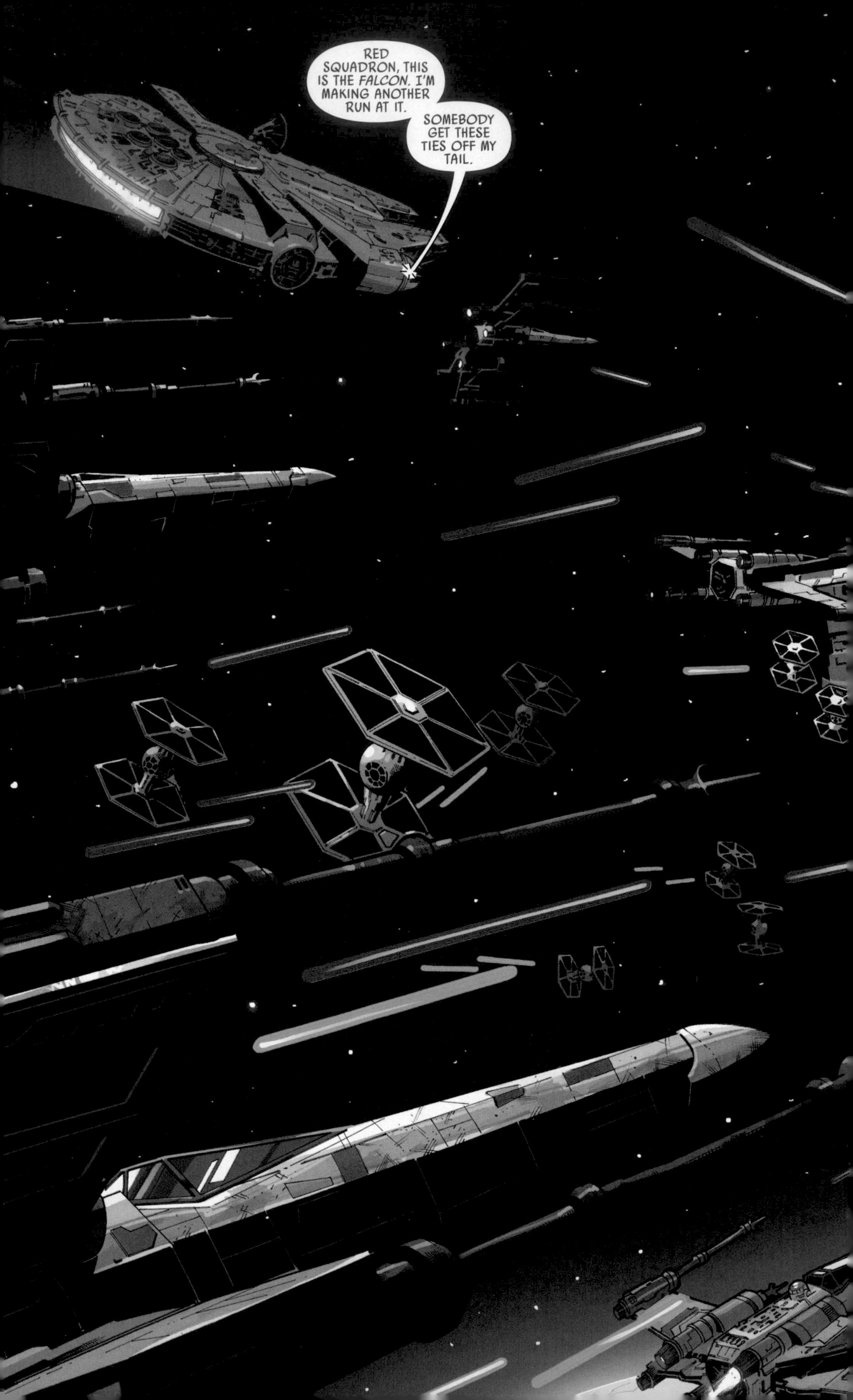
RED SQUADRON, THIS IS THE *FALCON*. I'M MAKING ANOTHER RUN AT IT.
SOMEBODY GET THESE TIES OFF MY TAIL.

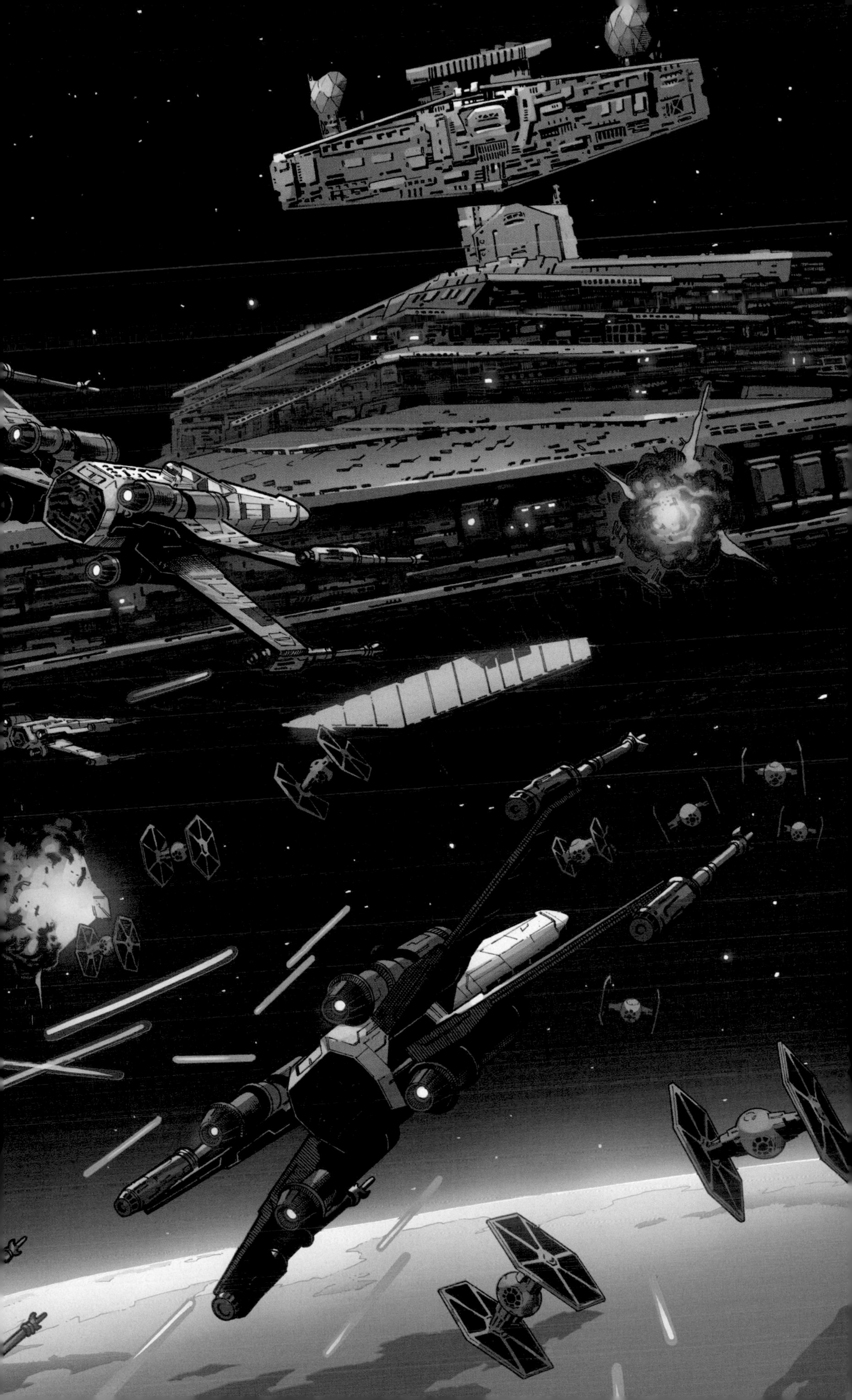

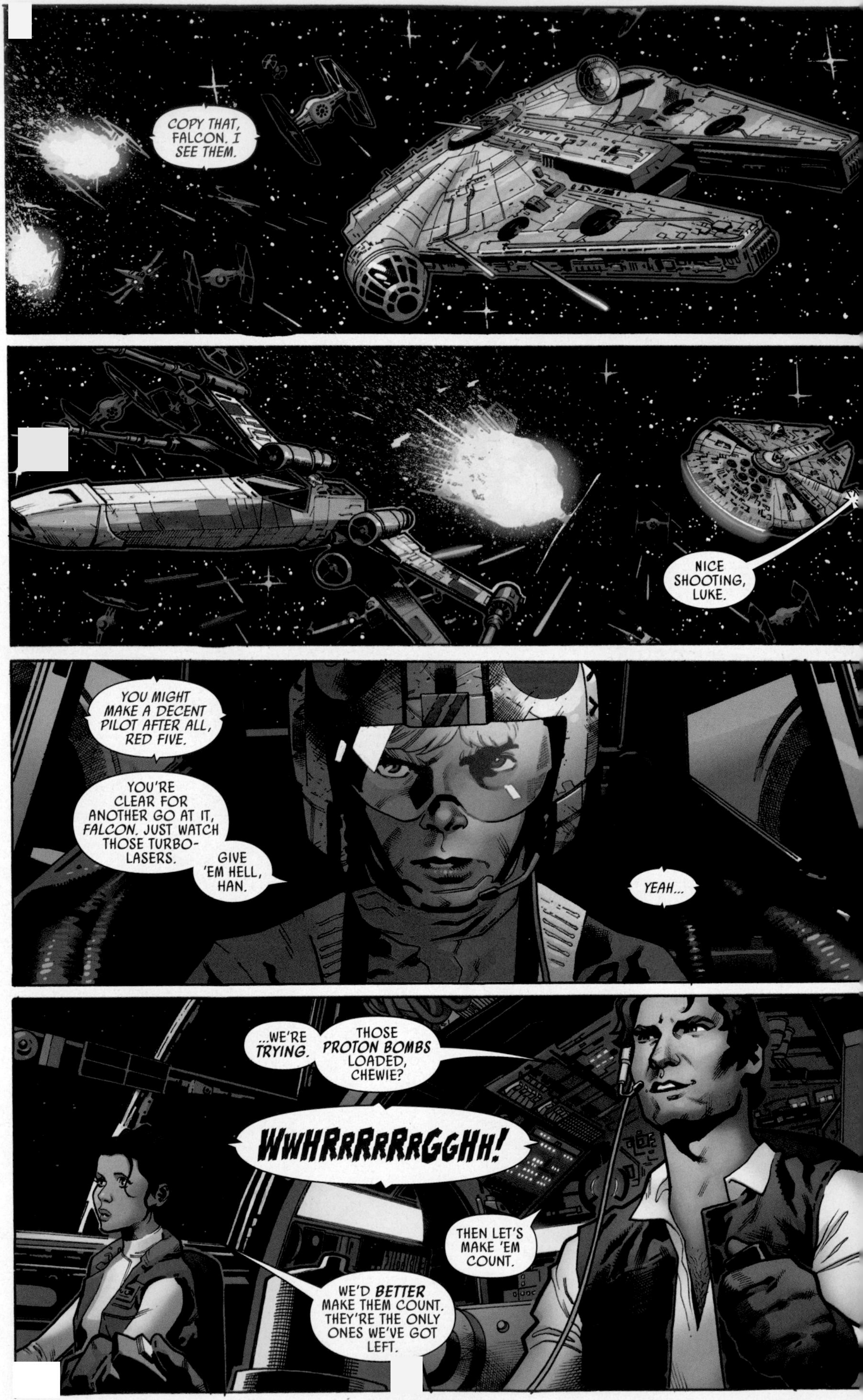
COPY THAT, FALCON. I SEE THEM.
NICE SHOOTING, LUKE.
YOU MIGHT MAKE A DECENT PILOT AFTER ALL, RED FIVE.
YOU'RE CLEAR FOR ANOTHER GO AT IT, FALCON. JUST WATCH THOSE TURBO-LASERS.
GIVE 'EM HELL, HAN.
YEAH...
...WE'RE TRYING.
THOSE PROTON BOMBS LOADED, CHEWIE?
WWHRRRRRRRGGHH!
THEN LET'S MAKE 'EM COUNT.
WE'D BETTER MAKE THEM COUNT. THEY'RE THE ONLY ONES WE'VE GOT LEFT.

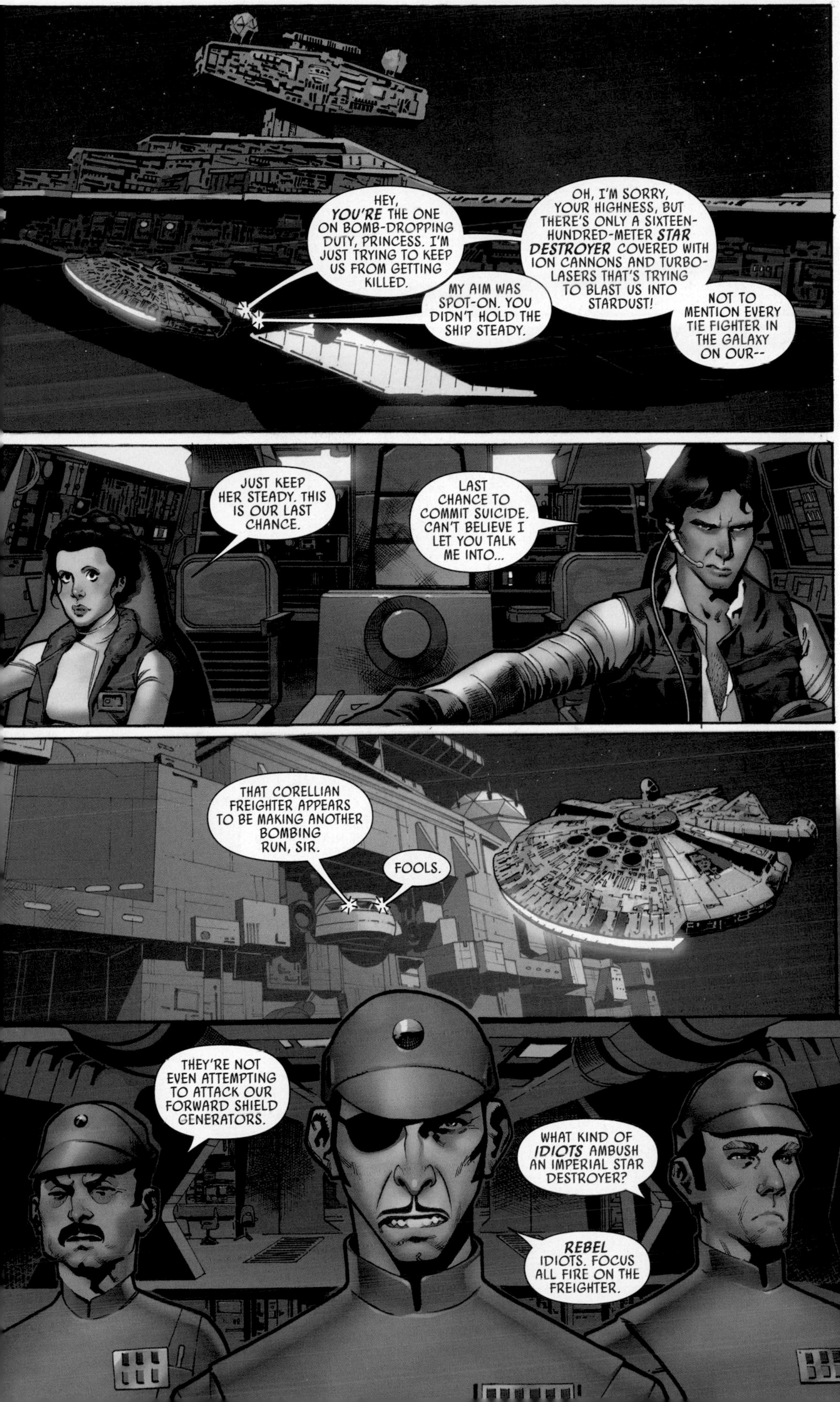
HEY, *YOU'RE* THE ONE ON BOMB-DROPPING DUTY, PRINCESS. I'M JUST TRYING TO KEEP US FROM GETTING KILLED.
MY AIM WAS SPOT-ON. YOU DIDN'T HOLD THE SHIP STEADY.
OH, I'M SORRY, YOUR HIGHNESS, BUT THERE'S ONLY A SIXTEEN-HUNDRED-METER *STAR DESTROYER* COVERED WITH ION CANNONS AND TURBO-LASERS THAT'S TRYING TO BLAST US INTO STARDUST!
NOT TO MENTION EVERY TIE FIGHTER IN THE GALAXY ON OUR--
JUST KEEP HER STEADY. THIS IS OUR LAST CHANCE.
LAST CHANCE TO COMMIT SUICIDE. CAN'T BELIEVE I LET YOU TALK ME INTO...
THAT CORELLIAN FREIGHTER APPEARS TO BE MAKING ANOTHER BOMBING RUN, SIR.
FOOLS.
THEY'RE NOT EVEN ATTEMPTING TO ATTACK OUR FORWARD SHIELD GENERATORS.
WHAT KIND OF *IDIOTS* AMBUSH AN IMPERIAL STAR DESTROYER?
REBEL IDIOTS. FOCUS ALL FIRE ON THE FREIGHTER.

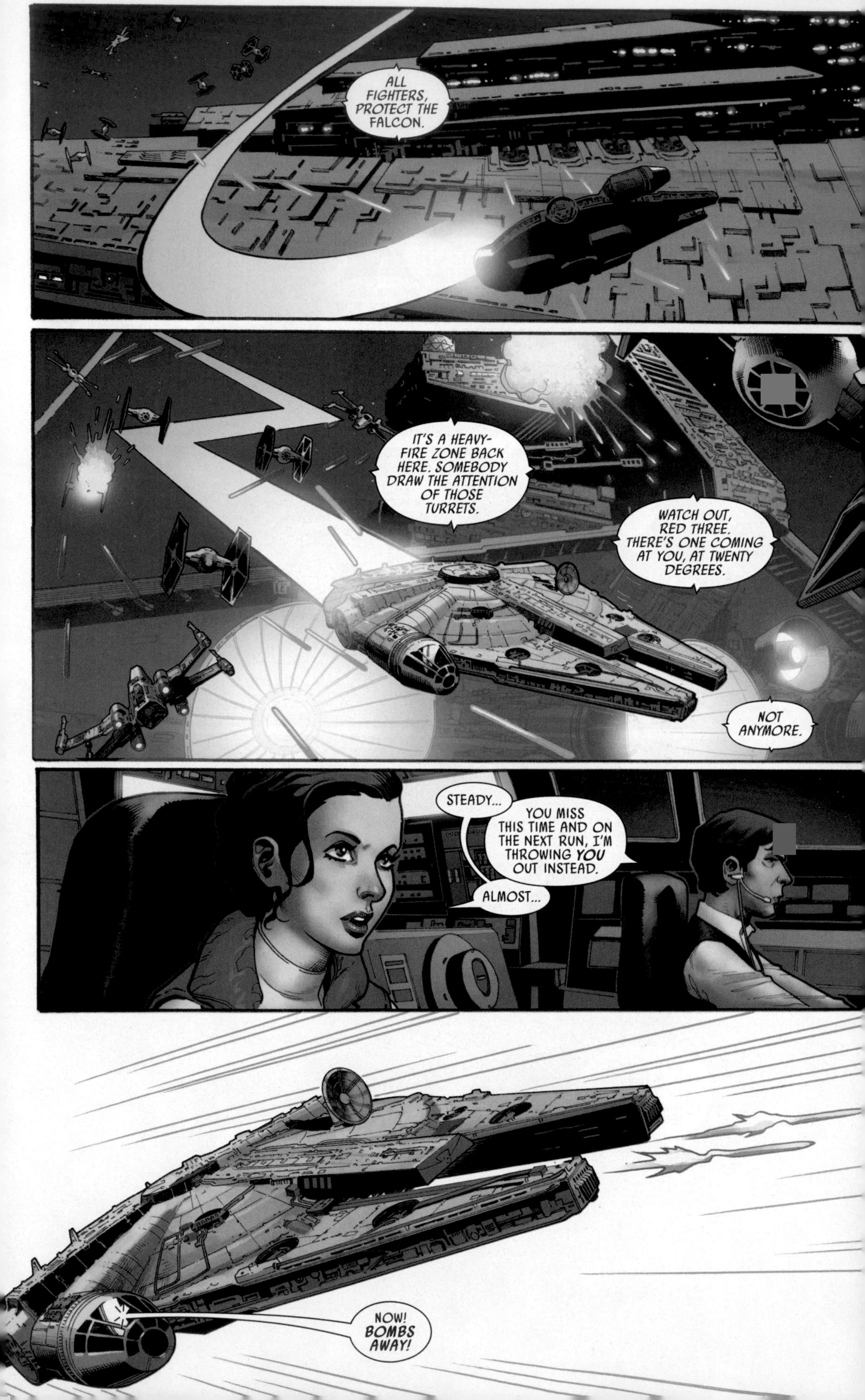
ALL FIGHTERS, PROTECT THE FALCON.
IT'S A HEAVY-FIRE ZONE BACK HERE. SOMEBODY DRAW THE ATTENTION OF THOSE TURRETS.
WATCH OUT, RED THREE. THERE'S ONE COMING AT YOU, AT TWENTY DEGREES.
NOT ANYMORE.
STEADY...
ALMOST...
YOU MISS THIS TIME AND ON THE NEXT RUN, I'M THROWING *YOU* OUT INSTEAD.
NOW! BOMBS AWAY!

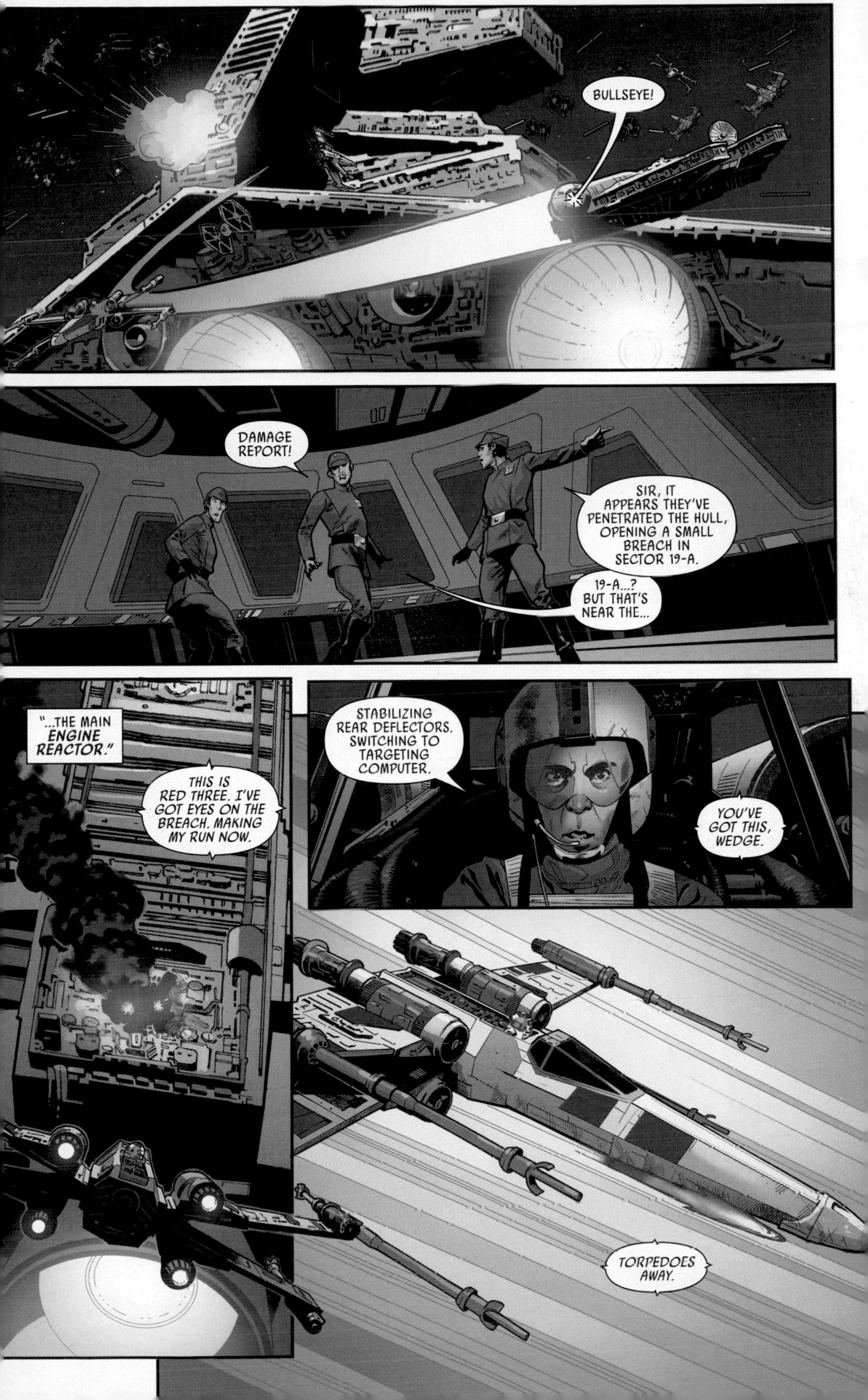
BULLSEYE!
DAMAGE REPORT!
SIR, IT APPEARS THEY'VE PENETRATED THE HULL, OPENING A SMALL BREACH IN SECTOR 19-A.
19-A...? BUT THAT'S NEAR THE...
"...THE MAIN ENGINE REACTOR."
THIS IS RED THREE. I'VE GOT EYES ON THE BREACH. MAKING MY RUN NOW.
STABILIZING REAR DEFLECTORS. SWITCHING TO TARGETING COMPUTER.
YOU'VE GOT THIS, WEDGE.
TORPEDOES AWAY.

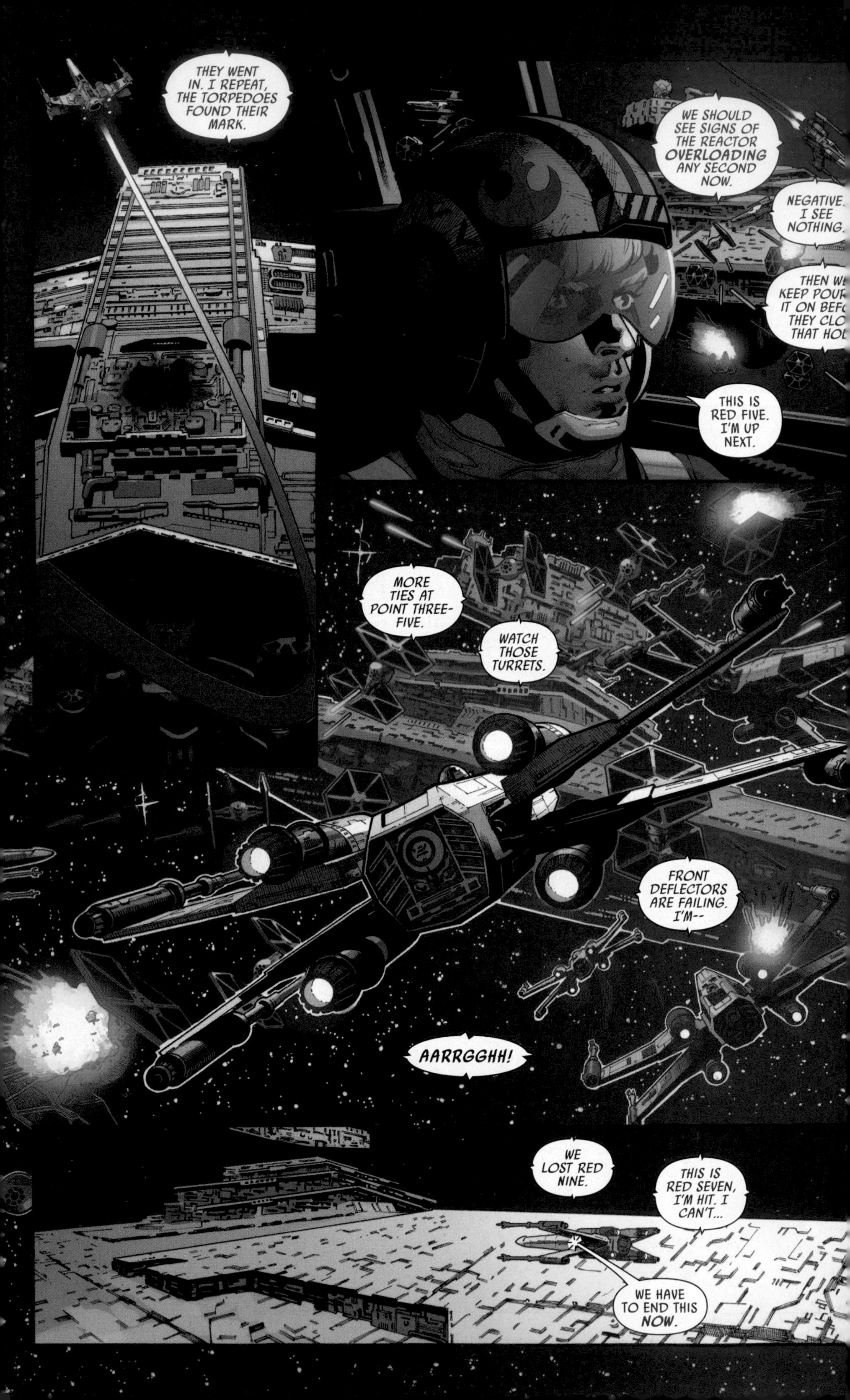

THEY WENT IN. I REPEAT, THE TORPEDOES FOUND THEIR MARK.
WE SHOULD SEE SIGNS OF THE REACTOR OVERLOADING ANY SECOND NOW.
NEGATIVE. I SEE NOTHING.
THEN WE KEEP POUR IT ON BEF THEY CLO THAT HO
THIS IS RED FIVE. I'M UP NEXT.
MORE TIES AT POINT THREE-FIVE.
WATCH THOSE TURRETS.
FRONT DEFLECTORS ARE FAILING. I'M--
AARRGGHH!
WE LOST RED NINE.
THIS IS RED SEVEN, I'M HIT. I CAN'T...
WE HAVE TO END THIS NOW.

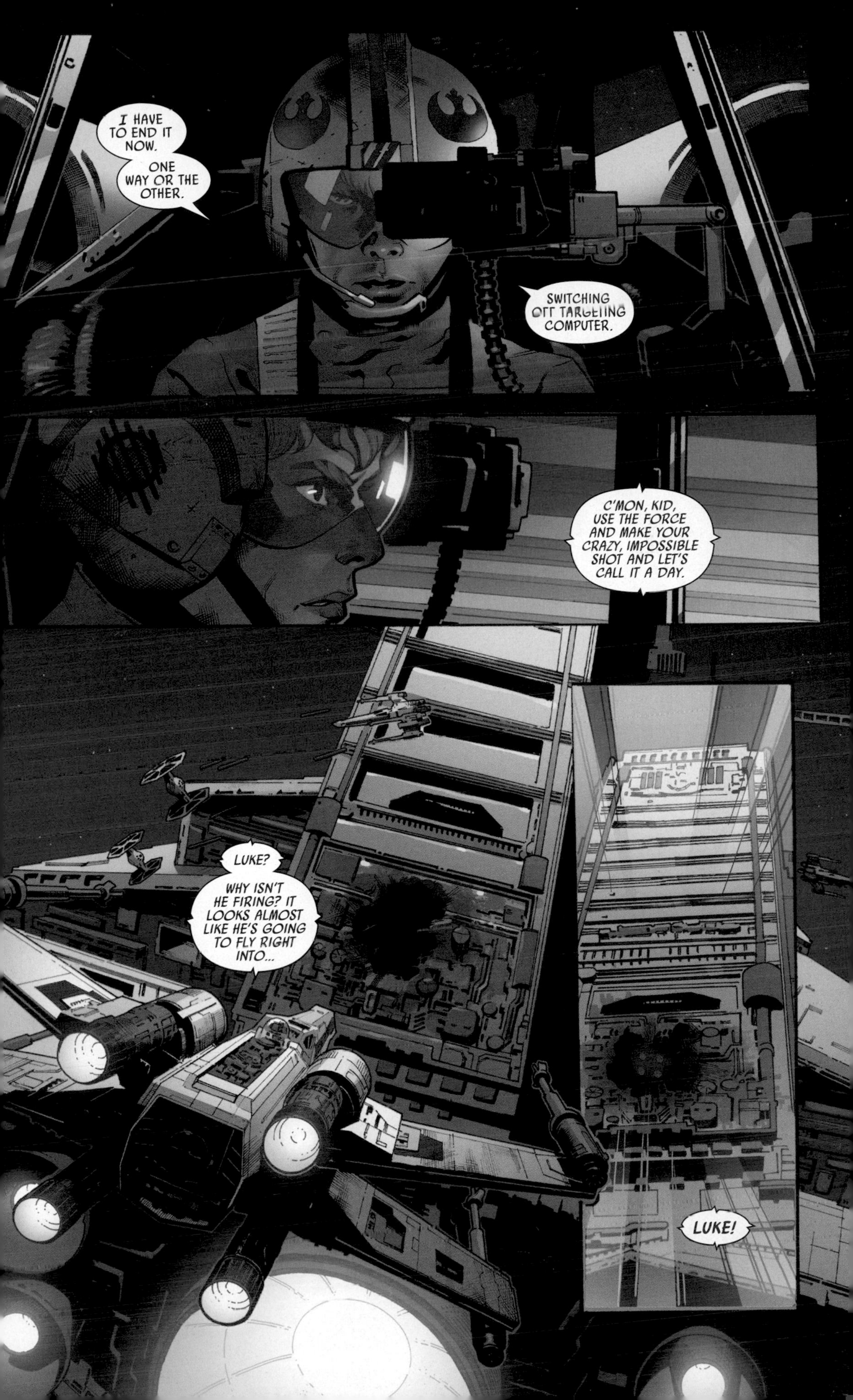
I HAVE TO END IT NOW.
ONE WAY OR THE OTHER.
SWITCHING OFF TARGETING COMPUTER.
C'MON, KID, USE THE FORCE AND MAKE YOUR CRAZY, IMPOSSIBLE SHOT AND LET'S CALL IT A DAY.
LUKE?
WHY ISN'T HE FIRING? IT LOOKS ALMOST LIKE HE'S GOING TO FLY RIGHT INTO...
LUKE!

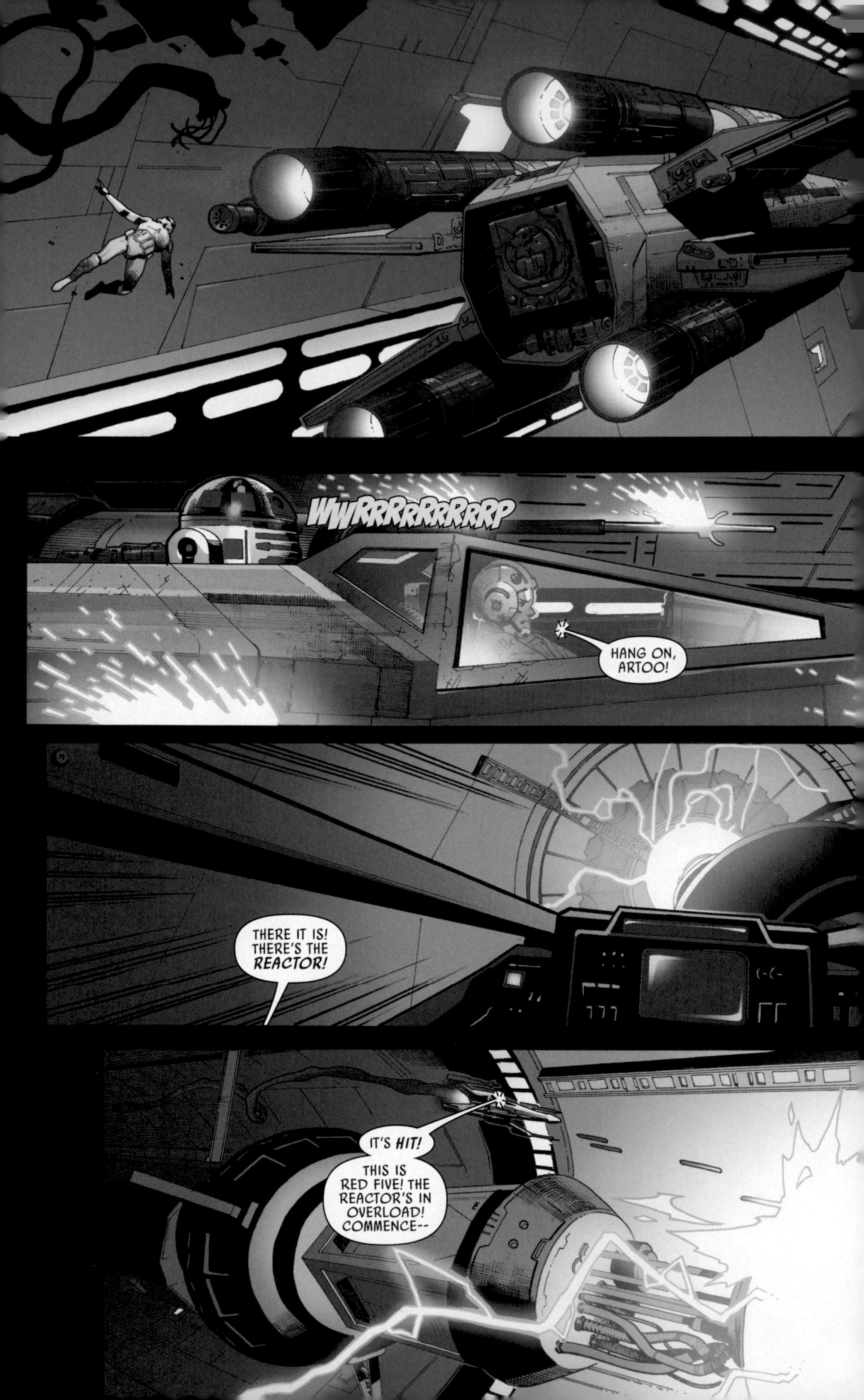
WWRRRRRRRRRP
HANG ON, ARTOO!
THERE IT IS! THERE'S THE REACTOR!
IT'S HIT!
THIS IS RED FIVE! THE REACTOR'S IN OVERLOAD! COMMENCE--

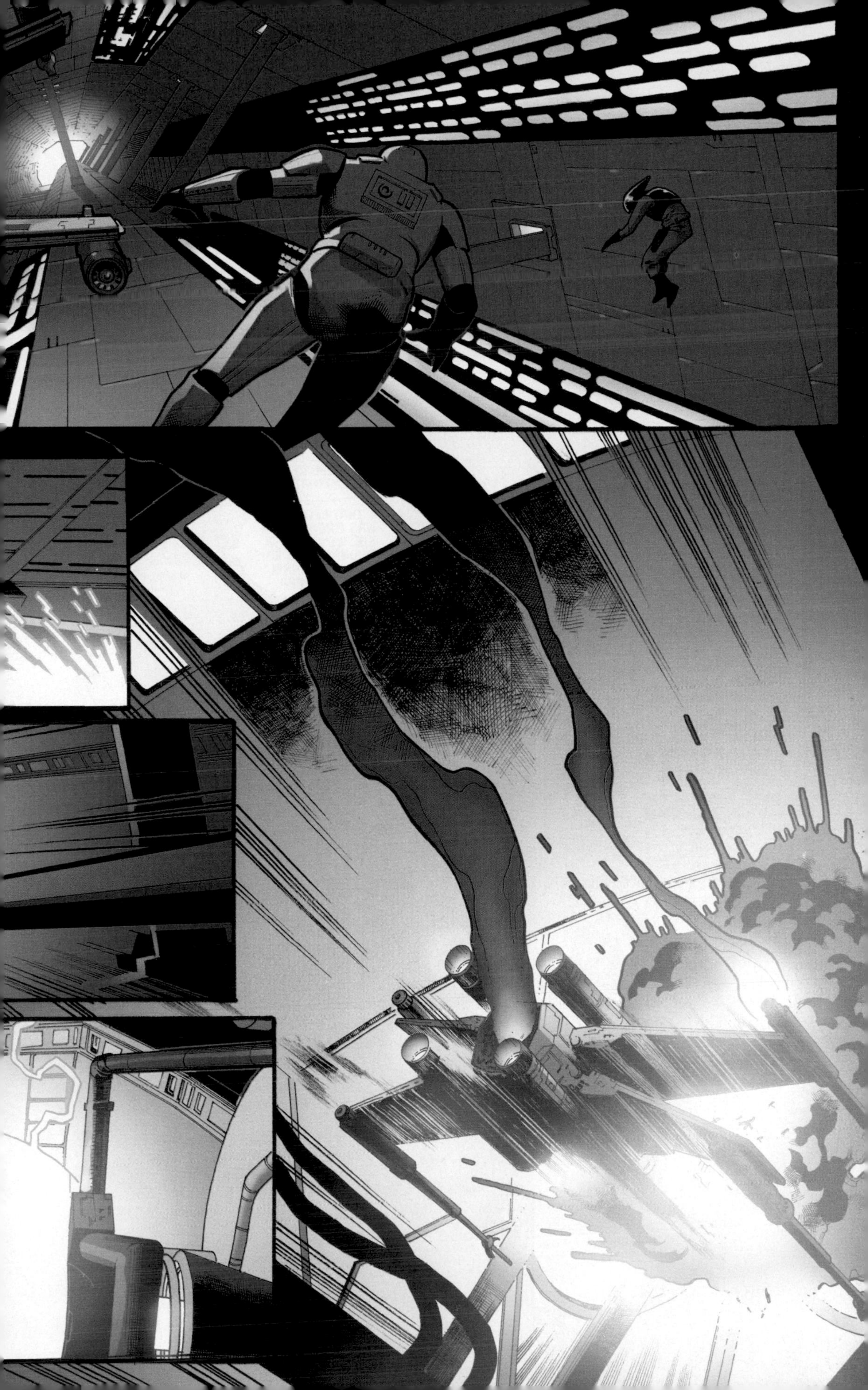

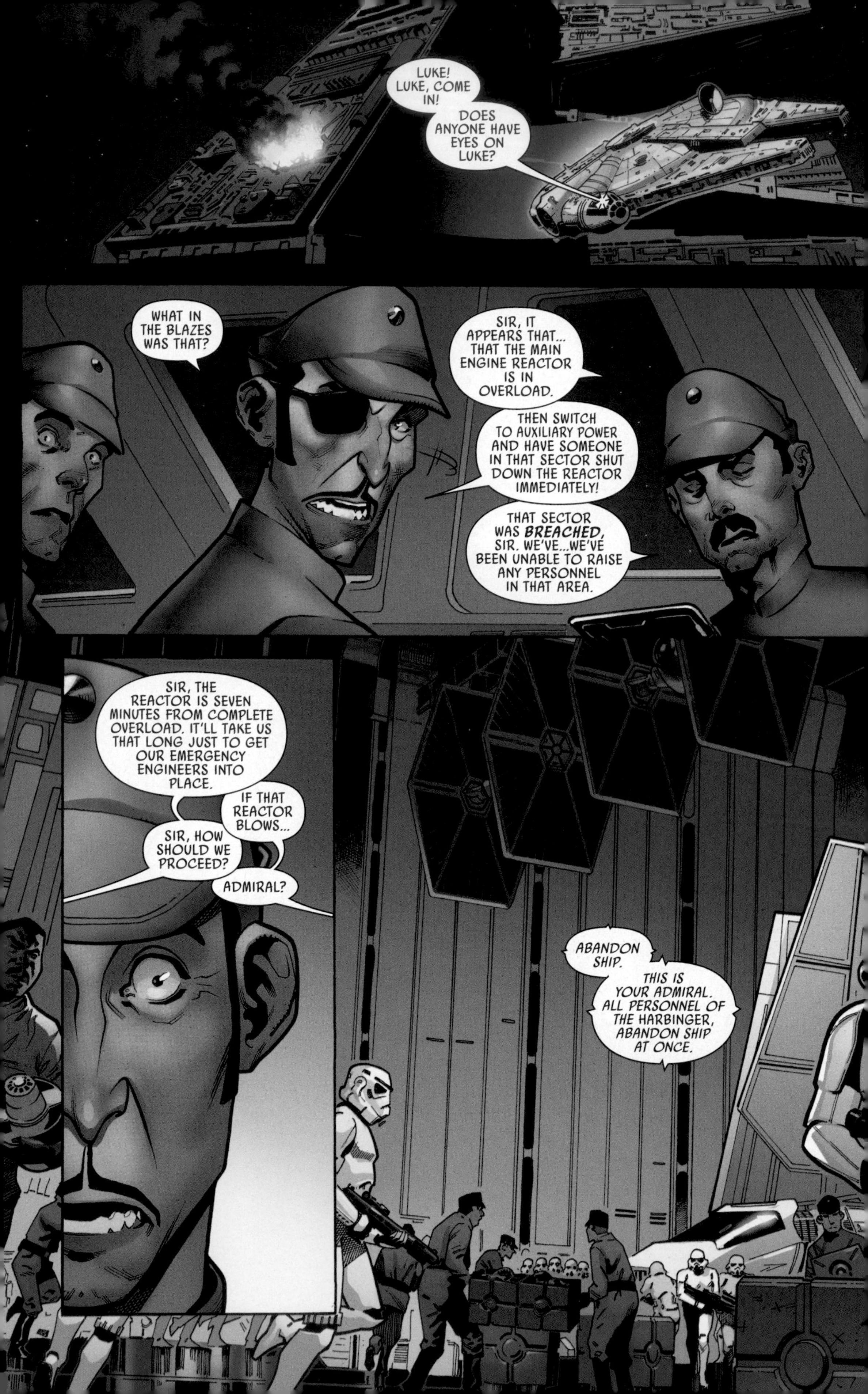
LUKE! LUKE, COME IN!
DOES ANYONE HAVE EYES ON LUKE?
WHAT IN THE BLAZES WAS THAT?
SIR, IT APPEARS THAT... THAT THE MAIN ENGINE REACTOR IS IN OVERLOAD.
THEN SWITCH TO AUXILIARY POWER AND HAVE SOMEONE IN THAT SECTOR SHUT DOWN THE REACTOR IMMEDIATELY!
THAT SECTOR WAS BREACHED, SIR. WE'VE...WE'VE BEEN UNABLE TO RAISE ANY PERSONNEL IN THAT AREA.
SIR, THE REACTOR IS SEVEN MINUTES FROM COMPLETE OVERLOAD. IT'LL TAKE US THAT LONG JUST TO GET OUR EMERGENCY ENGINEERS INTO PLACE.
IF THAT REACTOR BLOWS...
SIR, HOW SHOULD WE PROCEED?
ADMIRAL?
ABANDON SHIP.
THIS IS YOUR ADMIRAL. ALL PERSONNEL OF THE HARBINGER, ABANDON SHIP AT ONCE.

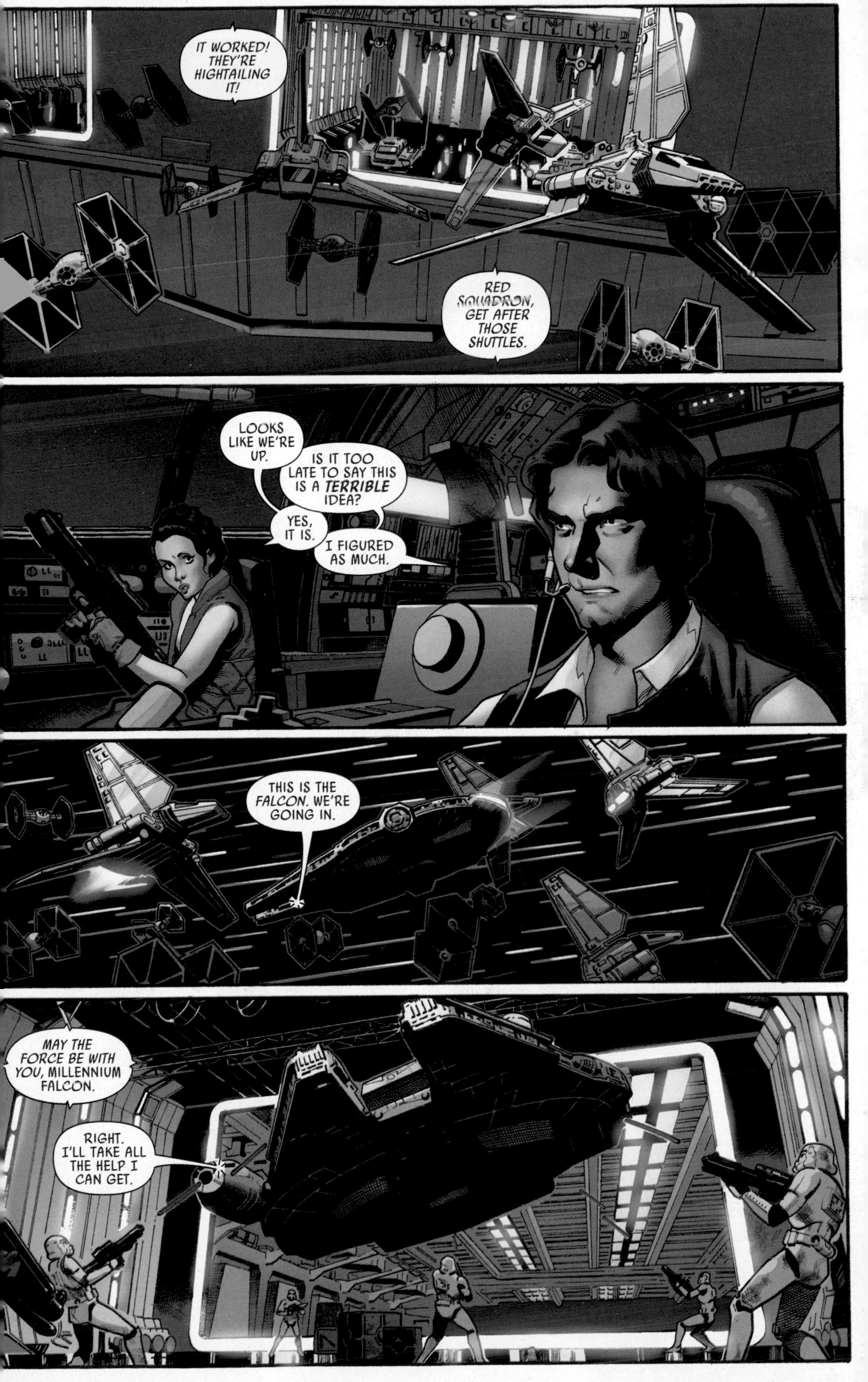
IT WORKED! THEY'RE HIGHTAILING IT!
RED SQUADRON, GET AFTER THOSE SHUTTLES.
LOOKS LIKE WE'RE UP.
IS IT TOO LATE TO SAY THIS IS A TERRIBLE IDEA?
YES, IT IS.
I FIGURED AS MUCH.
THIS IS THE FALCON. WE'RE GOING IN.
MAY THE FORCE BE WITH YOU, MILLENNIUM FALCON.
RIGHT. I'LL TAKE ALL THE HELP I CAN GET.

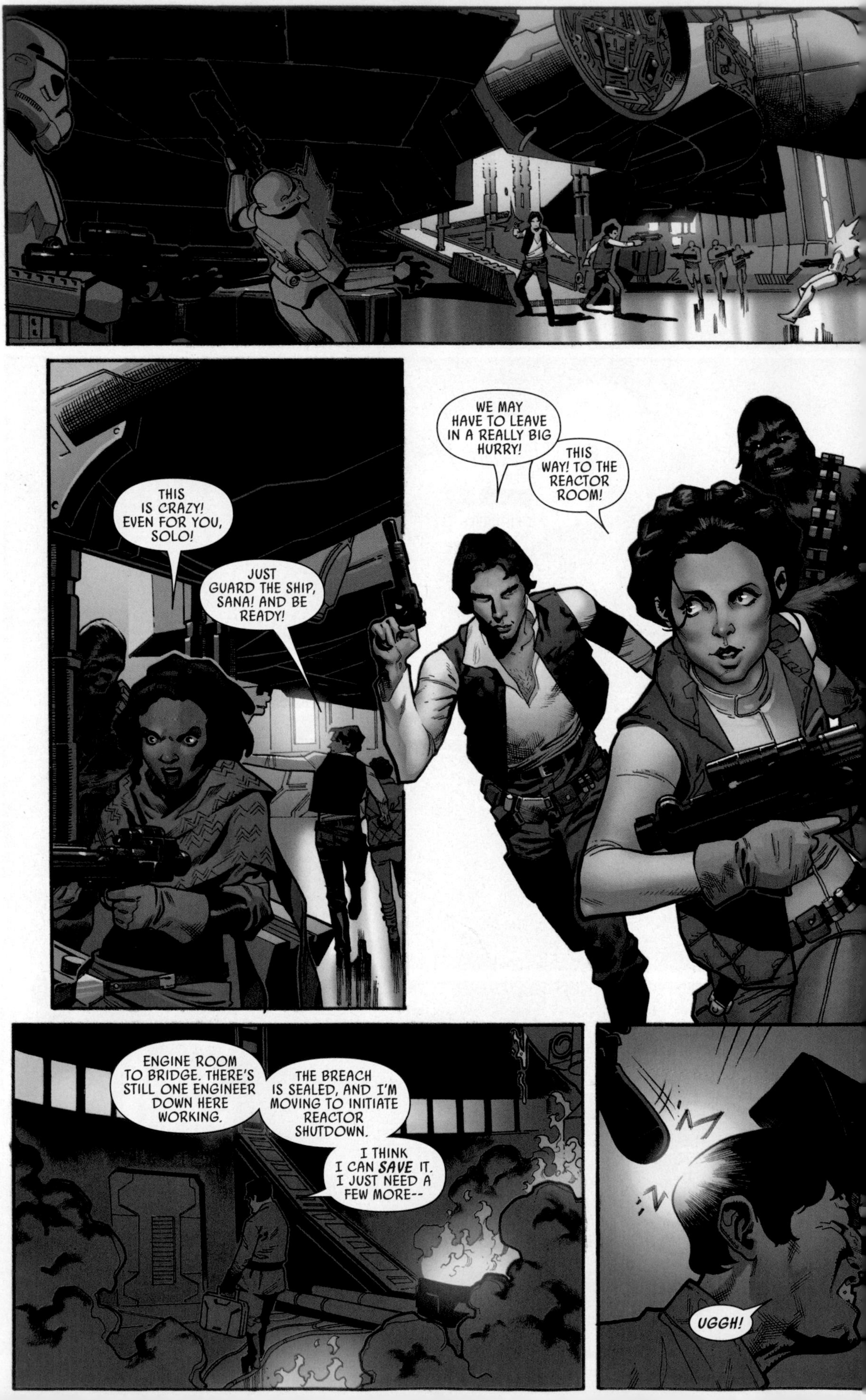
THIS IS CRAZY! EVEN FOR YOU, SOLO!
JUST GUARD THE SHIP, SANA! AND BE READY!
WE MAY HAVE TO LEAVE IN A REALLY BIG HURRY!
THIS WAY! TO THE REACTOR ROOM!
ENGINE ROOM TO BRIDGE. THERE'S STILL ONE ENGINEER DOWN HERE WORKING.
THE BREACH IS SEALED, AND I'M MOVING TO INITIATE REACTOR SHUTDOWN.
I THINK I CAN *SAVE* IT. I JUST NEED A FEW MORE--
UGGH!

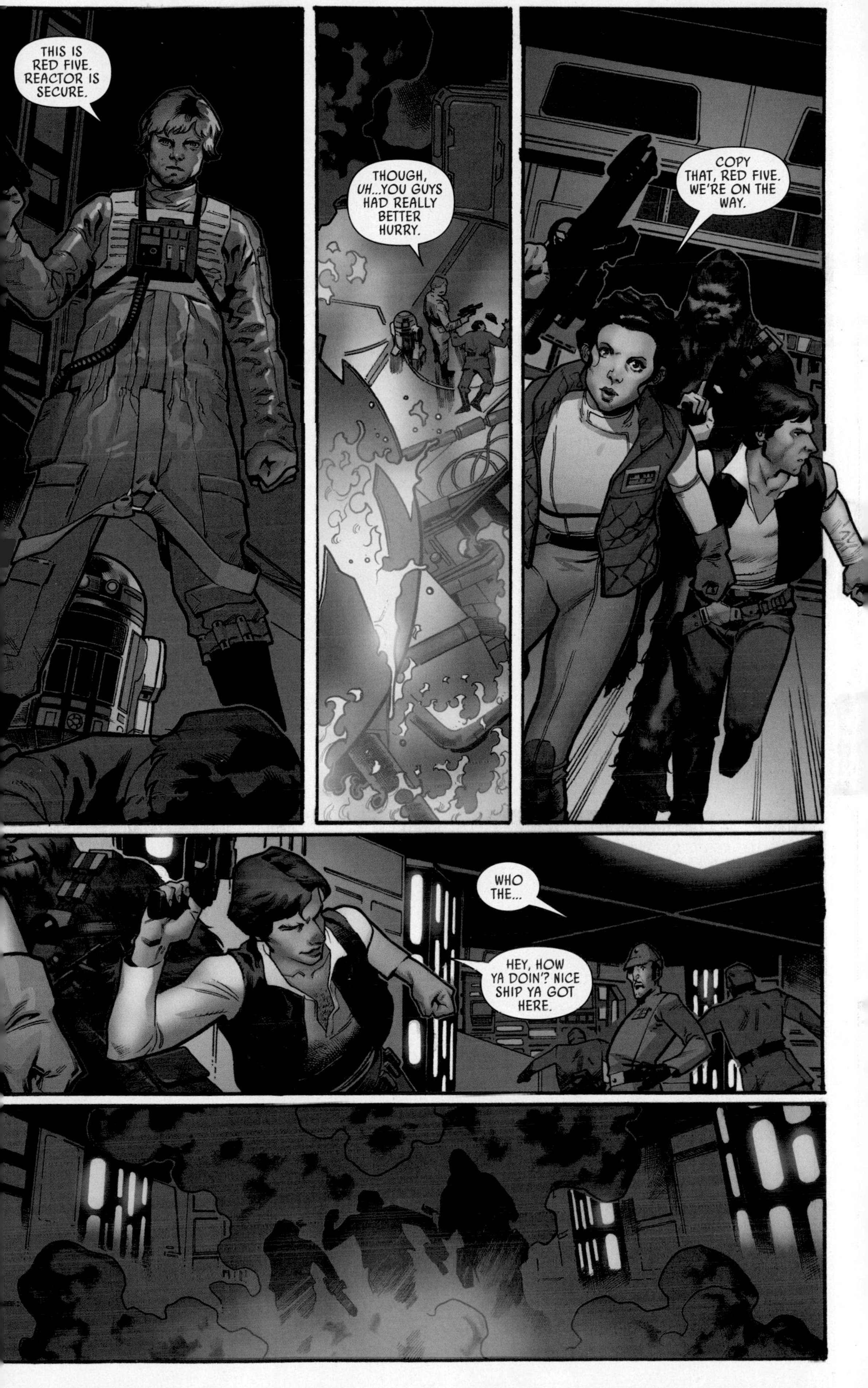
THIS IS RED FIVE. REACTOR IS SECURE.
THOUGH, UH...YOU GUYS HAD REALLY BETTER HURRY.
COPY THAT, RED FIVE. WE'RE ON THE WAY.
WHO THE...
HEY, HOW YA DOIN'? NICE SHIP YA GOT HERE.

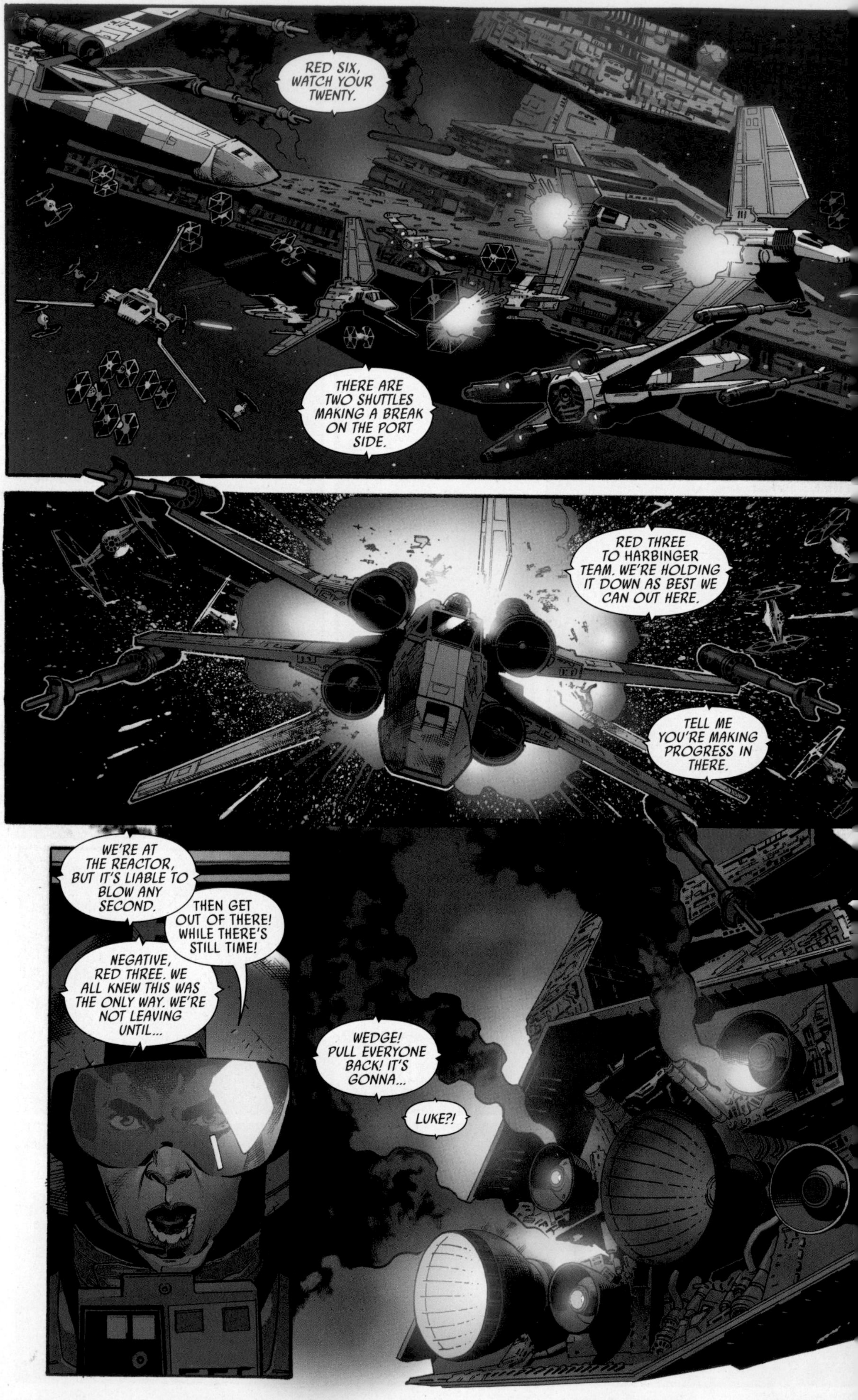
RED SIX, WATCH YOUR TWENTY.
THERE ARE TWO SHUTTLES MAKING A BREAK ON THE PORT SIDE.
RED THREE TO HARBINGER TEAM. WE'RE HOLDING IT DOWN AS BEST WE CAN OUT HERE.
TELL ME YOU'RE MAKING PROGRESS IN THERE.
WE'RE AT THE REACTOR, BUT IT'S LIABLE TO BLOW ANY SECOND.
THEN GET OUT OF THERE! WHILE THERE'S STILL TIME!
NEGATIVE, RED THREE. WE ALL KNEW THIS WAS THE ONLY WAY. WE'RE NOT LEAVING UNTIL...
WEDGE! PULL EVERYONE BACK! IT'S GONNA...
LUKE?!

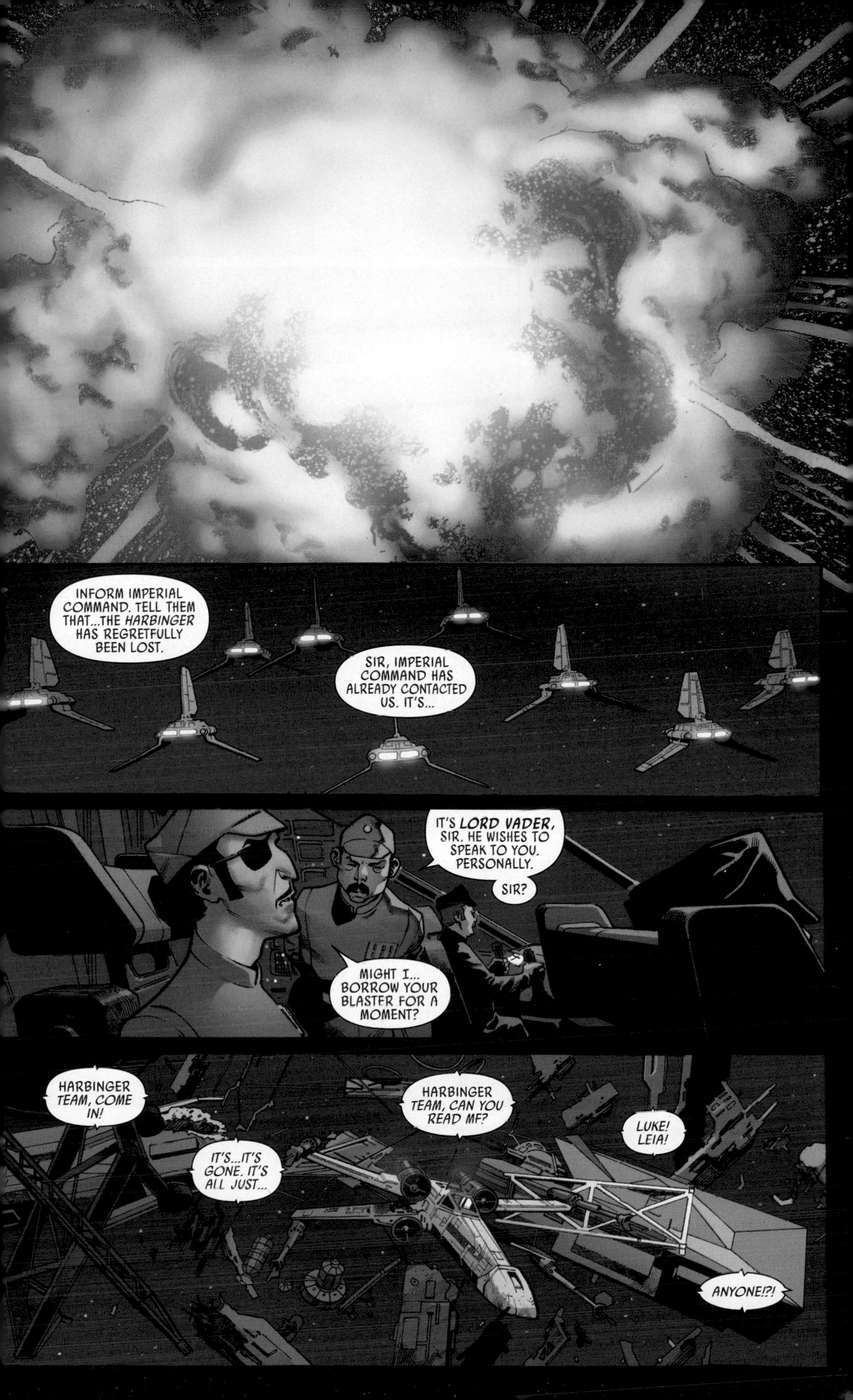
INFORM IMPERIAL COMMAND. TELL THEM THAT...THE *HARBINGER* HAS REGRETFULLY BEEN LOST.
SIR, IMPERIAL COMMAND HAS ALREADY CONTACTED US. IT'S...
IT'S ***LORD VADER***, SIR. HE WISHES TO SPEAK TO YOU. PERSONALLY.
SIR?
MIGHT I... BORROW YOUR BLASTER FOR A MOMENT?
HARBINGER TEAM, COME IN!
IT'S...IT'S GONE. IT'S ALL JUST...
HARBINGER TEAM, CAN YOU READ MF?
LUKE! LEIA!
ANYONE!?!

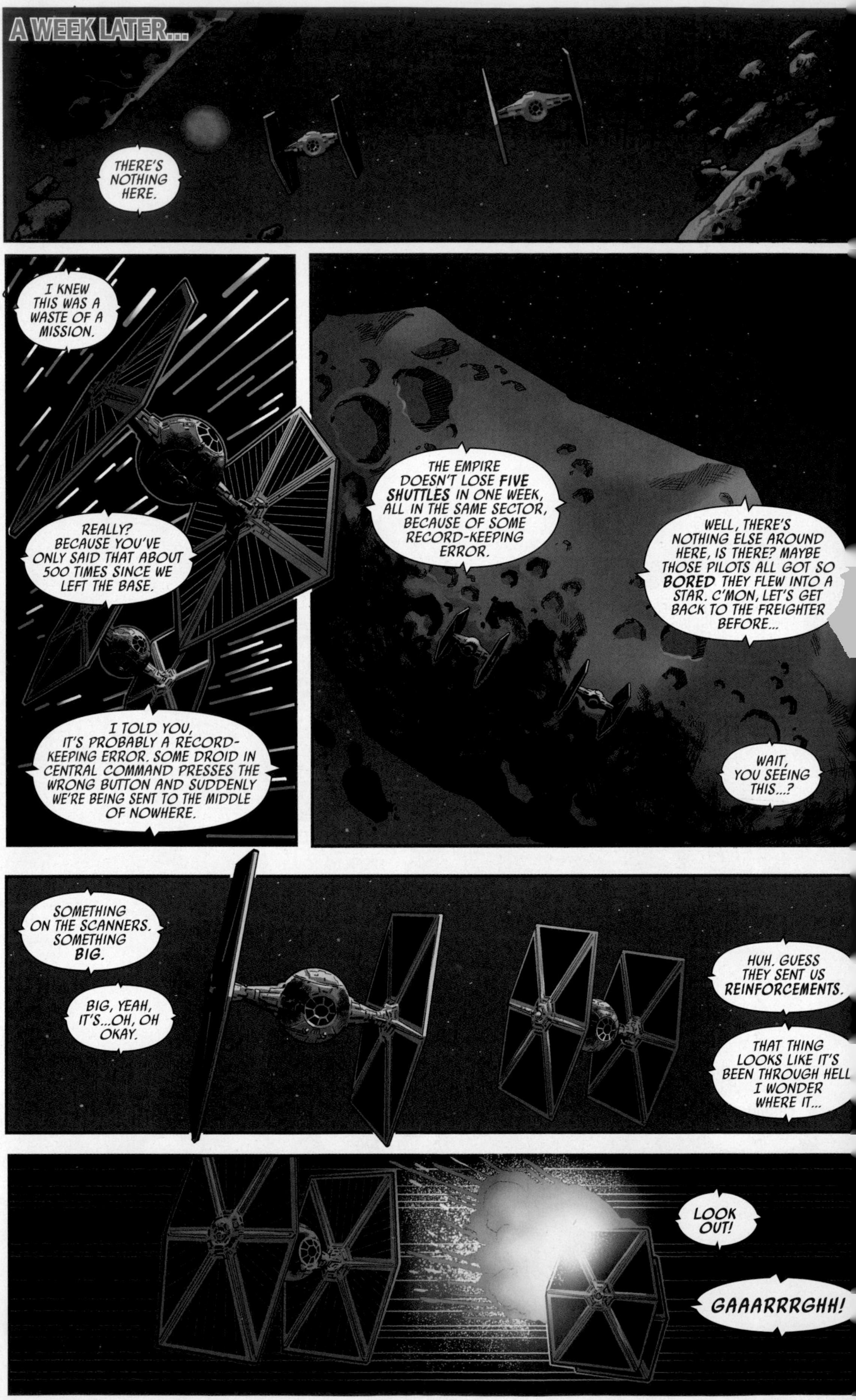
A WEEK LATER...
THERE'S NOTHING HERE.
I KNEW THIS WAS A WASTE OF A MISSION.
REALLY? BECAUSE YOU'VE ONLY SAID THAT ABOUT 500 TIMES SINCE WE LEFT THE BASE.
I TOLD YOU, IT'S PROBABLY A RECORD-KEEPING ERROR. SOME DROID IN CENTRAL COMMAND PRESSES THE WRONG BUTTON AND SUDDENLY WE'RE BEING SENT TO THE MIDDLE OF NOWHERE.
THE EMPIRE DOESN'T LOSE FIVE SHUTTLES IN ONE WEEK, ALL IN THE SAME SECTOR, BECAUSE OF SOME RECORD-KEEPING ERROR.
WELL, THERE'S NOTHING ELSE AROUND HERE, IS THERE? MAYBE THOSE PILOTS ALL GOT SO BORED THEY FLEW INTO A STAR. C'MON, LET'S GET BACK TO THE FREIGHTER BEFORE...
WAIT, YOU SEEING THIS...?
SOMETHING ON THE SCANNERS. SOMETHING BIG.
BIG, YEAH, IT'S...OH, OH OKAY.
HUH. GUESS THEY SENT US REINFORCEMENTS.
THAT THING LOOKS LIKE IT'S BEEN THROUGH HELL I WONDER WHERE IT...
LOOK OUT!
GAAARRRGHH!

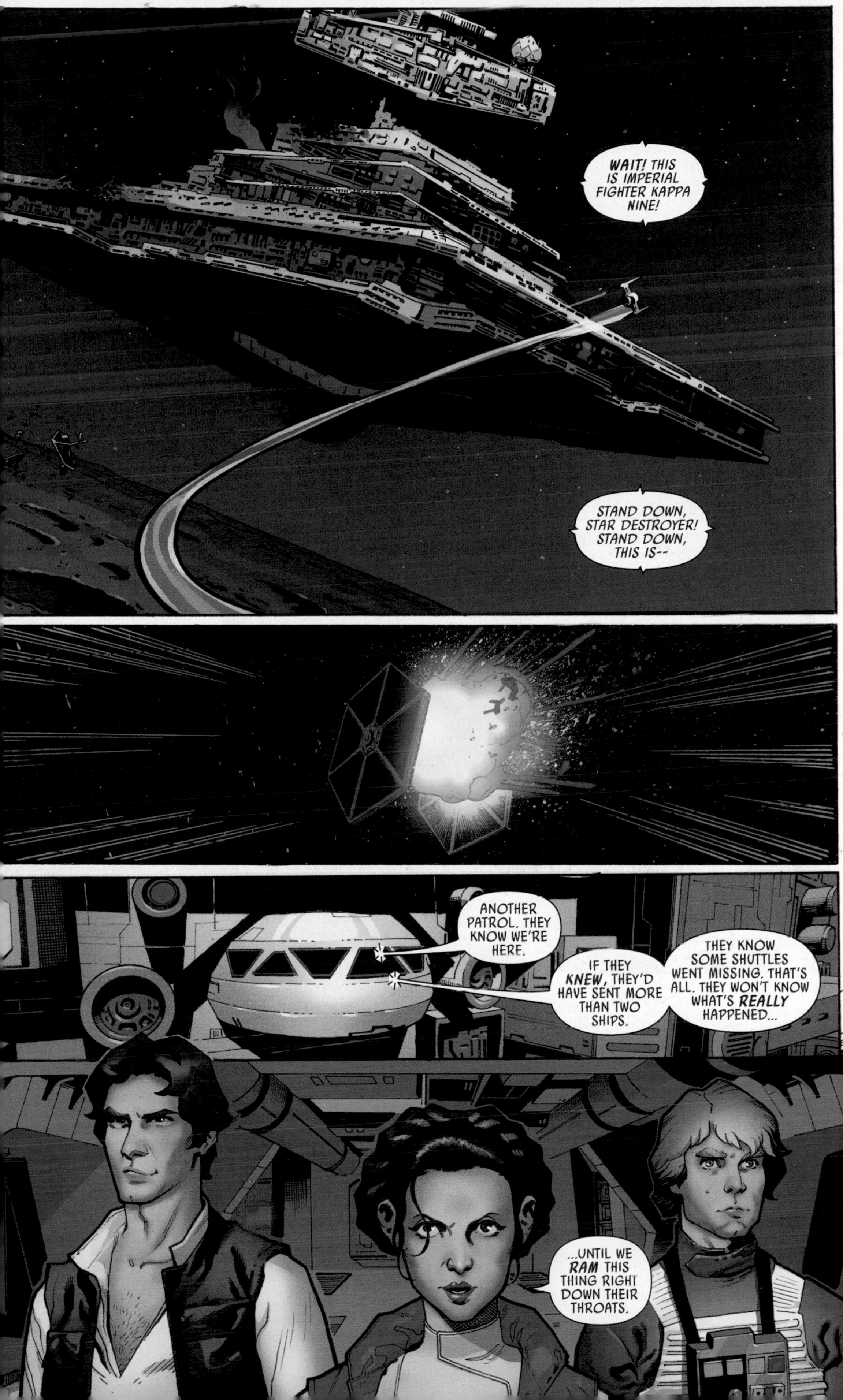
WAIT! THIS IS IMPERIAL FIGHTER KAPPA NINE!
STAND DOWN, STAR DESTROYER! STAND DOWN, THIS IS--
ANOTHER PATROL. THEY KNOW WE'RE HERE.
IF THEY KNEW, THEY'D HAVE SENT MORE THAN TWO SHIPS.
THEY KNOW SOME SHUTTLES WENT MISSING. THAT'S ALL. THEY WON'T KNOW WHAT'S REALLY HAPPENED...
...UNTIL WE RAM THIS THING RIGHT DOWN THEIR THROATS.

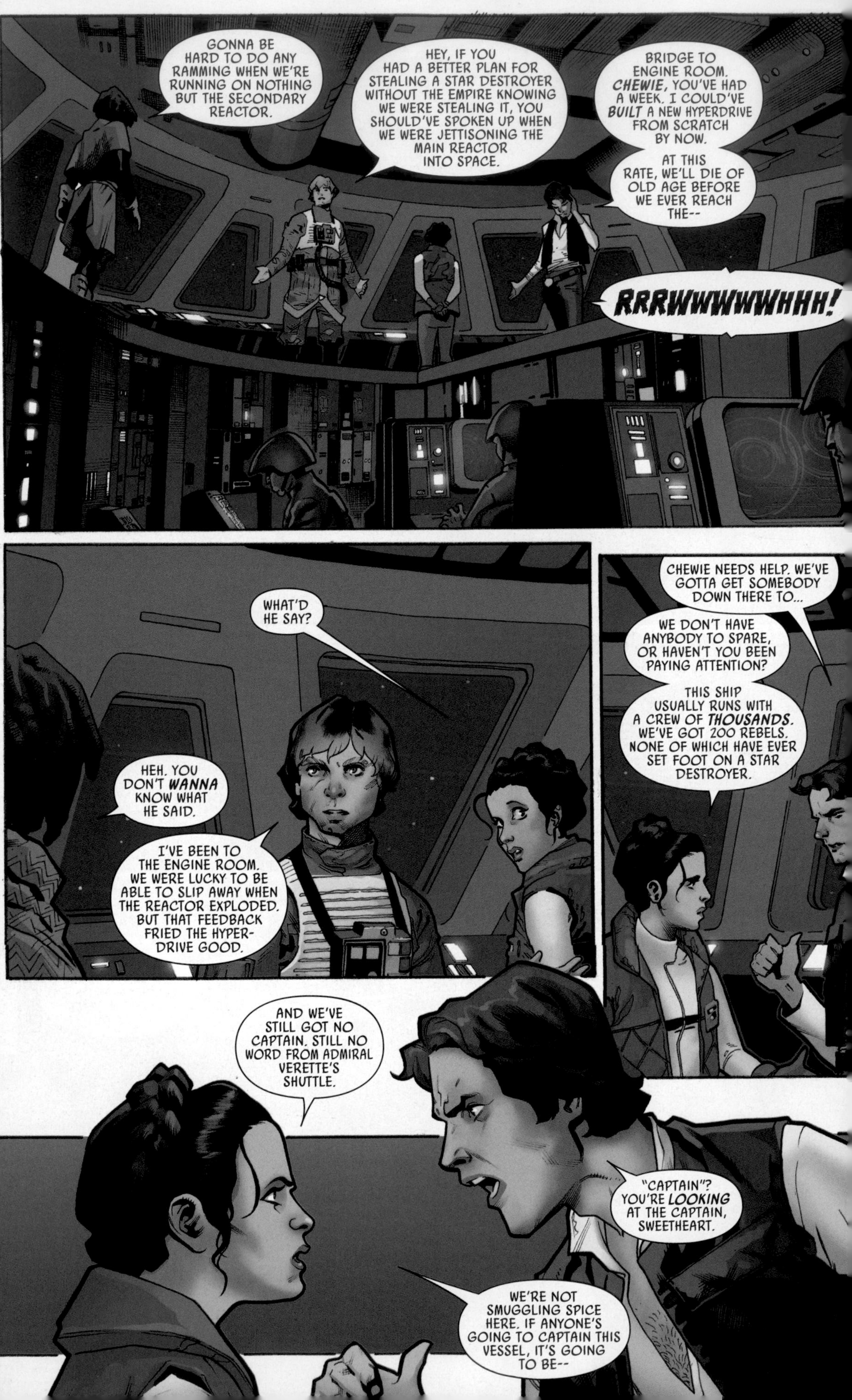
GONNA BE HARD TO DO ANY RAMMING WHEN WE'RE RUNNING ON NOTHING BUT THE SECONDARY REACTOR.
HEY, IF YOU HAD A BETTER PLAN FOR STEALING A STAR DESTROYER WITHOUT THE EMPIRE KNOWING WE WERE STEALING IT, YOU SHOULD'VE SPOKEN UP WHEN WE WERE JETTISONING THE MAIN REACTOR INTO SPACE.
BRIDGE TO ENGINE ROOM. CHEWIE, YOU'VE HAD A WEEK. I COULD'VE BUILT A NEW HYPERDRIVE FROM SCRATCH BY NOW.
AT THIS RATE, WE'LL DIE OF OLD AGE BEFORE WE EVER REACH THE--
RRRWWWWWHHH!
WHAT'D HE SAY?
HEH. YOU DON'T WANNA KNOW WHAT HE SAID.
I'VE BEEN TO THE ENGINE ROOM. WE WERE LUCKY TO BE ABLE TO SLIP AWAY WHEN THE REACTOR EXPLODED. BUT THAT FEEDBACK FRIED THE HYPER-DRIVE GOOD.
CHEWIE NEEDS HELP. WE'VE GOTTA GET SOMEBODY DOWN THERE TO...
WE DON'T HAVE ANYBODY TO SPARE, OR HAVEN'T YOU BEEN PAYING ATTENTION?
THIS SHIP USUALLY RUNS WITH A CREW OF THOUSANDS. WE'VE GOT 200 REBELS. NONE OF WHICH HAVE EVER SET FOOT ON A STAR DESTROYER.
AND WE'VE STILL GOT NO CAPTAIN. STILL NO WORD FROM ADMIRAL VERETTE'S SHUTTLE.
"CAPTAIN"? YOU'RE LOOKING AT THE CAPTAIN, SWEETHEART.
WE'RE NOT SMUGGLING SPICE HERE. IF ANYONE'S GOING TO CAPTAIN THIS VESSEL, IT'S GOING TO BE--

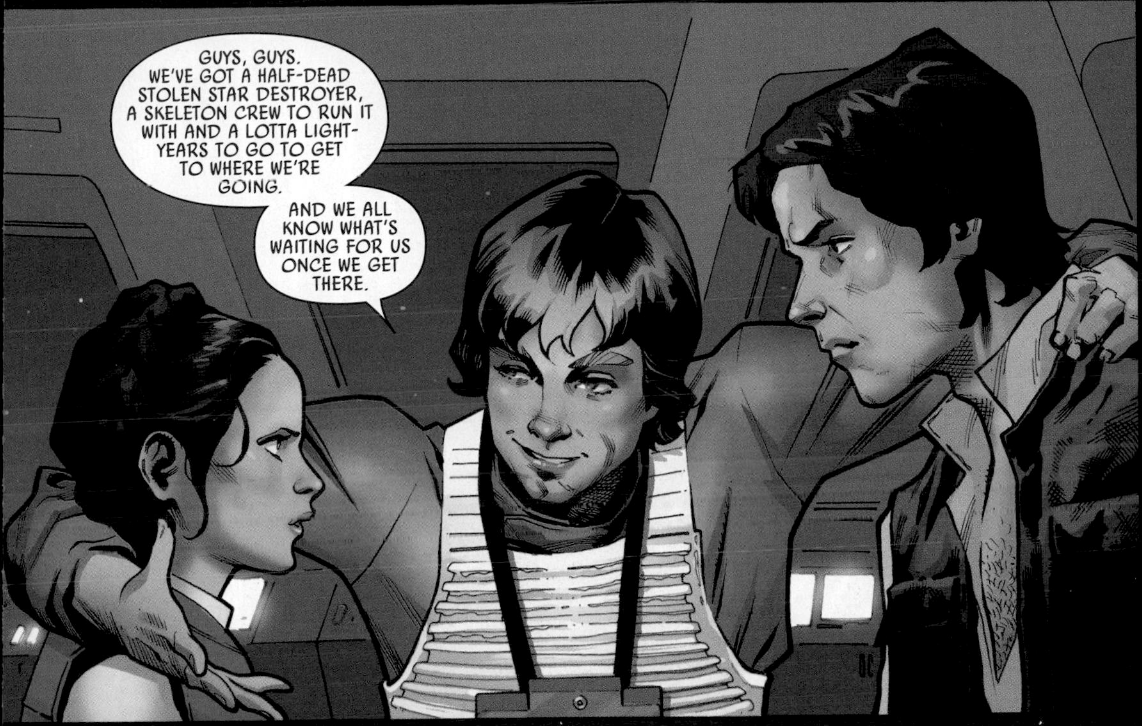
GUYS, GUYS. WE'VE GOT A HALF-DEAD STOLEN STAR DESTROYER, A SKELETON CREW TO RUN IT WITH AND A LOTTA LIGHT-YEARS TO GO TO GET TO WHERE WE'RE GOING.
AND WE ALL KNOW WHAT'S WAITING FOR US ONCE WE GET THERE.

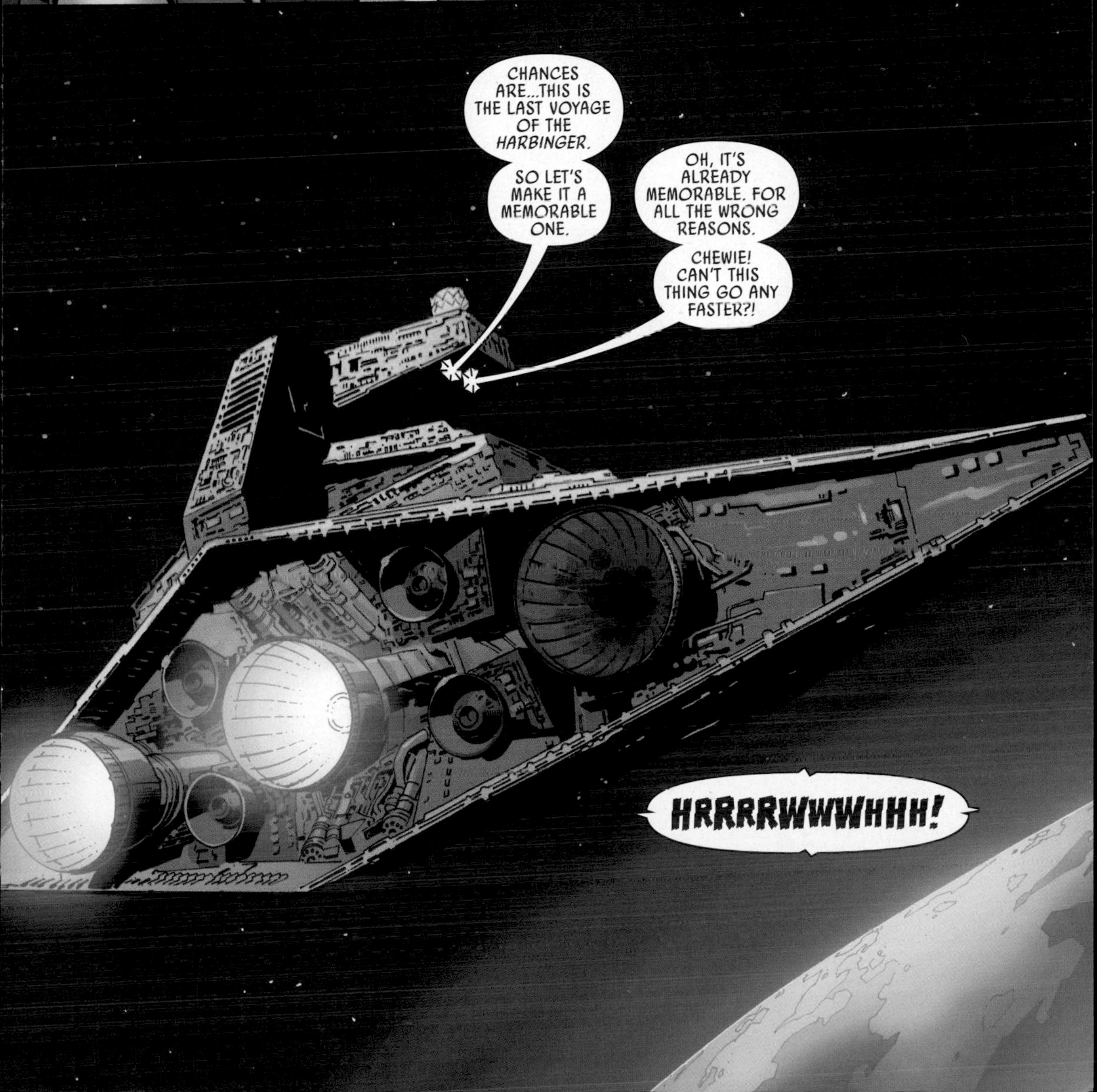
CHANCES ARE...THIS IS THE LAST VOYAGE OF THE *HARBINGER*.
SO LET'S MAKE IT A MEMORABLE ONE.
OH, IT'S ALREADY MEMORABLE. FOR ALL THE WRONG REASONS.
CHEWIE! CAN'T THIS THING GO ANY FASTER?!
HRRRRWWWHHH!

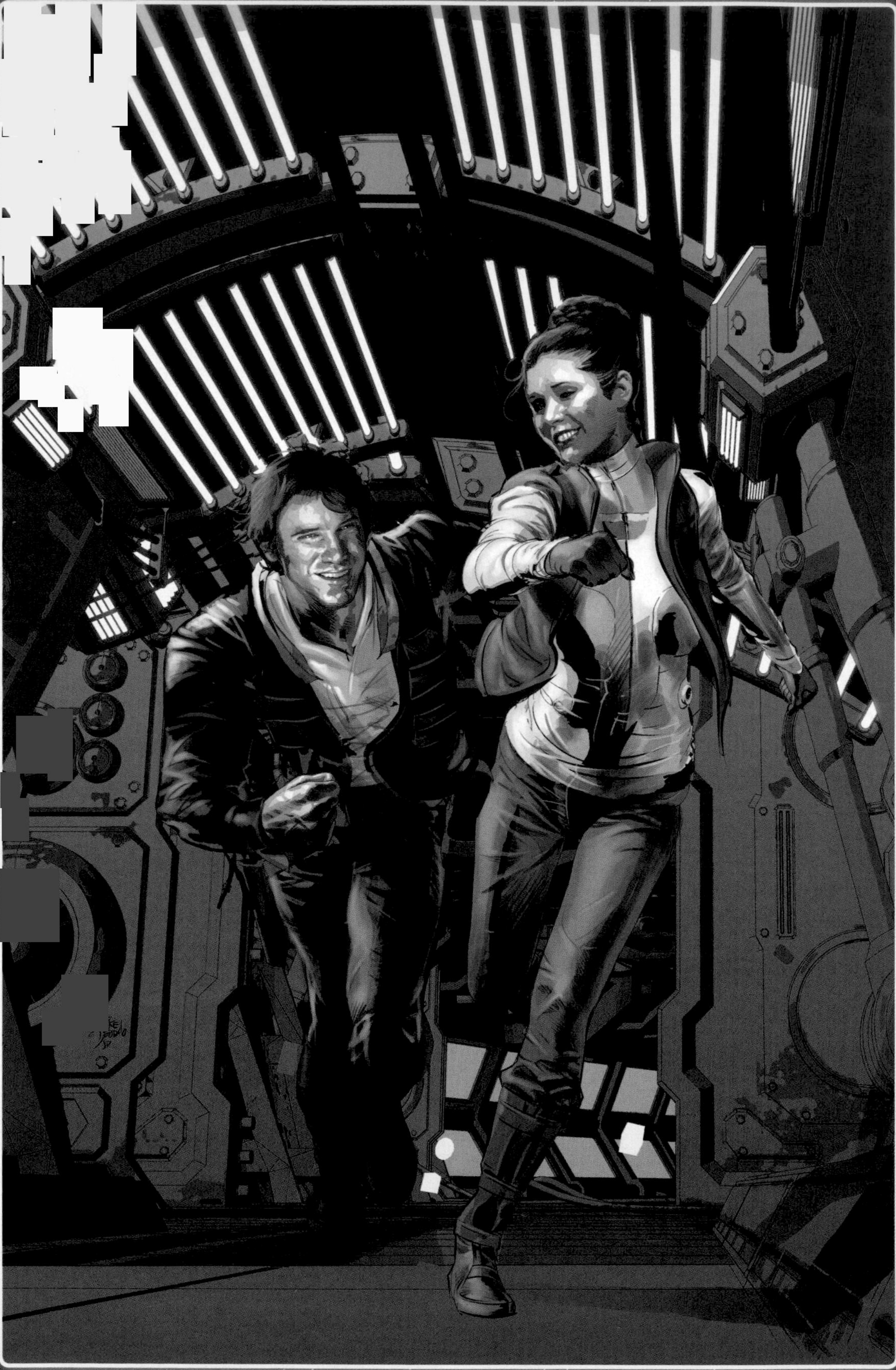

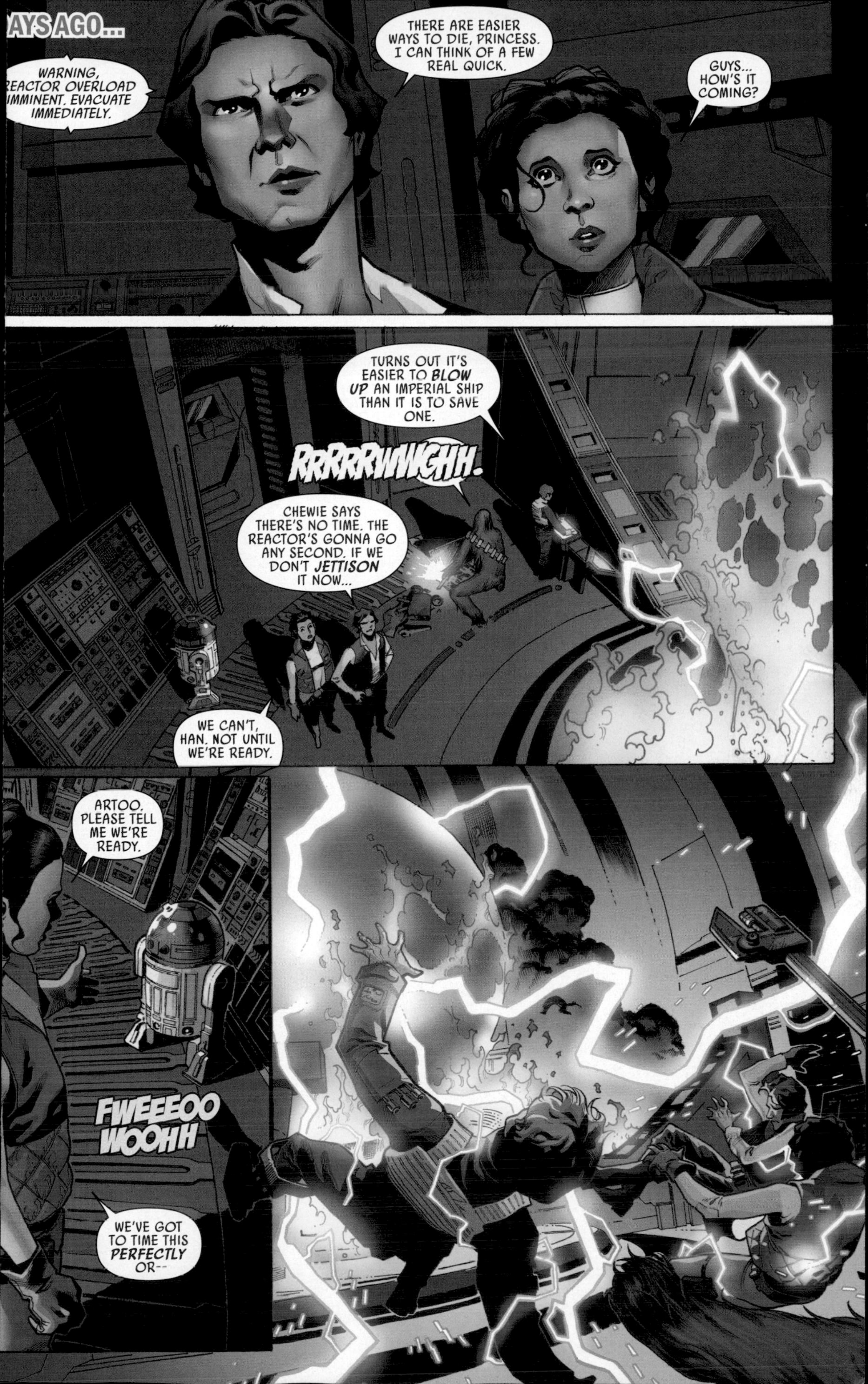
AYS AGO...
WARNING, REACTOR OVERLOAD IMMINENT. EVACUATE IMMEDIATELY.
THERE ARE EASIER WAYS TO DIE, PRINCESS. I CAN THINK OF A FEW REAL QUICK.
GUYS... HOW'S IT COMING?
TURNS OUT IT'S EASIER TO BLOW UP AN IMPERIAL SHIP THAN IT IS TO SAVE ONE.
RRRRRWWGHH.
CHEWIE SAYS THERE'S NO TIME. THE REACTOR'S GONNA GO ANY SECOND. IF WE DON'T JETTISON IT NOW...
WE CAN'T, HAN. NOT UNTIL WE'RE READY.
ARTOO, PLEASE TELL ME WE'RE READY.
FWEEEOO WOOHH
WE'VE GOT TO TIME THIS PERFECTLY OR--

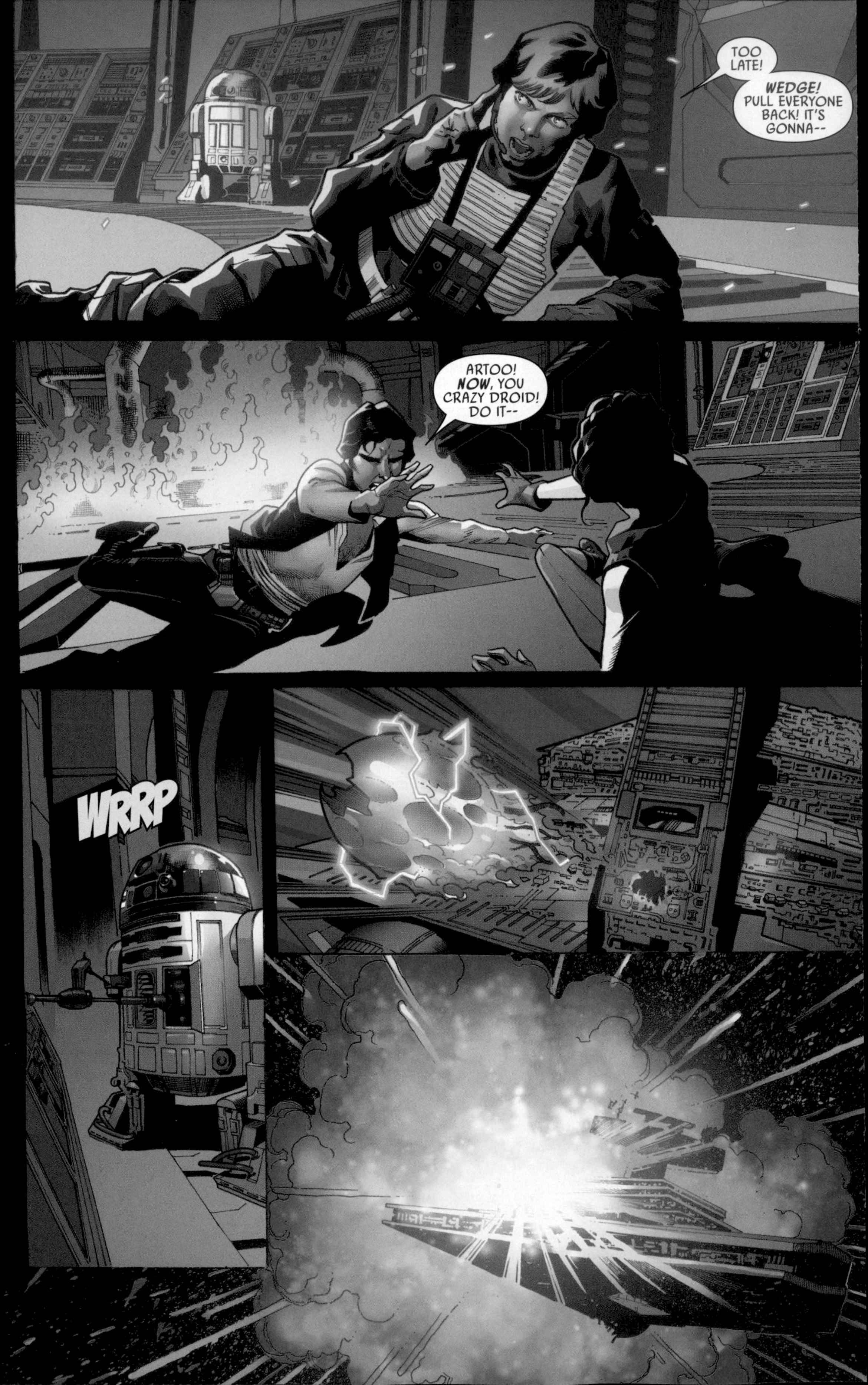
TOO LATE!
WEDGE! PULL EVERYONE BACK! IT'S GONNA--
ARTOO! NOW, YOU CRAZY DROID! DO IT--
WRRP

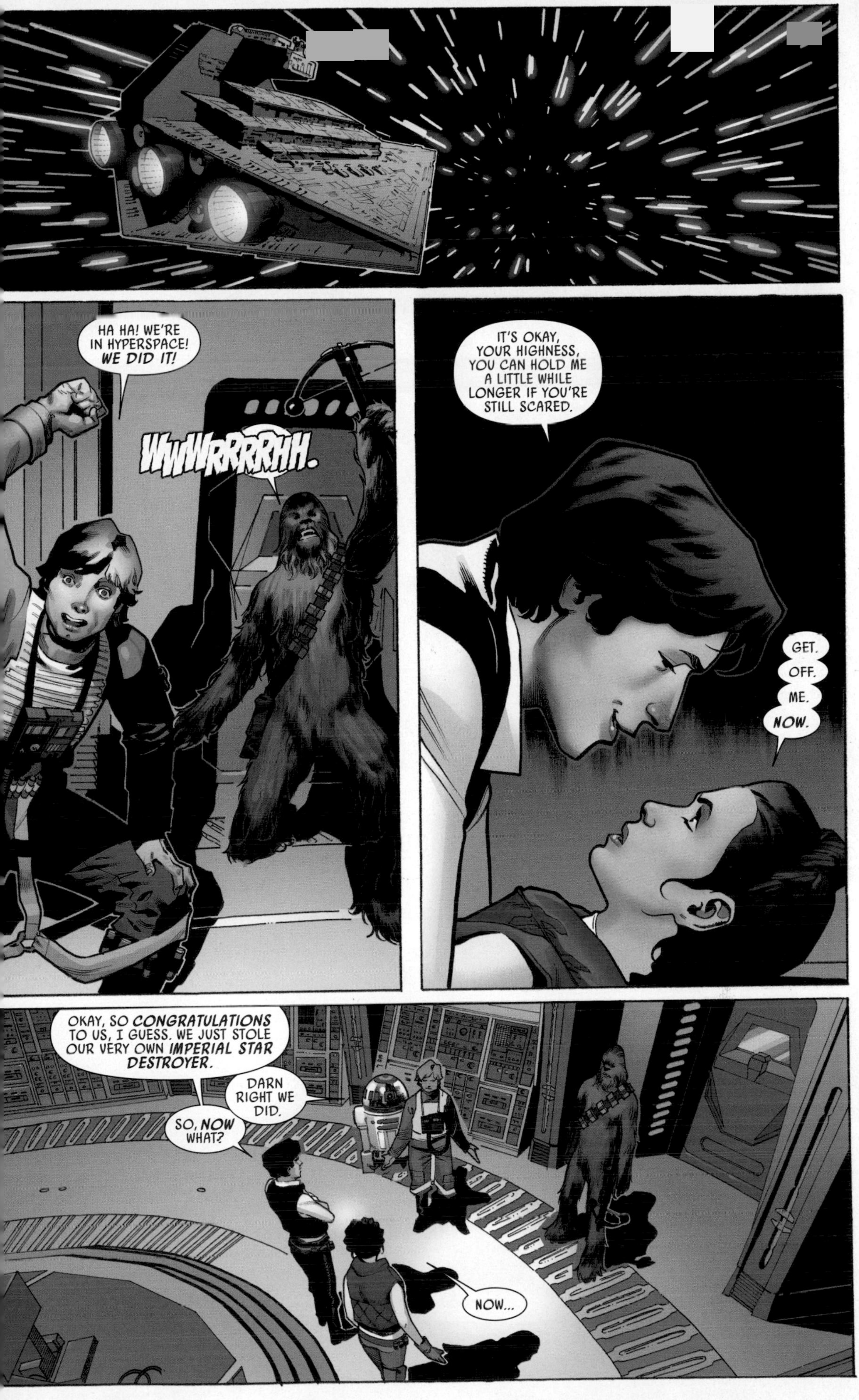
HA HA! WE'RE IN HYPERSPACE! WE DID IT!
WWWRRRRHH.
IT'S OKAY, YOUR HIGHNESS, YOU CAN HOLD ME A LITTLE WHILE LONGER IF YOU'RE STILL SCARED.
GET. OFF. ME. NOW.
OKAY, SO CONGRATULATIONS TO US, I GUESS. WE JUST STOLE OUR VERY OWN IMPERIAL STAR DESTROYER.
DARN RIGHT WE DID.
SO, NOW WHAT?
NOW...

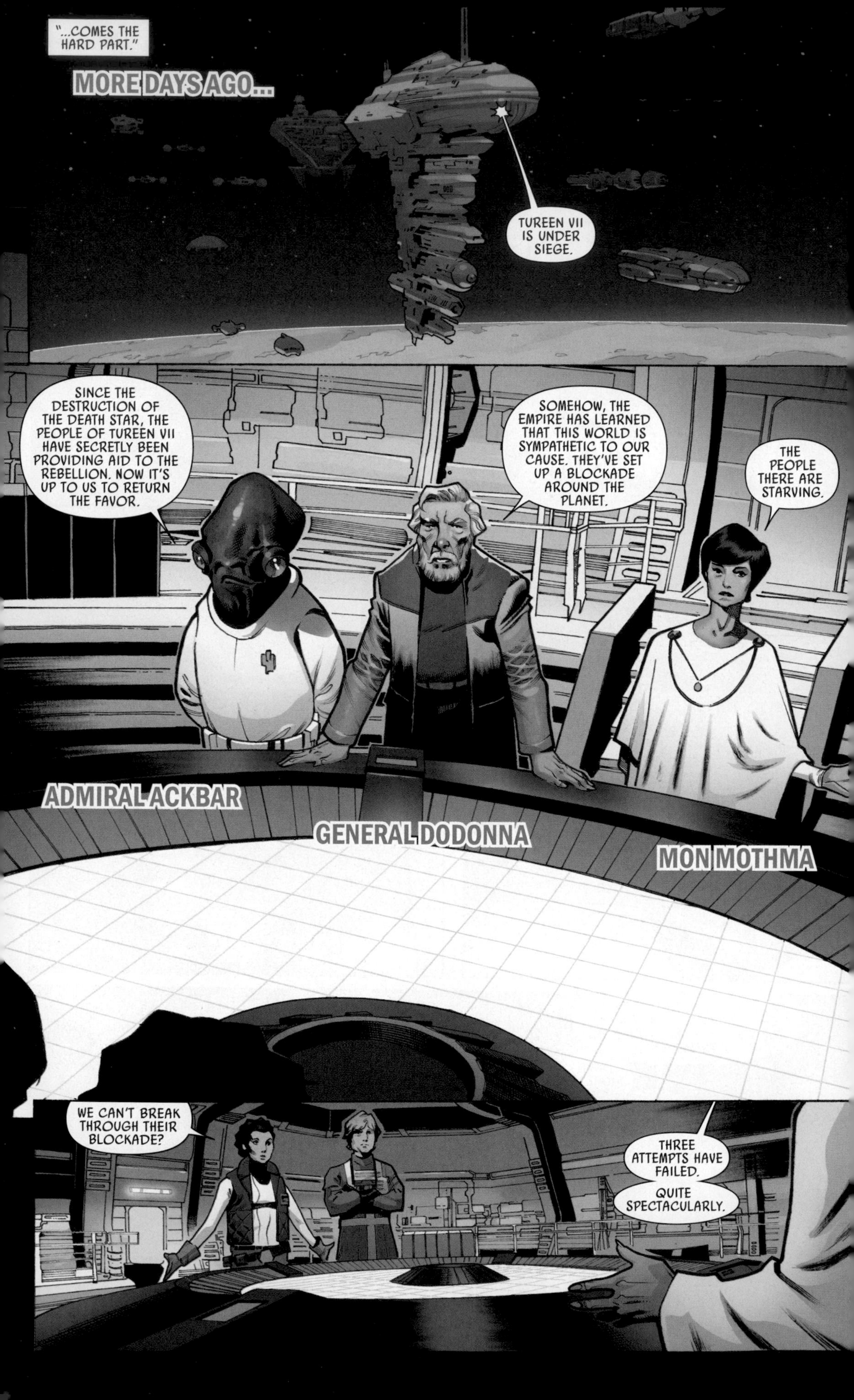
"...COMES THE HARD PART."
MORE DAYS AGO...
TUREEN VII IS UNDER SIEGE.
SINCE THE DESTRUCTION OF THE DEATH STAR, THE PEOPLE OF TUREEN VII HAVE SECRETLY BEEN PROVIDING AID TO THE REBELLION. NOW IT'S UP TO US TO RETURN THE FAVOR.
SOMEHOW, THE EMPIRE HAS LEARNED THAT THIS WORLD IS SYMPATHETIC TO OUR CAUSE. THEY'VE SET UP A BLOCKADE AROUND THE PLANET.
THE PEOPLE THERE ARE STARVING.
ADMIRAL ACKBAR
GENERAL DODONNA
MON MOTHMA
WE CAN'T BREAK THROUGH THEIR BLOCKADE?
THREE ATTEMPTS HAVE FAILED.
QUITE SPECTACULARLY.

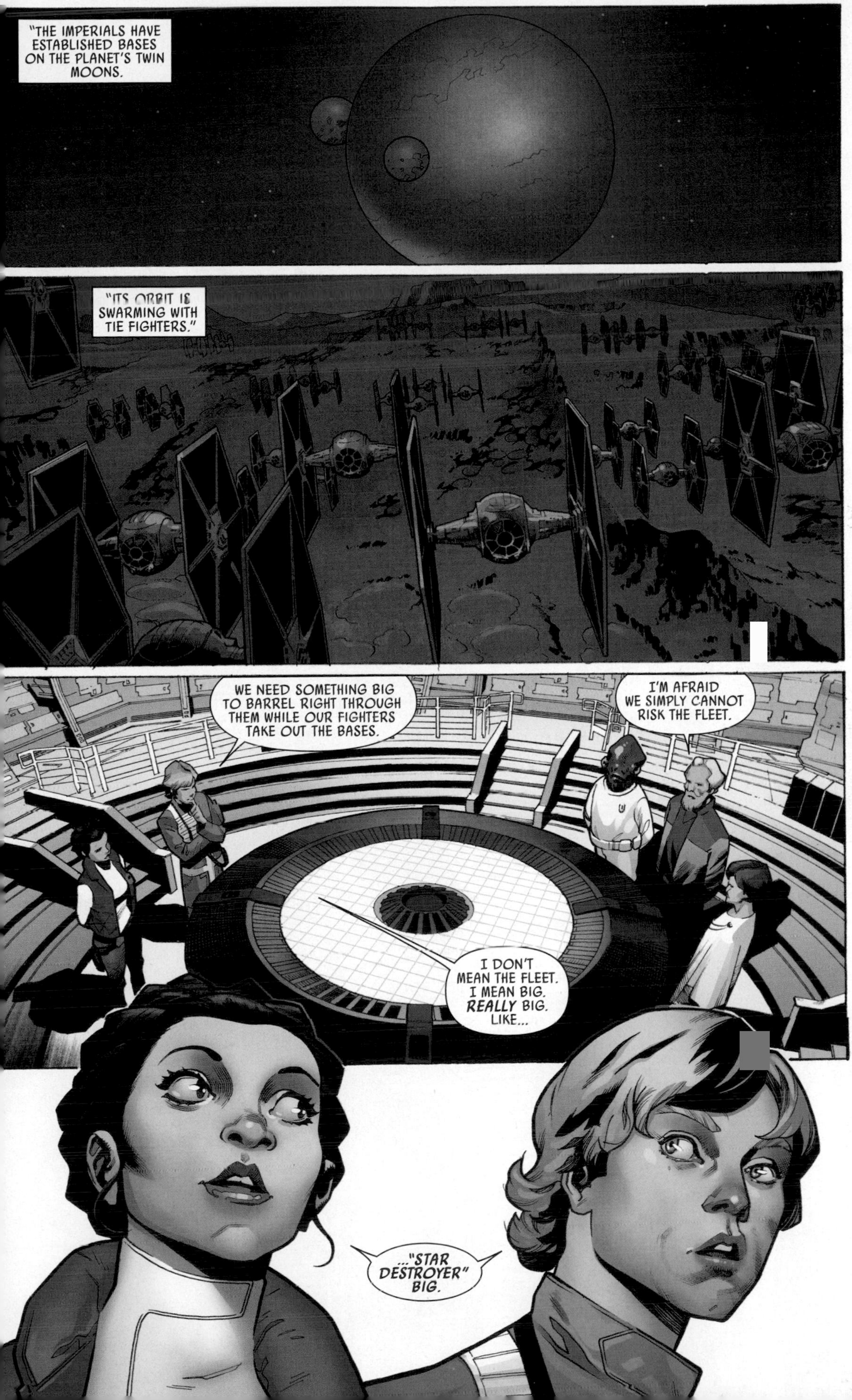
"THE IMPERIALS HAVE ESTABLISHED BASES ON THE PLANET'S TWIN MOONS.
"ITS ORBIT IS SWARMING WITH TIE FIGHTERS."
WE NEED SOMETHING BIG TO BARREL RIGHT THROUGH THEM WHILE OUR FIGHTERS TAKE OUT THE BASES.
I'M AFRAID WE SIMPLY CANNOT RISK THE FLEET.
I DON'T MEAN THE FLEET. I MEAN BIG. *REALLY* BIG. LIKE...
..."STAR DESTROYER" BIG.

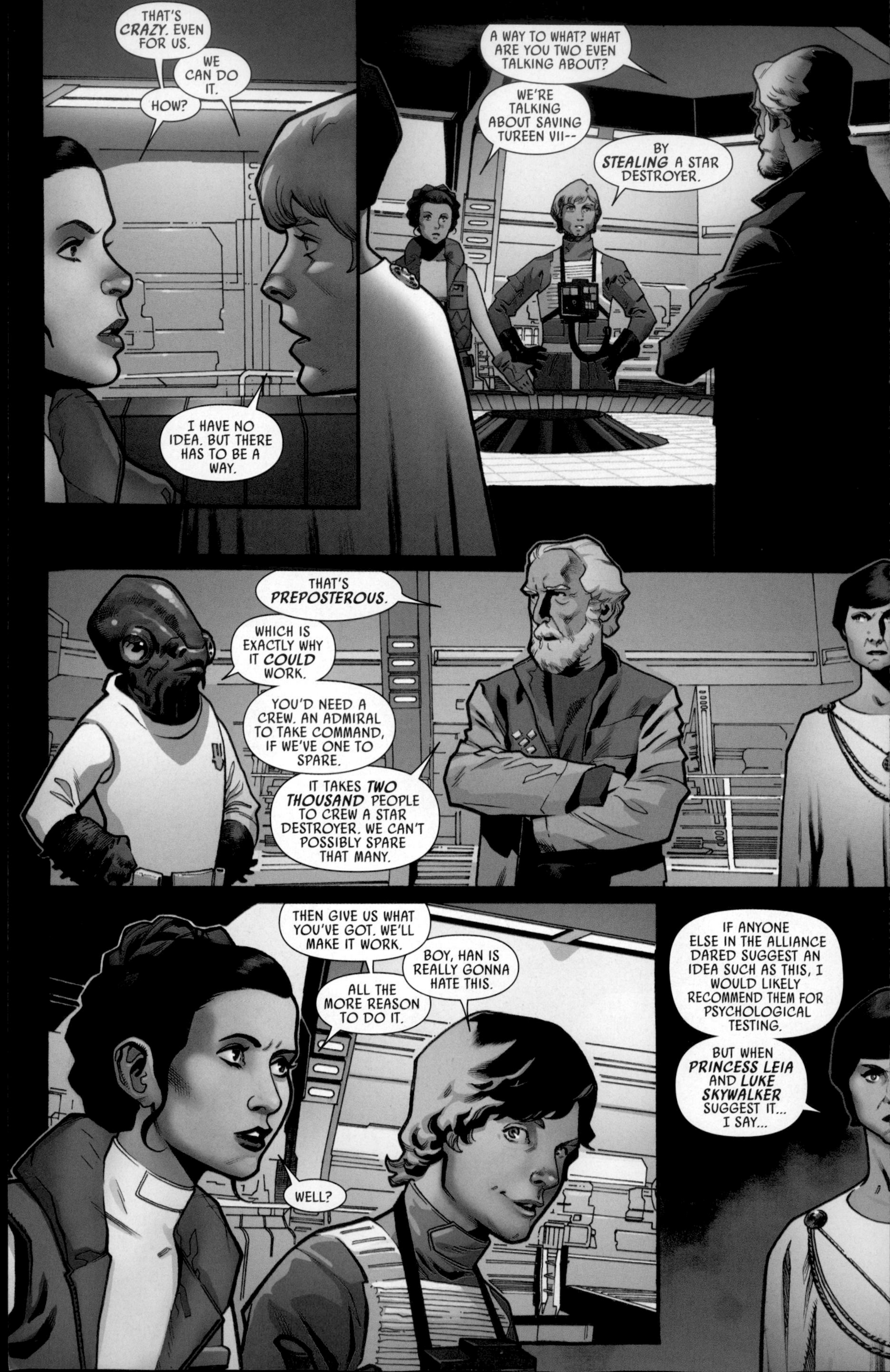
THAT'S CRAZY. EVEN FOR US.
WE CAN DO IT.
HOW?
I HAVE NO IDEA. BUT THERE HAS TO BE A WAY.
A WAY TO WHAT? WHAT ARE YOU TWO EVEN TALKING ABOUT?
WE'RE TALKING ABOUT SAVING TUREEN VII--
BY STEALING A STAR DESTROYER.
THAT'S PREPOSTEROUS.
WHICH IS EXACTLY WHY IT COULD WORK.
YOU'D NEED A CREW. AN ADMIRAL TO TAKE COMMAND, IF WE'VE ONE TO SPARE.
IT TAKES TWO THOUSAND PEOPLE TO CREW A STAR DESTROYER. WE CAN'T POSSIBLY SPARE THAT MANY.
THEN GIVE US WHAT YOU'VE GOT. WE'LL MAKE IT WORK.
BOY, HAN IS REALLY GONNA HATE THIS.
ALL THE MORE REASON TO DO IT.
IF ANYONE ELSE IN THE ALLIANCE DARED SUGGEST AN IDEA SUCH AS THIS, I WOULD LIKELY RECOMMEND THEM FOR PSYCHOLOGICAL TESTING.
BUT WHEN PRINCESS LEIA AND LUKE SKYWALKER SUGGEST IT... I SAY...
WELL?

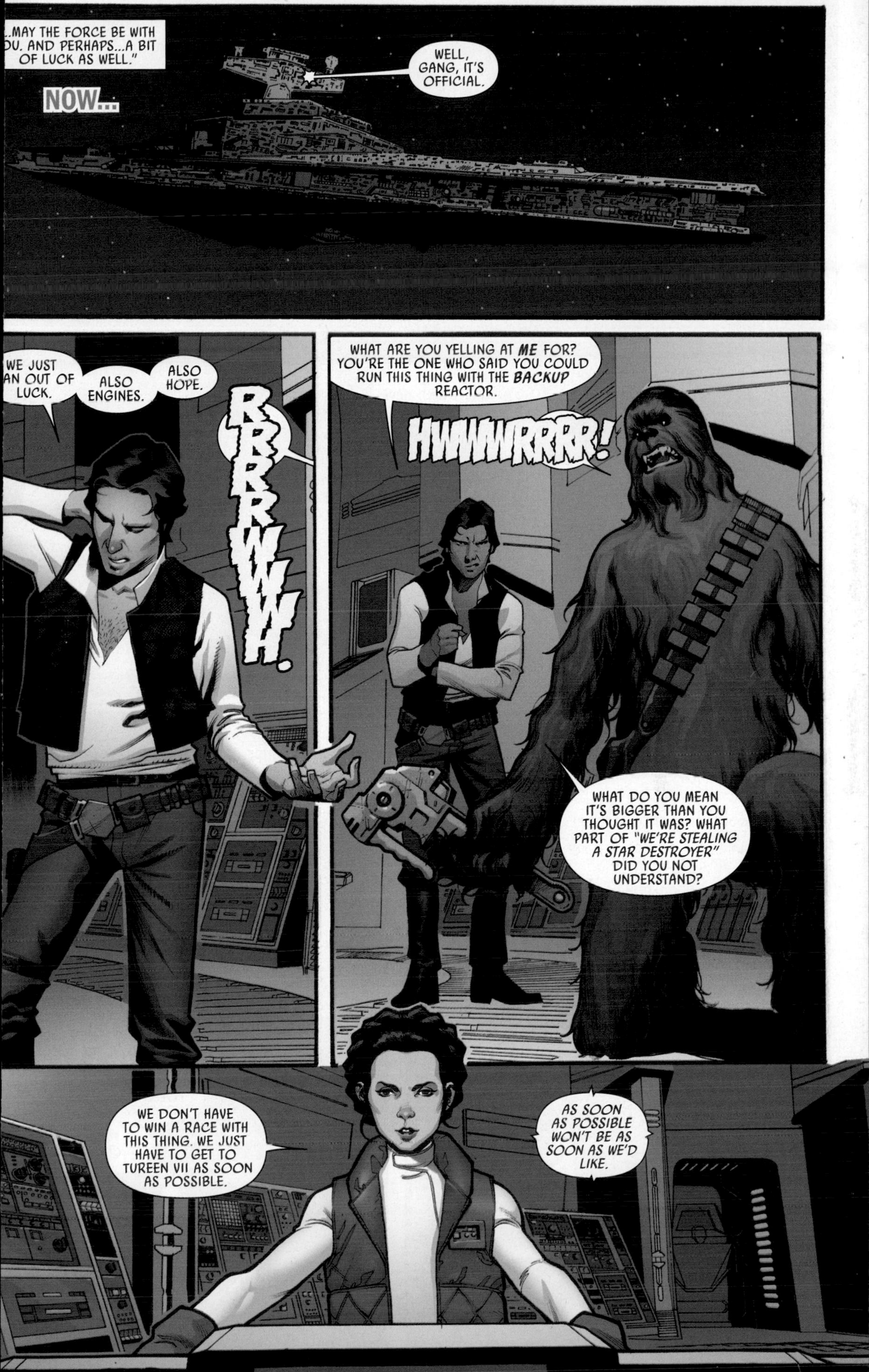
..MAY THE FORCE BE WITH OU. AND PERHAPS...A BIT OF LUCK AS WELL."
NOW...
WELL, GANG, IT'S OFFICIAL.
WE JUST AN OUT OF LUCK.
ALSO ENGINES.
ALSO HOPE.
RRRRWWH.
WHAT ARE YOU YELLING AT ME FOR? YOU'RE THE ONE WHO SAID YOU COULD RUN THIS THING WITH THE BACKUP REACTOR.
HWWWRRRR!
WHAT DO YOU MEAN IT'S BIGGER THAN YOU THOUGHT IT WAS? WHAT PART OF "WE'RE STEALING A STAR DESTROYER" DID YOU NOT UNDERSTAND?
WE DON'T HAVE TO WIN A RACE WITH THIS THING. WE JUST HAVE TO GET TO TUREEN VII AS SOON AS POSSIBLE.
AS SOON AS POSSIBLE WON'T BE AS SOON AS WE'D LIKE.

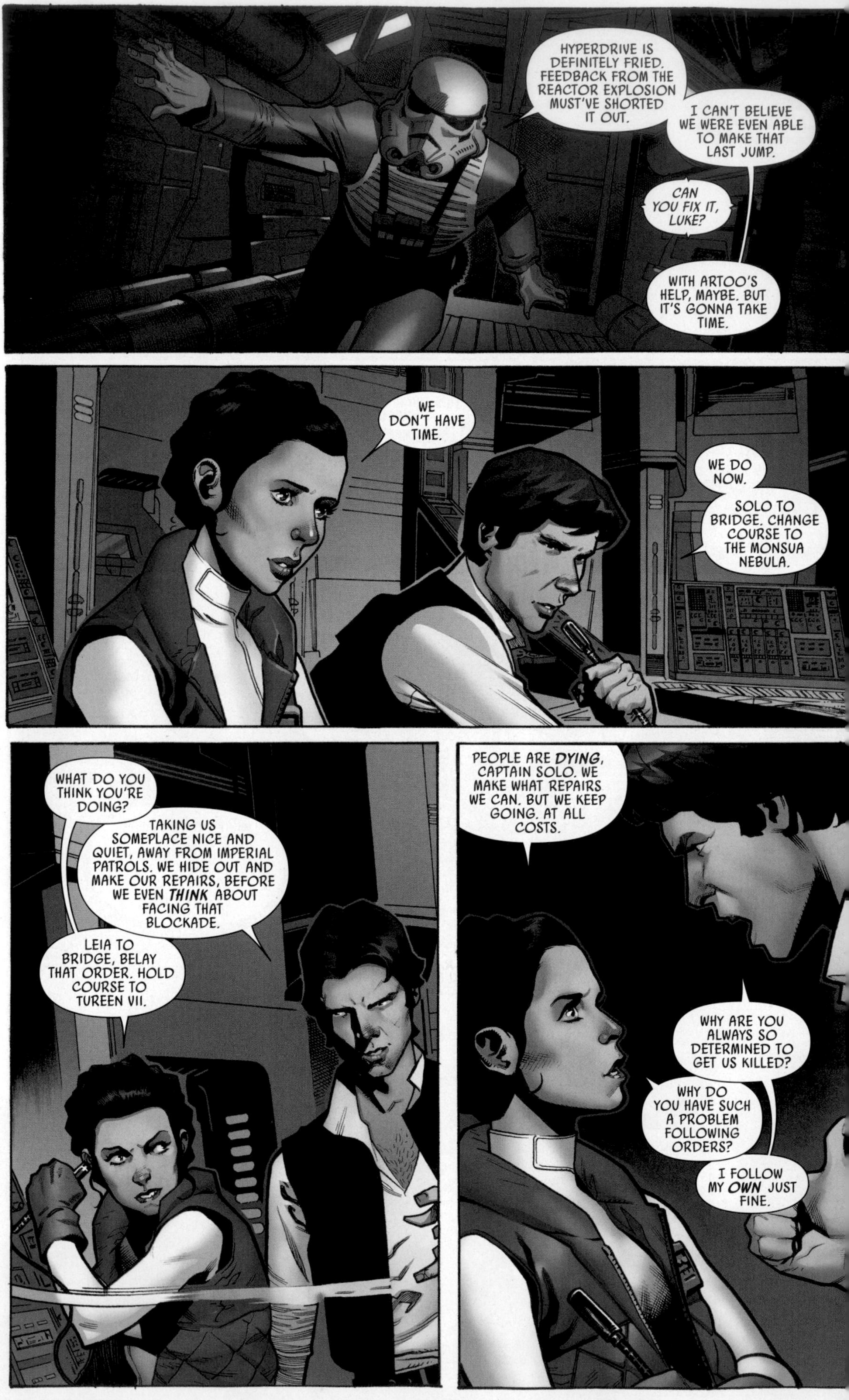
HYPERDRIVE IS DEFINITELY FRIED. FEEDBACK FROM THE REACTOR EXPLOSION MUST'VE SHORTED IT OUT.
I CAN'T BELIEVE WE WERE EVEN ABLE TO MAKE THAT LAST JUMP.
CAN YOU FIX IT, LUKE?
WITH ARTOO'S HELP, MAYBE. BUT IT'S GONNA TAKE TIME.
WE DON'T HAVE TIME.
WE DO NOW.
SOLO TO BRIDGE. CHANGE COURSE TO THE MONSUA NEBULA.
WHAT DO YOU THINK YOU'RE DOING?
TAKING US SOMEPLACE NICE AND QUIET, AWAY FROM IMPERIAL PATROLS. WE HIDE OUT AND MAKE OUR REPAIRS, BEFORE WE EVEN ***THINK*** ABOUT FACING THAT BLOCKADE.
LEIA TO BRIDGE, BELAY THAT ORDER. HOLD COURSE TO TUREEN VII.
PEOPLE ARE ***DYING***, CAPTAIN SOLO. WE MAKE WHAT REPAIRS WE CAN. BUT WE KEEP GOING. AT ALL COSTS.
WHY ARE YOU ALWAYS SO DETERMINED TO GET US KILLED?
WHY DO YOU HAVE SUCH A PROBLEM FOLLOWING ORDERS?
I FOLLOW MY ***OWN*** JUST FINE.

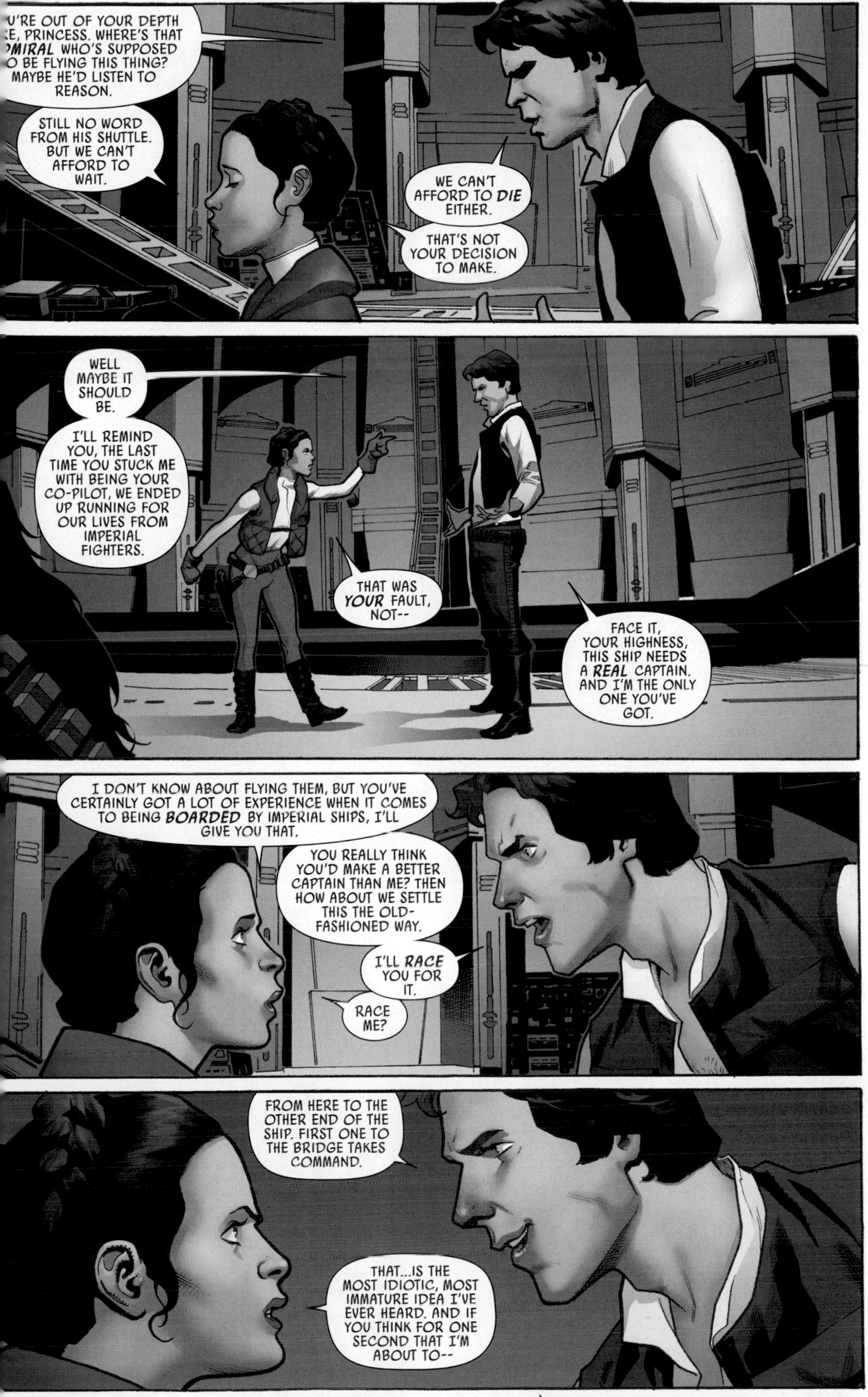
U'RE OUT OF YOUR DEPTH E, PRINCESS. WHERE'S THAT MIRAL WHO'S SUPPOSED O BE FLYING THIS THING? MAYBE HE'D LISTEN TO REASON.
STILL NO WORD FROM HIS SHUTTLE. BUT WE CAN'T AFFORD TO WAIT.
WE CAN'T AFFORD TO DIE EITHER.
THAT'S NOT YOUR DECISION TO MAKE.
WELL MAYBE IT SHOULD BE.
I'LL REMIND YOU, THE LAST TIME YOU STUCK ME WITH BEING YOUR CO-PILOT, WE ENDED UP RUNNING FOR OUR LIVES FROM IMPERIAL FIGHTERS.
THAT WAS YOUR FAULT, NOT--
FACE IT, YOUR HIGHNESS, THIS SHIP NEEDS A REAL CAPTAIN. AND I'M THE ONLY ONE YOU'VE GOT.
I DON'T KNOW ABOUT FLYING THEM, BUT YOU'VE CERTAINLY GOT A LOT OF EXPERIENCE WHEN IT COMES TO BEING BOARDED BY IMPERIAL SHIPS, I'LL GIVE YOU THAT.
YOU REALLY THINK YOU'D MAKE A BETTER CAPTAIN THAN ME? THEN HOW ABOUT WE SETTLE THIS THE OLD-FASHIONED WAY.
I'LL RACE YOU FOR IT.
RACE ME?
FROM HERE TO THE OTHER END OF THE SHIP. FIRST ONE TO THE BRIDGE TAKES COMMAND.
THAT...IS THE MOST IDIOTIC, MOST IMMATURE IDEA I'VE EVER HEARD. AND IF YOU THINK FOR ONE SECOND THAT I'M ABOUT TO--

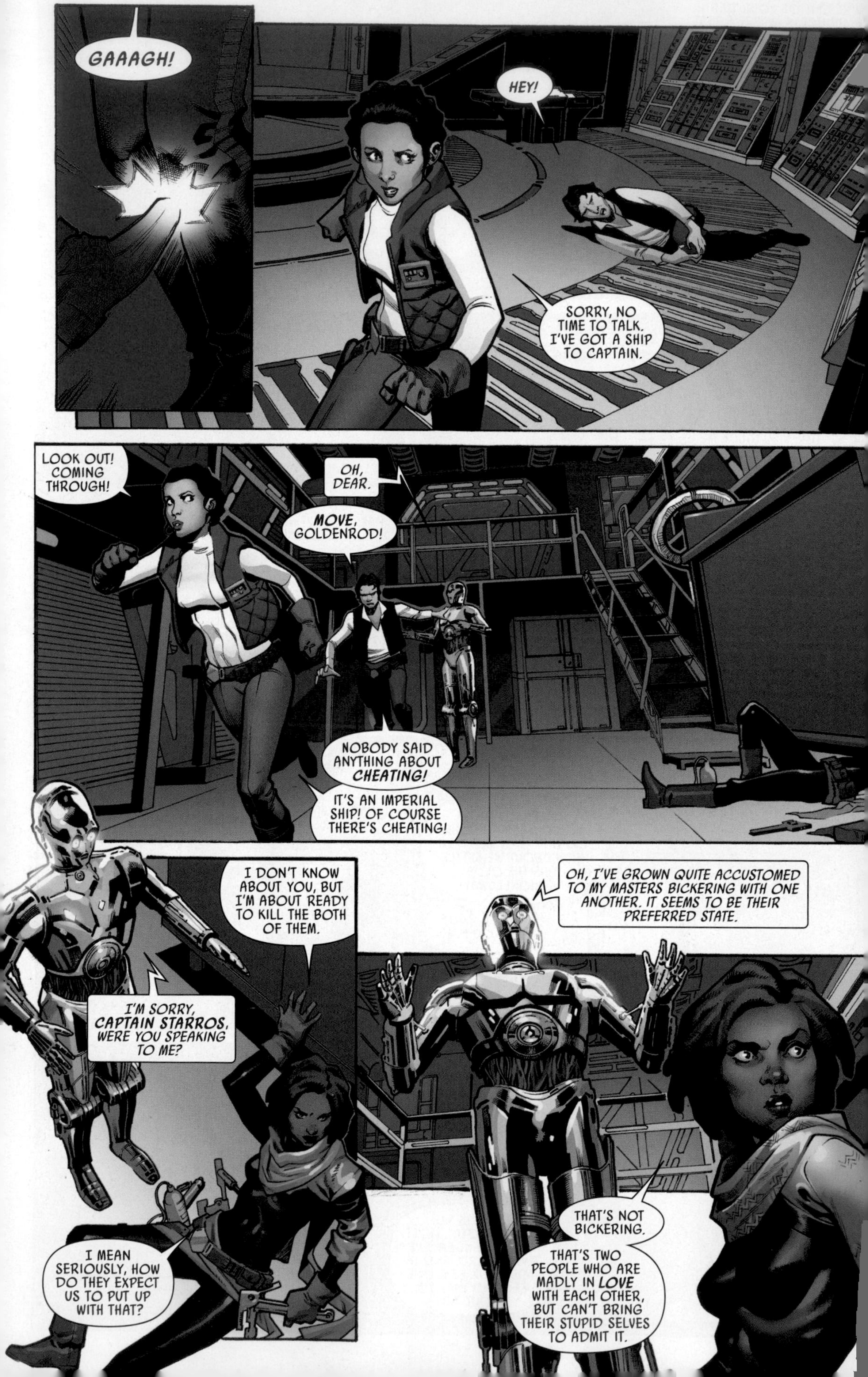
GAAAGH!
HEY!
SORRY, NO TIME TO TALK. I'VE GOT A SHIP TO CAPTAIN.
LOOK OUT! COMING THROUGH!
OH, DEAR.
MOVE, GOLDENROD!
NOBODY SAID ANYTHING ABOUT CHEATING!
IT'S AN IMPERIAL SHIP! OF COURSE THERE'S CHEATING!
I DON'T KNOW ABOUT YOU, BUT I'M ABOUT READY TO KILL THE BOTH OF THEM.
I'M SORRY, CAPTAIN STARROS, WERE YOU SPEAKING TO ME?
I MEAN SERIOUSLY, HOW DO THEY EXPECT US TO PUT UP WITH THAT?
OH, I'VE GROWN QUITE ACCUSTOMED TO MY MASTERS BICKERING WITH ONE ANOTHER. IT SEEMS TO BE THEIR PREFERRED STATE.
THAT'S NOT BICKERING.
THAT'S TWO PEOPLE WHO ARE MADLY IN LOVE WITH EACH OTHER, BUT CAN'T BRING THEIR STUPID SELVES TO ADMIT IT.

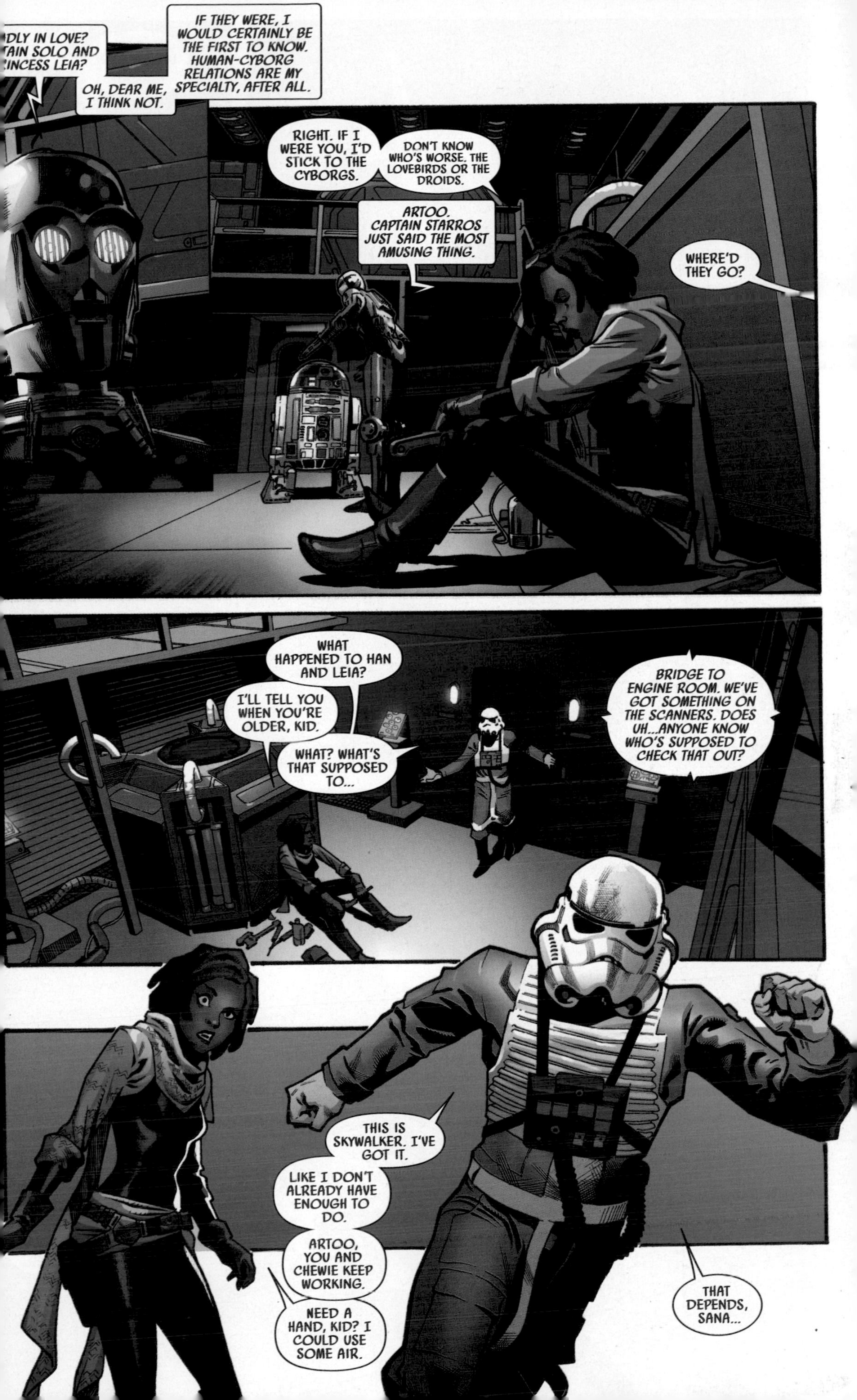

DLY IN LOVE? TAIN SOLO AND RINCESS LEIA?
OH, DEAR ME, I THINK NOT.
IF THEY WERE, I WOULD CERTAINLY BE THE FIRST TO KNOW. HUMAN-CYBORG RELATIONS ARE MY SPECIALTY, AFTER ALL.
RIGHT. IF I WERE YOU, I'D STICK TO THE CYBORGS.
DON'T KNOW WHO'S WORSE. THE LOVEBIRDS OR THE DROIDS.
ARTOO. CAPTAIN STARROS JUST SAID THE MOST AMUSING THING.
WHERE'D THEY GO?
WHAT HAPPENED TO HAN AND LEIA?
I'LL TELL YOU WHEN YOU'RE OLDER, KID.
WHAT? WHAT'S THAT SUPPOSED TO...
BRIDGE TO ENGINE ROOM. WE'VE GOT SOMETHING ON THE SCANNERS. DOES UH...ANYONE KNOW WHO'S SUPPOSED TO CHECK THAT OUT?
THIS IS SKYWALKER. I'VE GOT IT.
LIKE I DON'T ALREADY HAVE ENOUGH TO DO.
ARTOO, YOU AND CHEWIE KEEP WORKING.
NEED A HAND, KID? I COULD USE SOME AIR.
THAT DEPENDS, SANA...

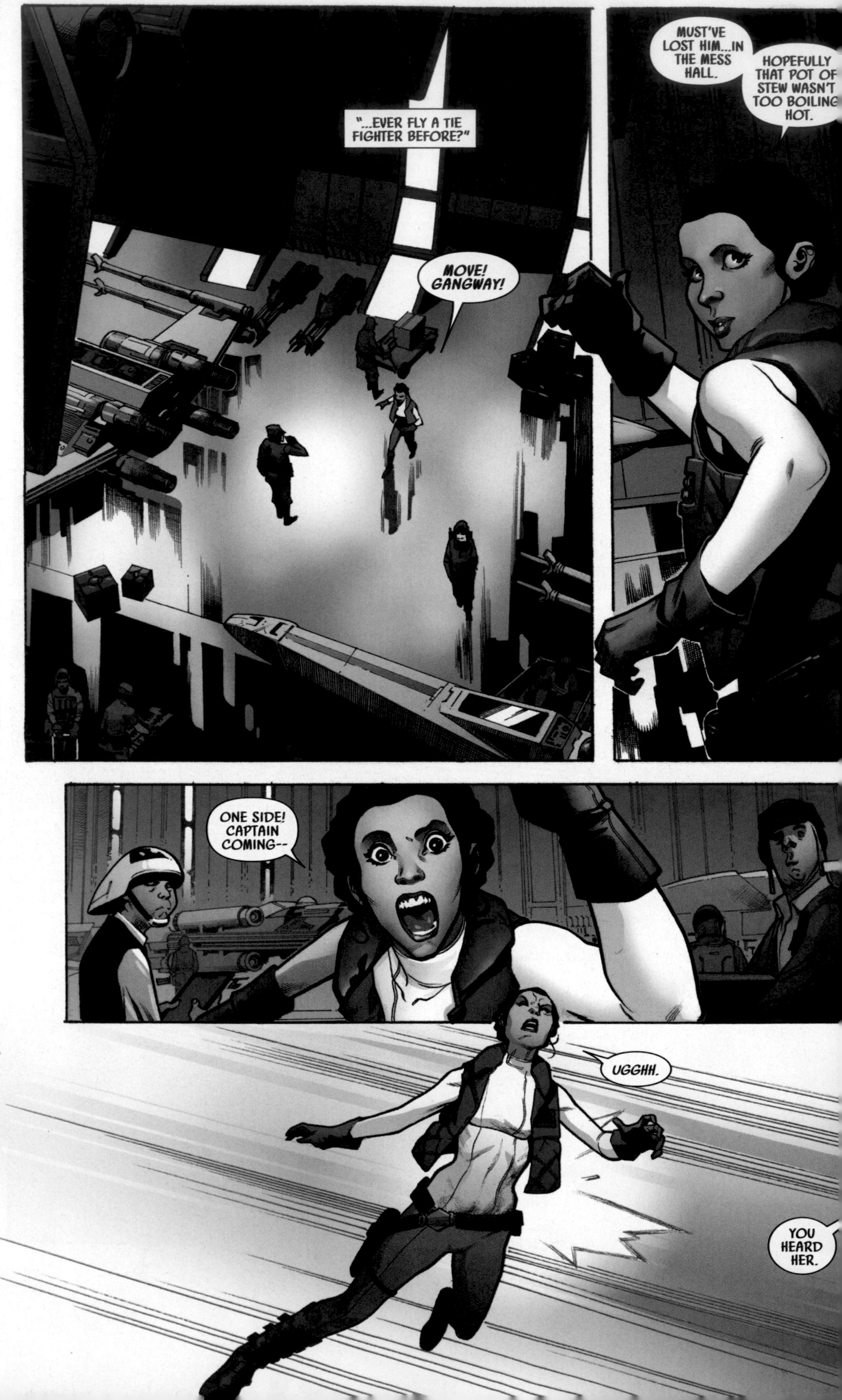
"...EVER FLY A TIE FIGHTER BEFORE?"
MOVE! GANGWAY!
MUST'VE LOST HIM...IN THE MESS HALL.
HOPEFULLY THAT POT OF STEW WASN'T TOO BOILING HOT.
ONE SIDE! CAPTAIN COMING--
UGGHH.
YOU HEARD HER.

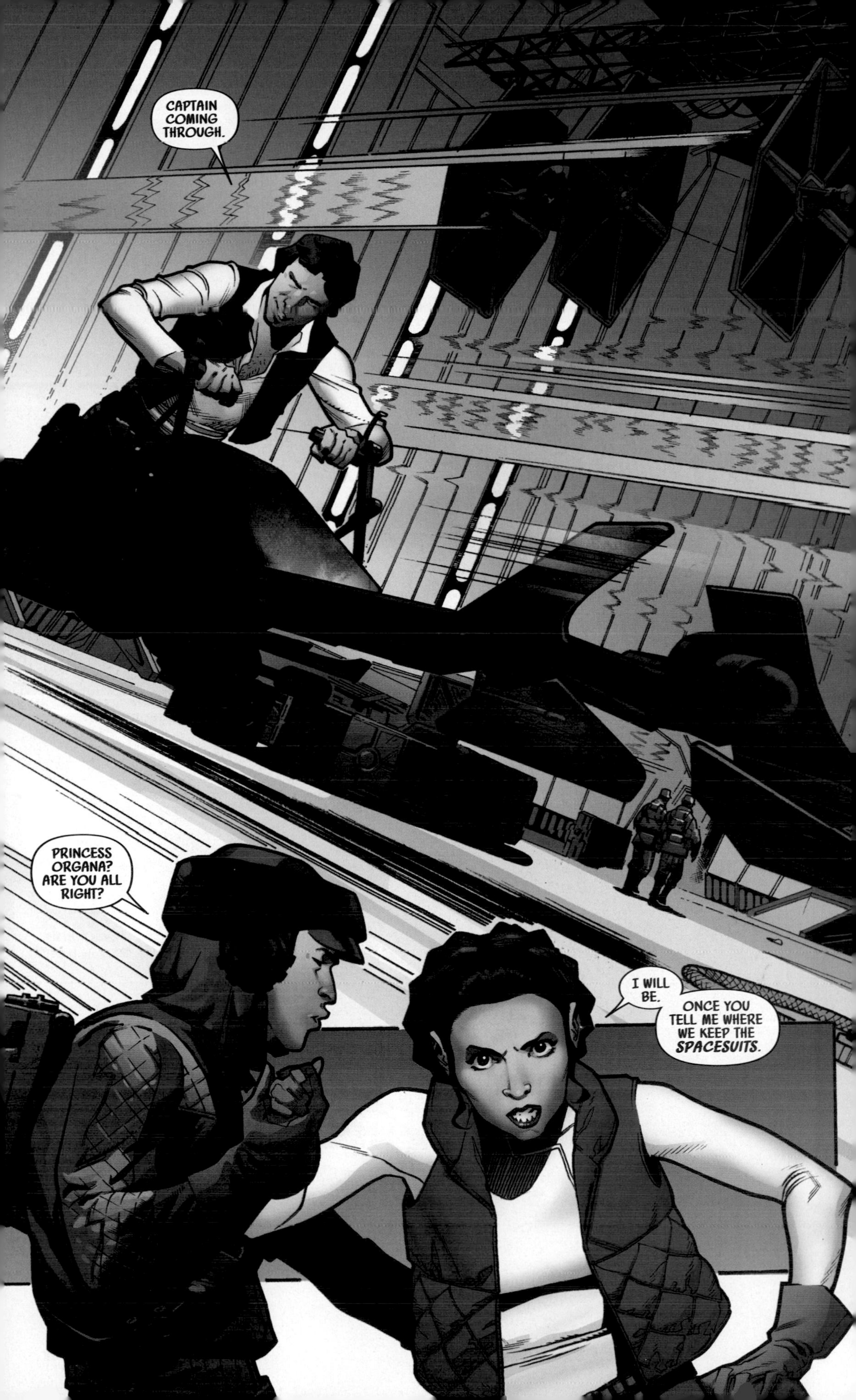
CAPTAIN COMING THROUGH.
PRINCESS ORGANA? ARE YOU ALL RIGHT?
I WILL BE.
ONCE YOU TELL ME WHERE WE KEEP THE SPACESUITS.

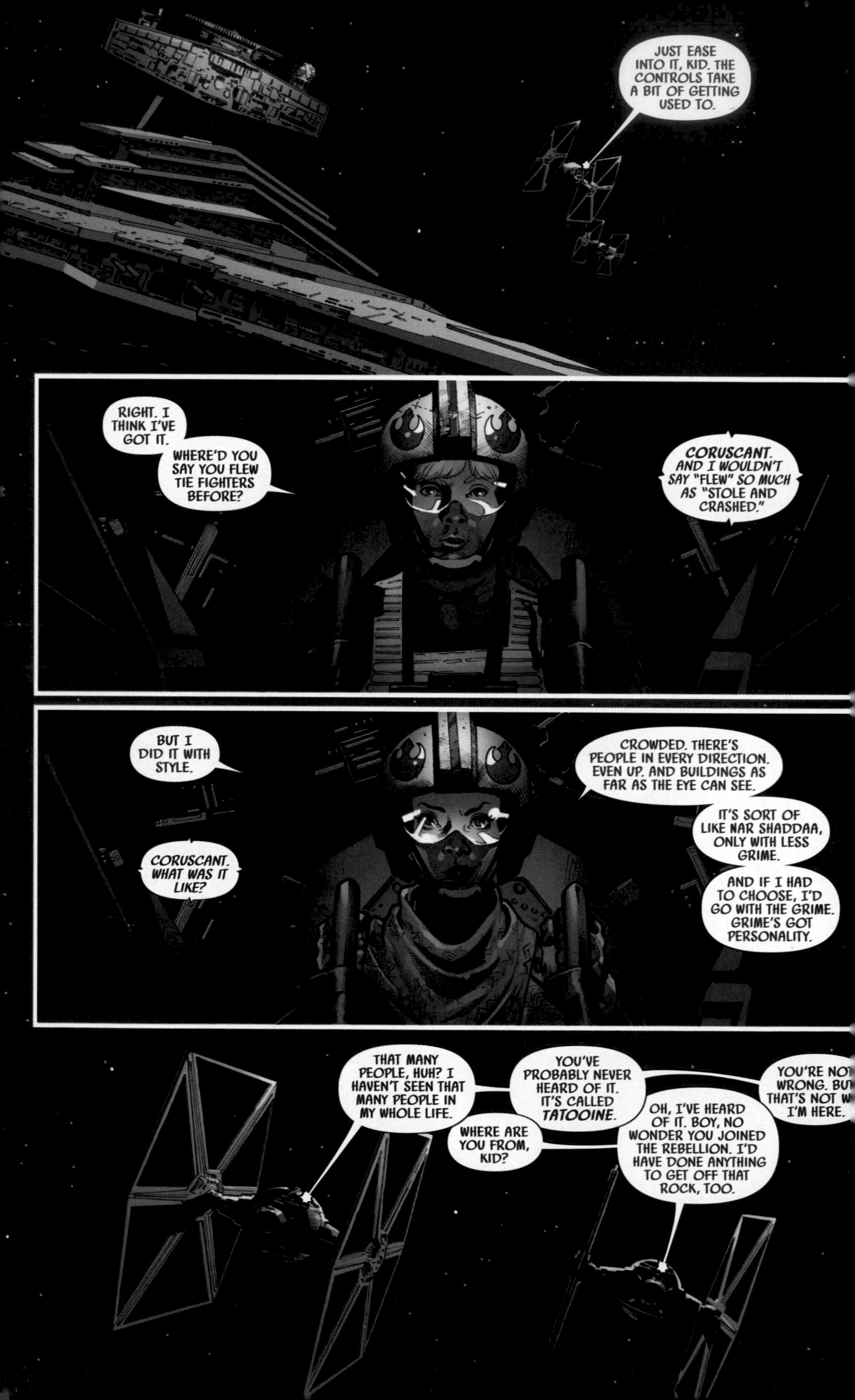

JUST EASE INTO IT, KID. THE CONTROLS TAKE A BIT OF GETTING USED TO.
RIGHT. I THINK I'VE GOT IT.
WHERE'D YOU SAY YOU FLEW TIE FIGHTERS BEFORE?
CORUSCANT. AND I WOULDN'T SAY "FLEW" SO MUCH AS "STOLE AND CRASHED."
BUT I DID IT WITH STYLE.
CORUSCANT. WHAT WAS IT LIKE?
CROWDED. THERE'S PEOPLE IN EVERY DIRECTION. EVEN UP. AND BUILDINGS AS FAR AS THE EYE CAN SEE.
IT'S SORT OF LIKE NAR SHADDAA, ONLY WITH LESS GRIME.
AND IF I HAD TO CHOOSE, I'D GO WITH THE GRIME. GRIME'S GOT PERSONALITY.
THAT MANY PEOPLE, HUH? I HAVEN'T SEEN THAT MANY PEOPLE IN MY WHOLE LIFE.
WHERE ARE YOU FROM, KID?
YOU'VE PROBABLY NEVER HEARD OF IT. IT'S CALLED *TATOOINE*.
OH, I'VE HEARD OF IT. BOY, NO WONDER YOU JOINED THE REBELLION. I'D HAVE DONE ANYTHING TO GET OFF THAT ROCK, TOO.
YOU'RE NOT WRONG. BUT THAT'S NOT W I'M HERE.

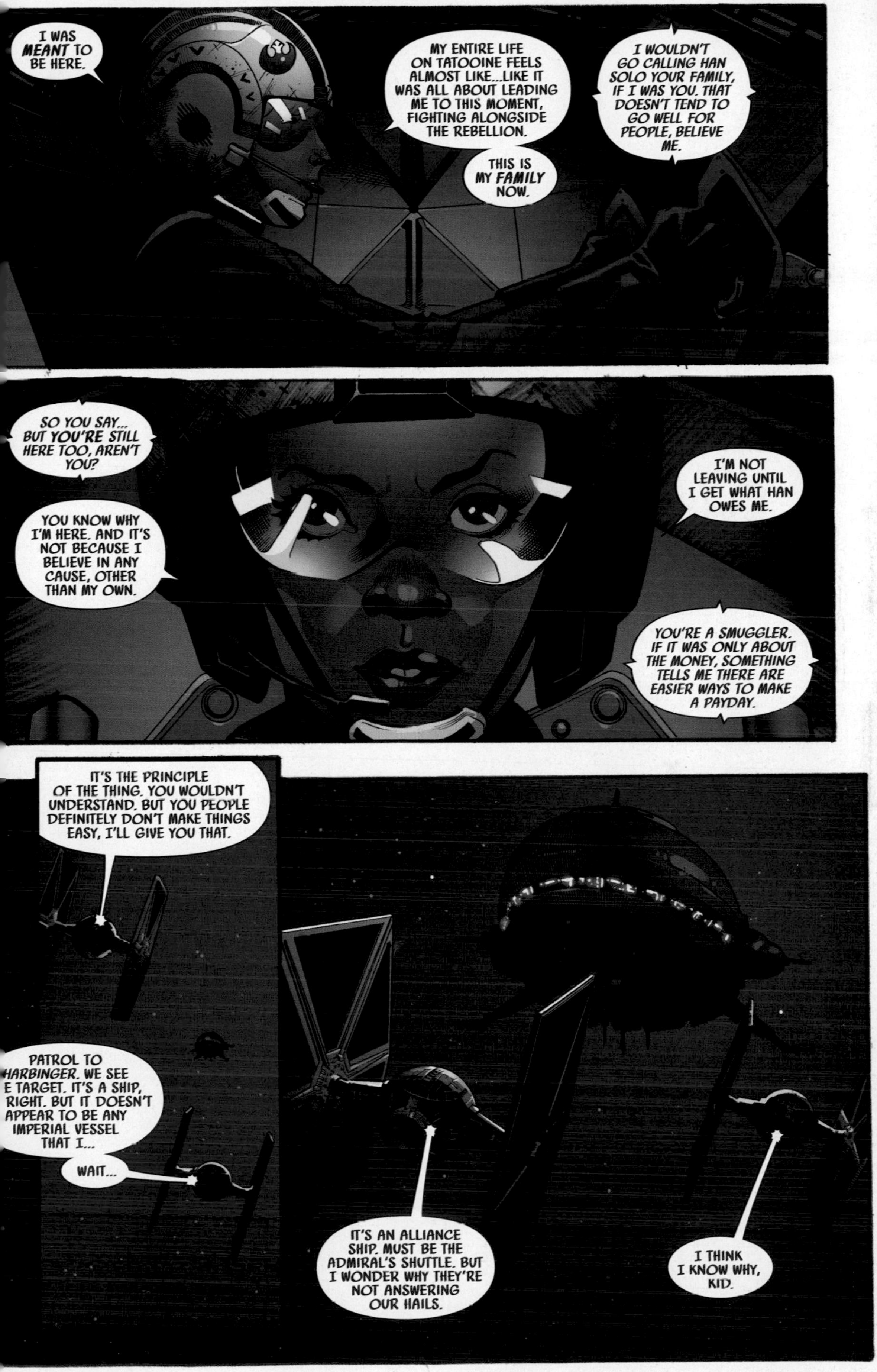

I WAS MEANT TO BE HERE.
MY ENTIRE LIFE ON TATOOINE FEELS ALMOST LIKE...LIKE IT WAS ALL ABOUT LEADING ME TO THIS MOMENT, FIGHTING ALONGSIDE THE REBELLION.
THIS IS MY FAMILY NOW.
I WOULDN'T GO CALLING HAN SOLO YOUR FAMILY, IF I WAS YOU. THAT DOESN'T TEND TO GO WELL FOR PEOPLE, BELIEVE ME.
SO YOU SAY... BUT YOU'RE STILL HERE TOO, AREN'T YOU?
YOU KNOW WHY I'M HERE. AND IT'S NOT BECAUSE I BELIEVE IN ANY CAUSE, OTHER THAN MY OWN.
I'M NOT LEAVING UNTIL I GET WHAT HAN OWES ME.
YOU'RE A SMUGGLER. IF IT WAS ONLY ABOUT THE MONEY, SOMETHING TELLS ME THERE ARE EASIER WAYS TO MAKE A PAYDAY.
IT'S THE PRINCIPLE OF THE THING. YOU WOULDN'T UNDERSTAND. BUT YOU PEOPLE DEFINITELY DON'T MAKE THINGS EASY, I'LL GIVE YOU THAT.
PATROL TO HARBINGER. WE SEE E TARGET. IT'S A SHIP, RIGHT. BUT IT DOESN'T APPEAR TO BE ANY IMPERIAL VESSEL THAT I...
WAIT...
IT'S AN ALLIANCE SHIP. MUST BE THE ADMIRAL'S SHUTTLE. BUT I WONDER WHY THEY'RE NOT ANSWERING OUR HAILS.
I THINK I KNOW WHY, KID.

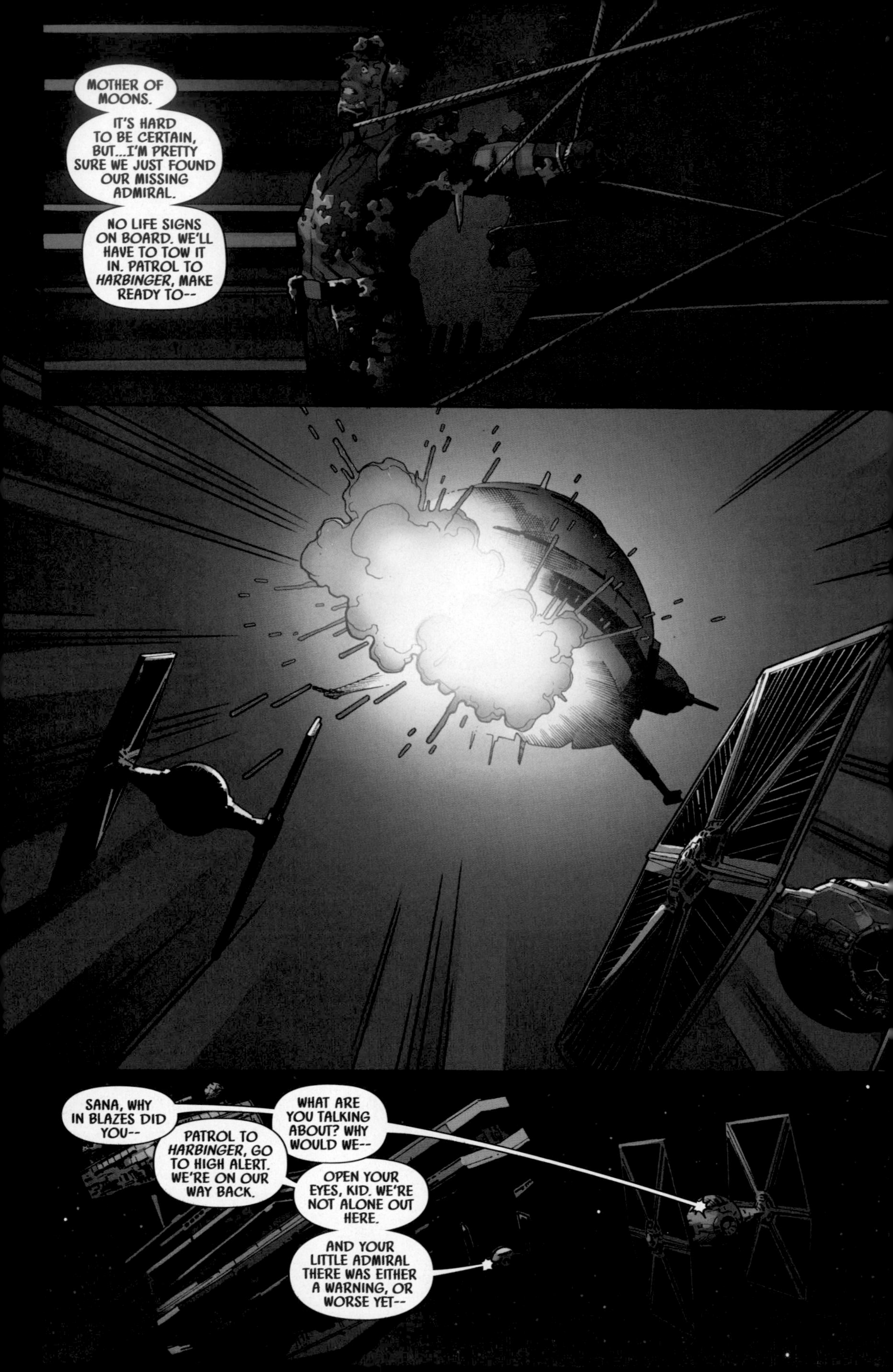

MOTHER OF MOONS.
IT'S HARD TO BE CERTAIN, BUT...I'M PRETTY SURE WE JUST FOUND OUR MISSING ADMIRAL.
NO LIFE SIGNS ON BOARD. WE'LL HAVE TO TOW IT IN. PATROL TO HARBINGER, MAKE READY TO--
SANA, WHY IN BLAZES DID YOU--
WHAT ARE YOU TALKING ABOUT? WHY WOULD WE--
PATROL TO HARBINGER, GO TO HIGH ALERT. WE'RE ON OUR WAY BACK.
OPEN YOUR EYES, KID. WE'RE NOT ALONE OUT HERE.
AND YOUR LITTLE ADMIRAL THERE WAS EITHER A WARNING, OR WORSE YET--

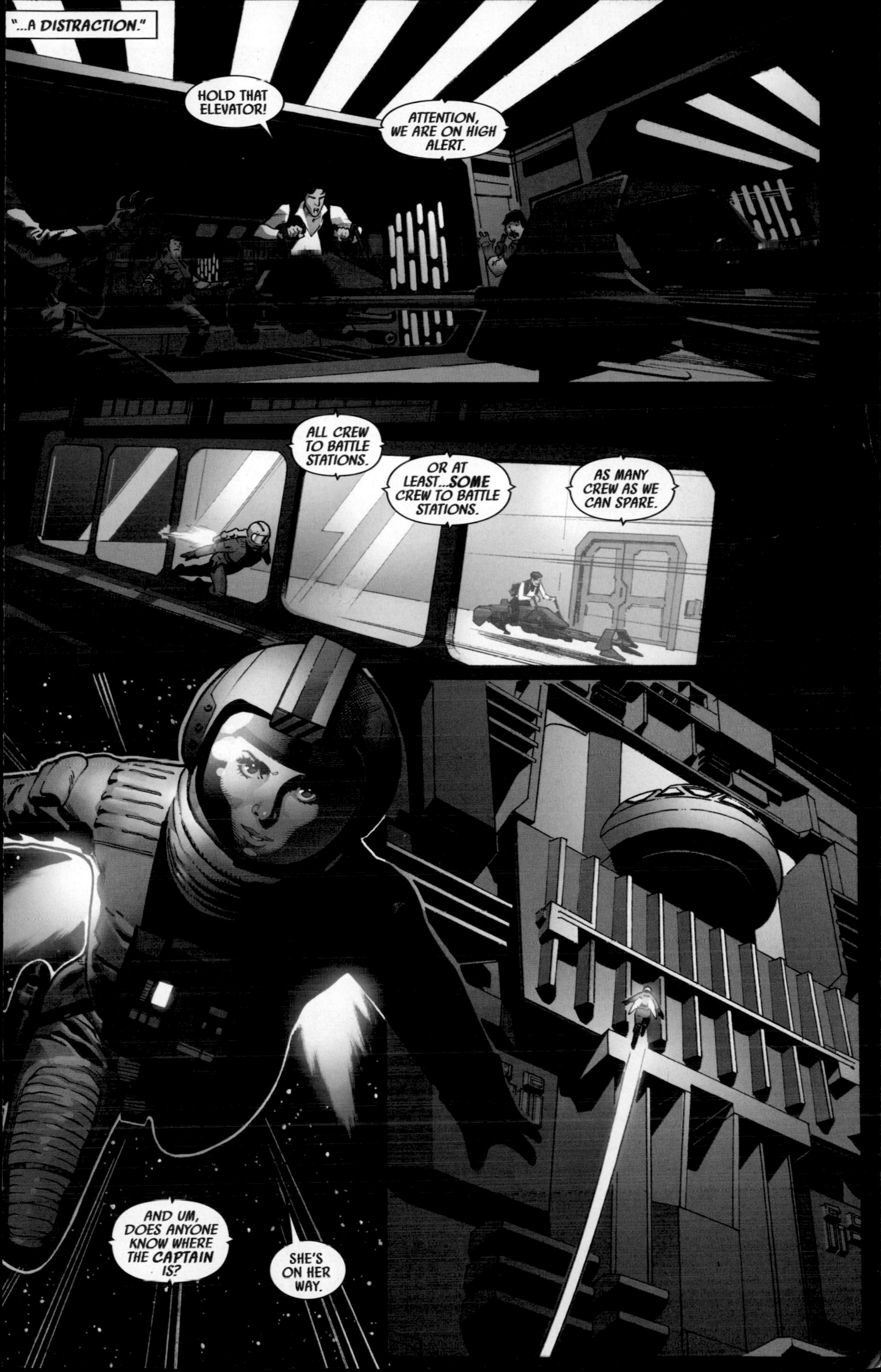
"...A DISTRACTION."
HOLD THAT ELEVATOR!
ATTENTION, WE ARE ON HIGH ALERT.
ALL CREW TO BATTLE STATIONS.
OR AT LEAST...SOME CREW TO BATTLE STATIONS.
AS MANY CREW AS WE CAN SPARE.
AND UM, DOES ANYONE KNOW WHERE THE CAPTAIN IS?
SHE'S ON HER WAY.

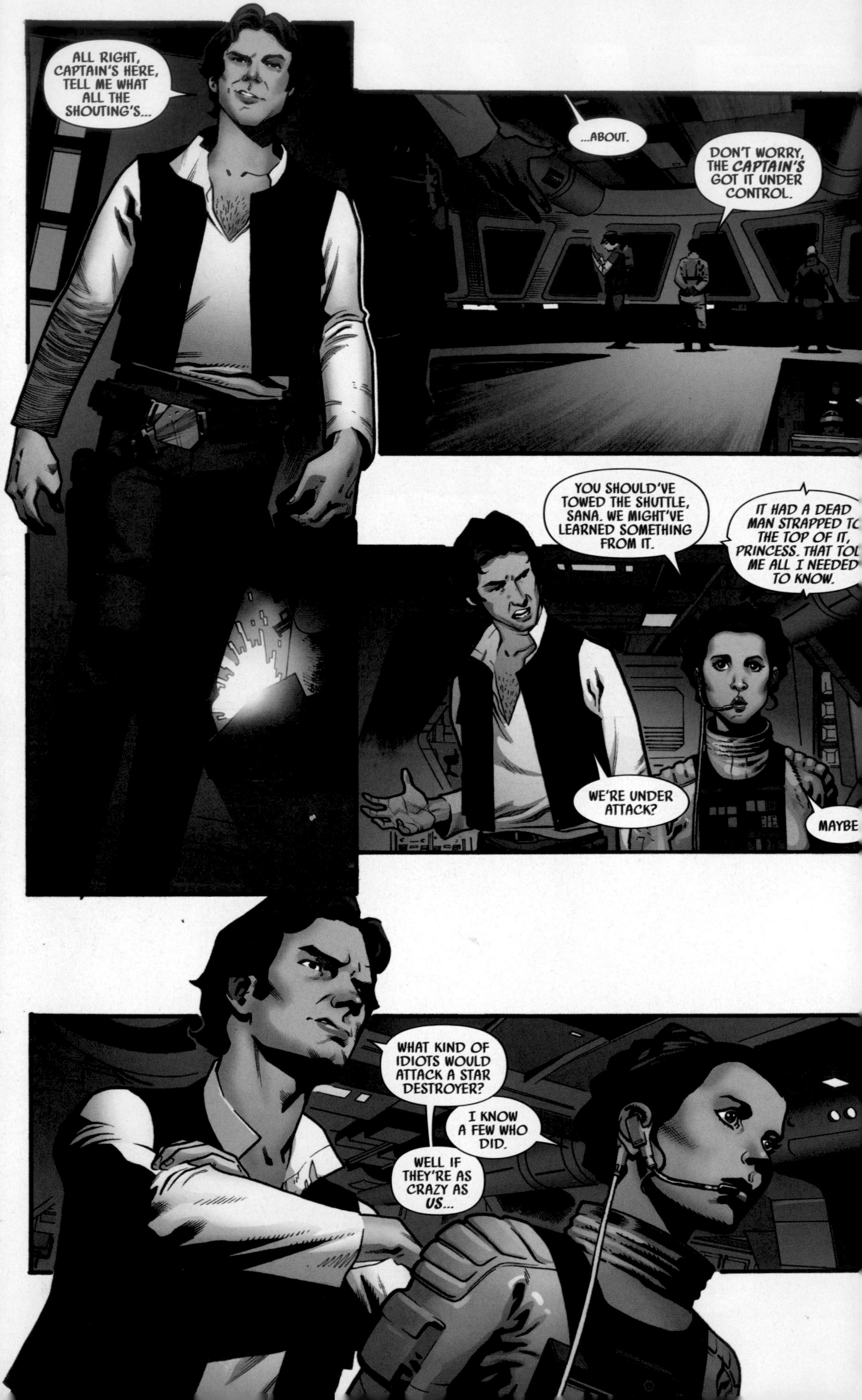
ALL RIGHT, CAPTAIN'S HERE, TELL ME WHAT ALL THE SHOUTING'S...
...ABOUT.
DON'T WORRY, THE *CAPTAIN'S* GOT IT UNDER CONTROL.
YOU SHOULD'VE TOWED THE SHUTTLE, SANA. WE MIGHT'VE LEARNED SOMETHING FROM IT.
IT HAD A DEAD MAN STRAPPED TO THE TOP OF IT, PRINCESS. THAT TOLD ME ALL I NEEDED TO KNOW.
WE'RE UNDER ATTACK?
MAYBE
WHAT KIND OF IDIOTS WOULD ATTACK A STAR DESTROYER?
I KNOW A FEW WHO DID.
WELL IF THEY'RE AS CRAZY AS *US*...

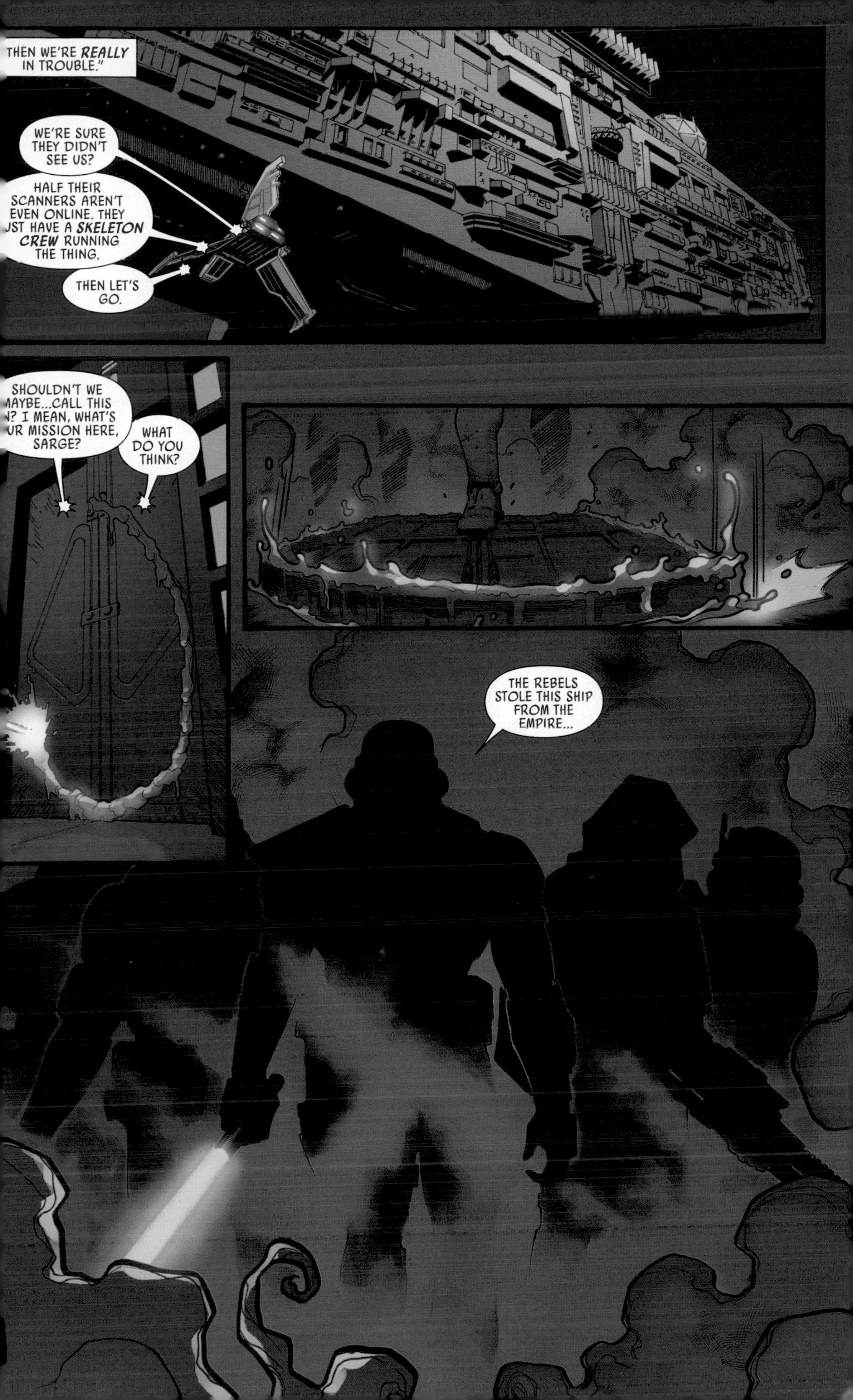
THEN WE'RE REALLY IN TROUBLE."
WE'RE SURE THEY DIDN'T SEE US?
HALF THEIR SCANNERS AREN'T EVEN ONLINE. THEY UST HAVE A SKELETON CREW RUNNING THE THING.
THEN LET'S GO.
SHOULDN'T WE MAYBE...CALL THIS N? I MEAN, WHAT'S UR MISSION HERE, SARGE?
WHAT DO YOU THINK?
THE REBELS STOLE THIS SHIP FROM THE EMPIRE...

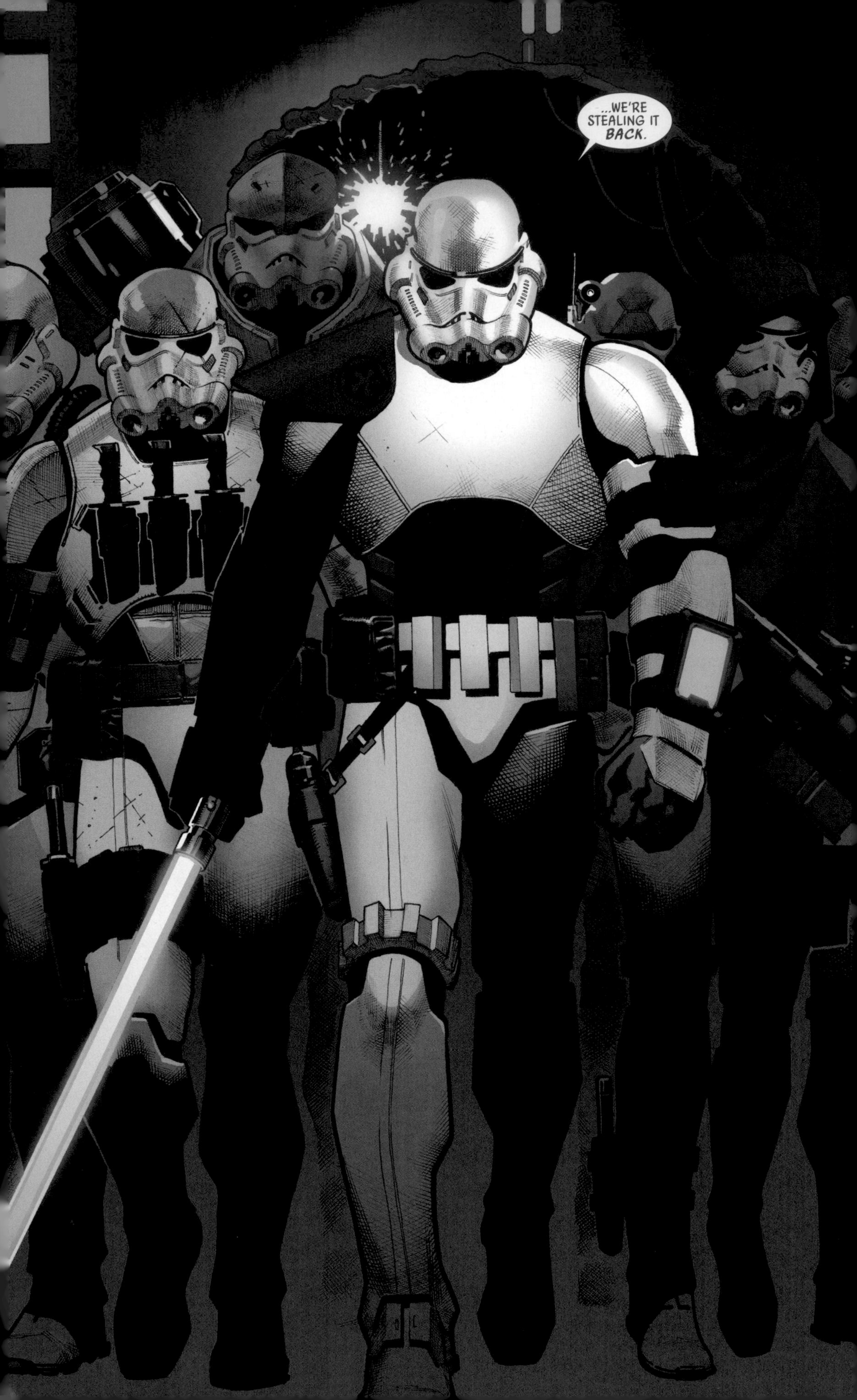
...WE'RE STEALING IT BACK.

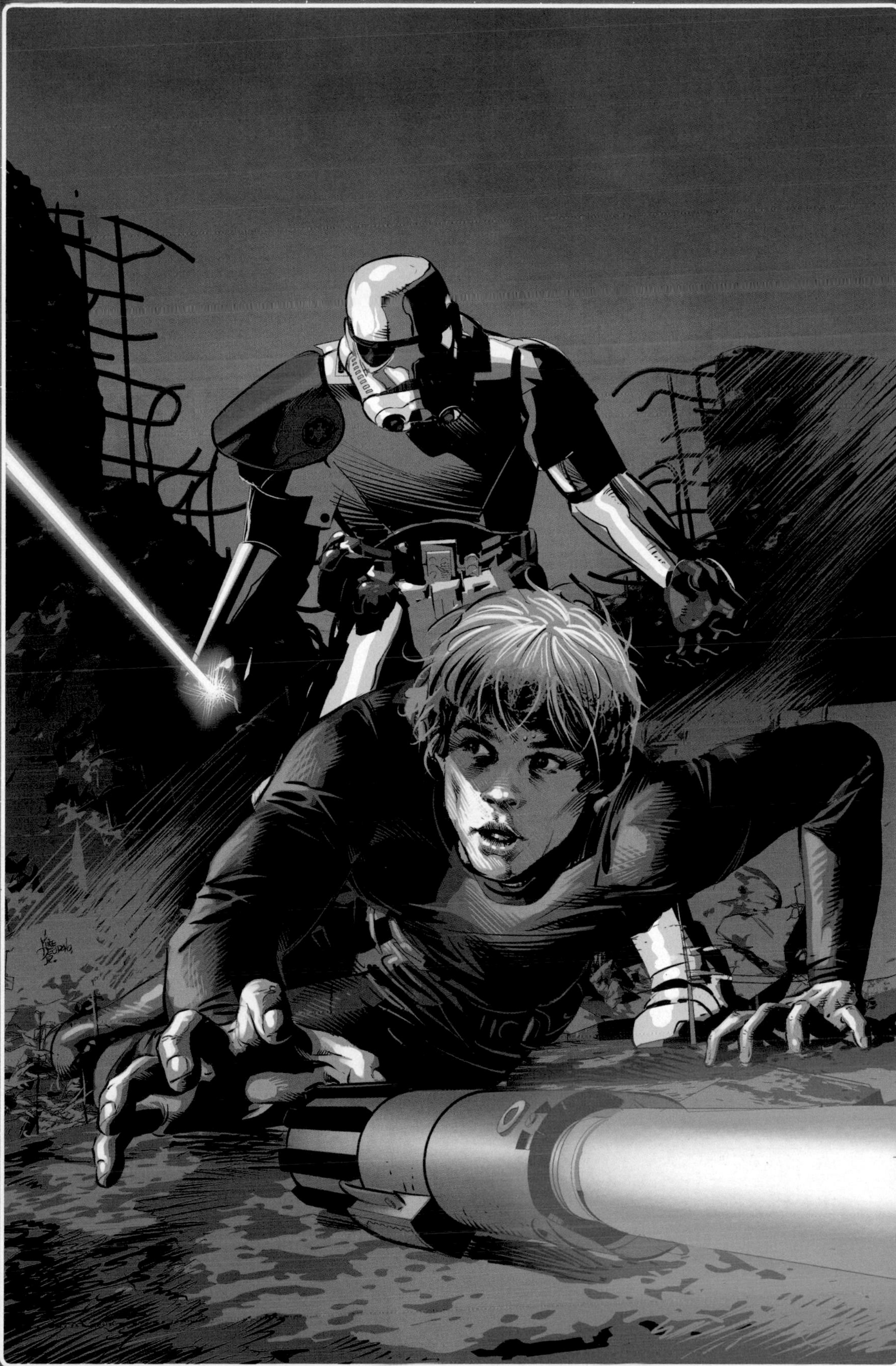

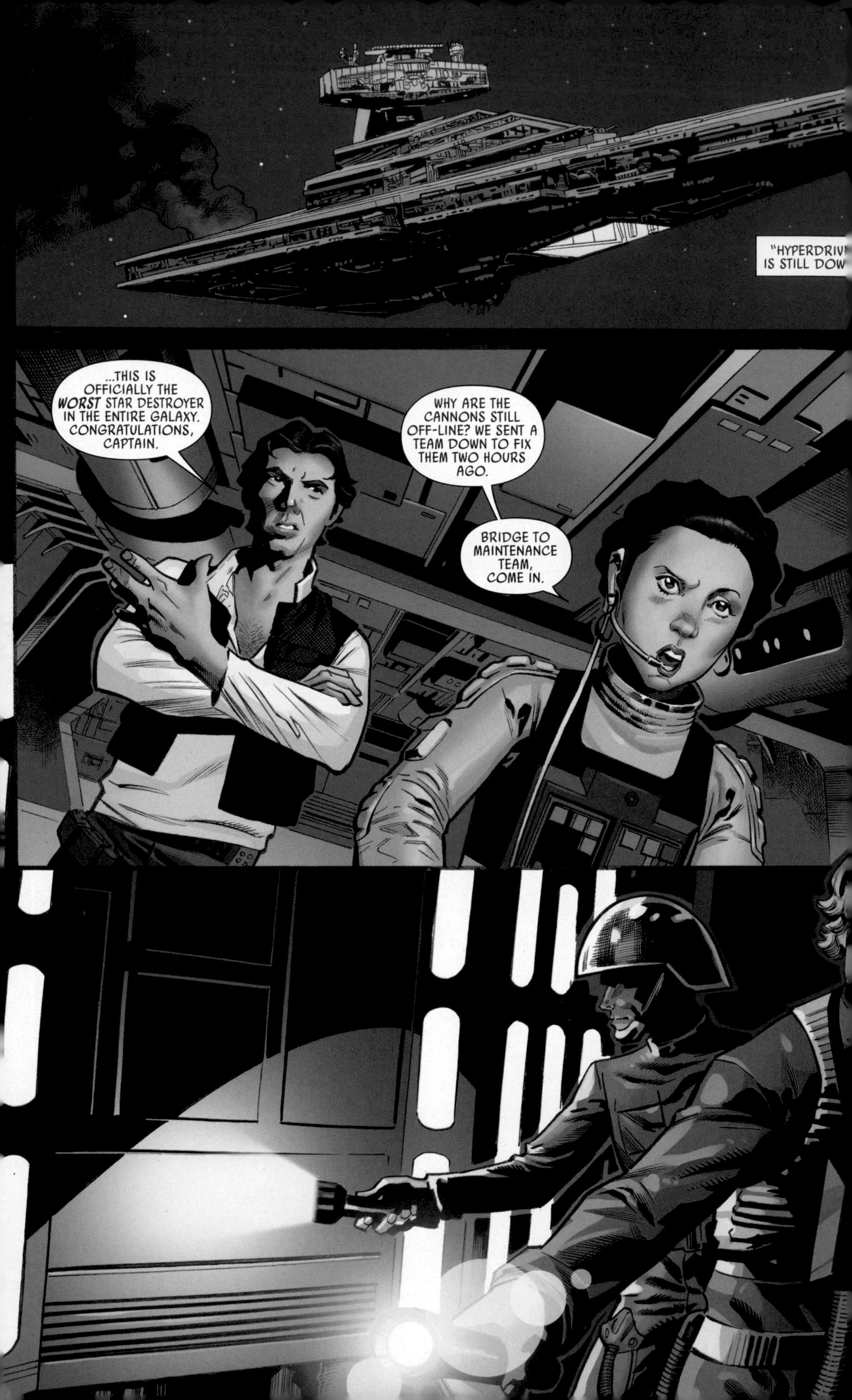

"HYPERDRIV
IS STILL DOW
...THIS IS OFFICIALLY THE *WORST* STAR DESTROYER IN THE ENTIRE GALAXY. CONGRATULATIONS, CAPTAIN.
WHY ARE THE CANNONS STILL OFF-LINE? WE SENT A TEAM DOWN TO FIX THEM TWO HOURS AGO.
BRIDGE TO MAINTENANCE TEAM, COME IN.

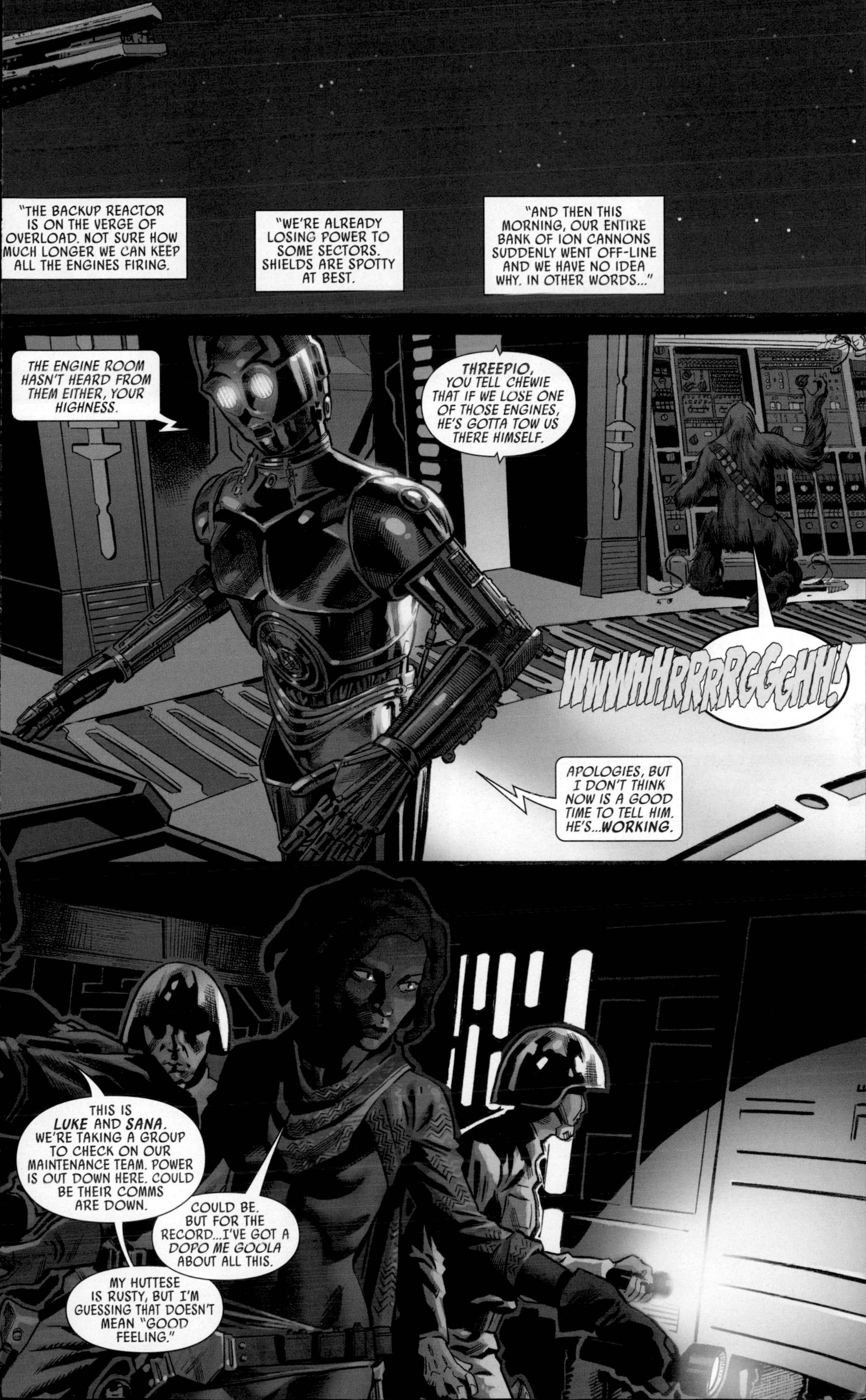
"THE BACKUP REACTOR IS ON THE VERGE OF OVERLOAD. NOT SURE HOW MUCH LONGER WE CAN KEEP ALL THE ENGINES FIRING.
"WE'RE ALREADY LOSING POWER TO SOME SECTORS. SHIELDS ARE SPOTTY AT BEST.
"AND THEN THIS MORNING, OUR ENTIRE BANK OF ION CANNONS SUDDENLY WENT OFF-LINE AND WE HAVE NO IDEA WHY. IN OTHER WORDS..."
THE ENGINE ROOM HASN'T HEARD FROM THEM EITHER, YOUR HIGHNESS.
THREEPIO, YOU TELL CHEWIE THAT IF WE LOSE ONE OF THOSE ENGINES, HE'S GOTTA TOW US THERE HIMSELF.
WWWHRRRRGGHH!
APOLOGIES, BUT I DON'T THINK NOW IS A GOOD TIME TO TELL HIM. HE'S...WORKING.
THIS IS LUKE AND SANA. WE'RE TAKING A GROUP TO CHECK ON OUR MAINTENANCE TEAM. POWER IS OUT DOWN HERE. COULD BE THEIR COMMS ARE DOWN.
COULD BE. BUT FOR THE RECORD...I'VE GOT A DOPO ME GOOLA ABOUT ALL THIS.
MY HUTTESE IS RUSTY, BUT I'M GUESSING THAT DOESN'T MEAN "GOOD FEELING."

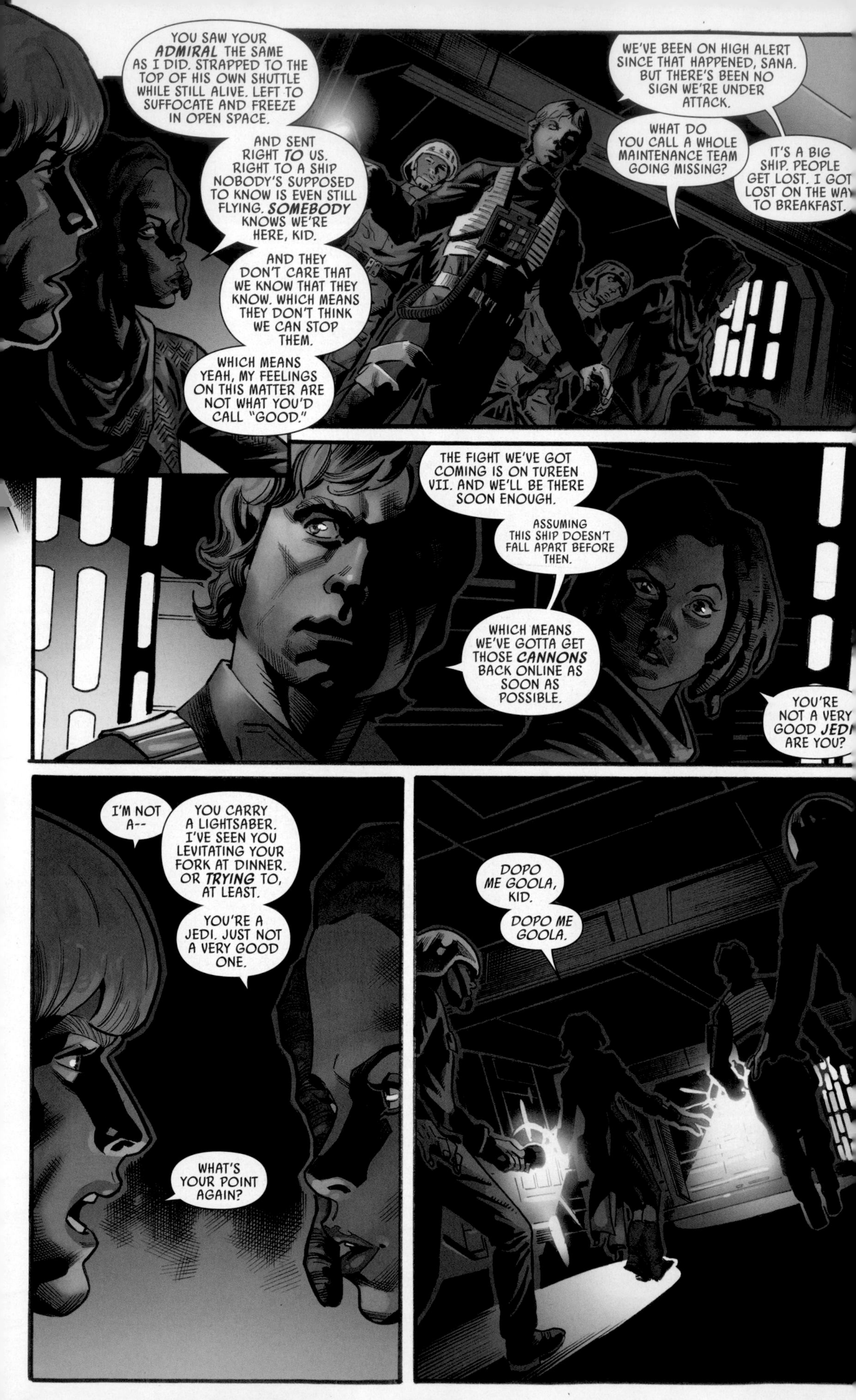
YOU SAW YOUR ADMIRAL THE SAME AS I DID. STRAPPED TO THE TOP OF HIS OWN SHUTTLE WHILE STILL ALIVE. LEFT TO SUFFOCATE AND FREEZE IN OPEN SPACE.
AND SENT RIGHT TO US. RIGHT TO A SHIP NOBODY'S SUPPOSED TO KNOW IS EVEN STILL FLYING. SOMEBODY KNOWS WE'RE HERE, KID.
AND THEY DON'T CARE THAT WE KNOW THAT THEY KNOW. WHICH MEANS THEY DON'T THINK WE CAN STOP THEM.
WHICH MEANS YEAH, MY FEELINGS ON THIS MATTER ARE NOT WHAT YOU'D CALL "GOOD."
WE'VE BEEN ON HIGH ALERT SINCE THAT HAPPENED, SANA. BUT THERE'S BEEN NO SIGN WE'RE UNDER ATTACK.
WHAT DO YOU CALL A WHOLE MAINTENANCE TEAM GOING MISSING?
IT'S A BIG SHIP. PEOPLE GET LOST. I GOT LOST ON THE WAY TO BREAKFAST.
THE FIGHT WE'VE GOT COMING IS ON TUREEN VII. AND WE'LL BE THERE SOON ENOUGH.
ASSUMING THIS SHIP DOESN'T FALL APART BEFORE THEN.
WHICH MEANS WE'VE GOTTA GET THOSE CANNONS BACK ONLINE AS SOON AS POSSIBLE.
YOU'RE NOT A VERY GOOD JEDI ARE YOU?
I'M NOT A--
YOU CARRY A LIGHTSABER. I'VE SEEN YOU LEVITATING YOUR FORK AT DINNER. OR TRYING TO, AT LEAST.
YOU'RE A JEDI. JUST NOT A VERY GOOD ONE.
WHAT'S YOUR POINT AGAIN?
DOPO ME GOOLA, KID.
DOPO ME GOOLA.

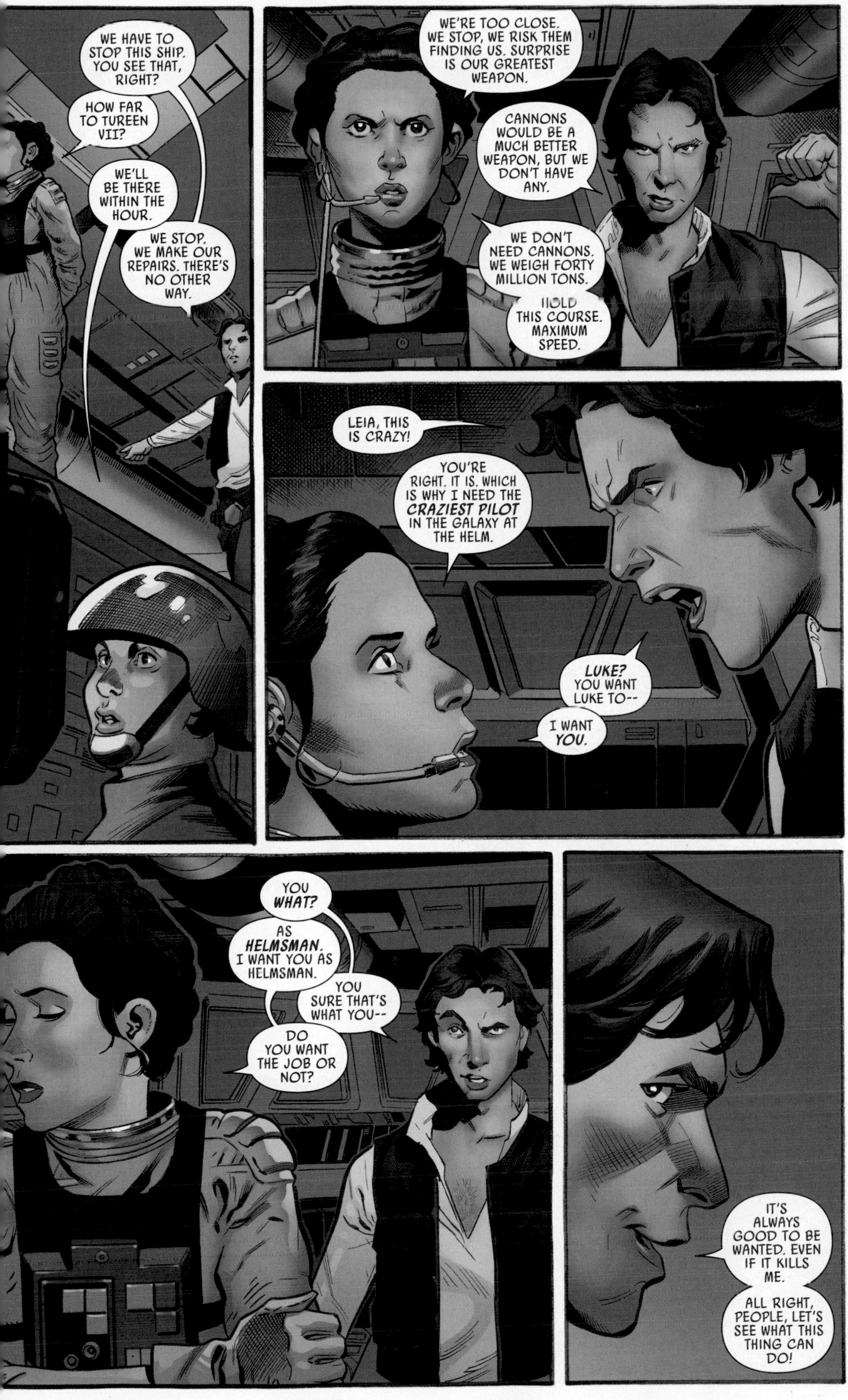

WE HAVE TO STOP THIS SHIP. YOU SEE THAT, RIGHT?
HOW FAR TO TUREEN VII?
WE'LL BE THERE WITHIN THE HOUR.
WE STOP. WE MAKE OUR REPAIRS. THERE'S NO OTHER WAY.
WE'RE TOO CLOSE. WE STOP, WE RISK THEM FINDING US. SURPRISE IS OUR GREATEST WEAPON.
CANNONS WOULD BE A MUCH BETTER WEAPON, BUT WE DON'T HAVE ANY.
WE DON'T NEED CANNONS. WE WEIGH FORTY MILLION TONS.
HOLD THIS COURSE. MAXIMUM SPEED.
LEIA, THIS IS CRAZY!
YOU'RE RIGHT. IT IS. WHICH IS WHY I NEED THE ***CRAZIEST PILOT*** IN THE GALAXY AT THE HELM.
LUKE? YOU WANT LUKE TO--
I WANT ***YOU.***
YOU ***WHAT?***
AS ***HELMSMAN.*** I WANT YOU AS HELMSMAN.
YOU SURE THAT'S WHAT YOU--
DO YOU WANT THE JOB OR NOT?
IT'S ALWAYS GOOD TO BE WANTED. EVEN IF IT KILLS ME.
ALL RIGHT, PEOPLE, LET'S SEE WHAT THIS THING CAN DO!

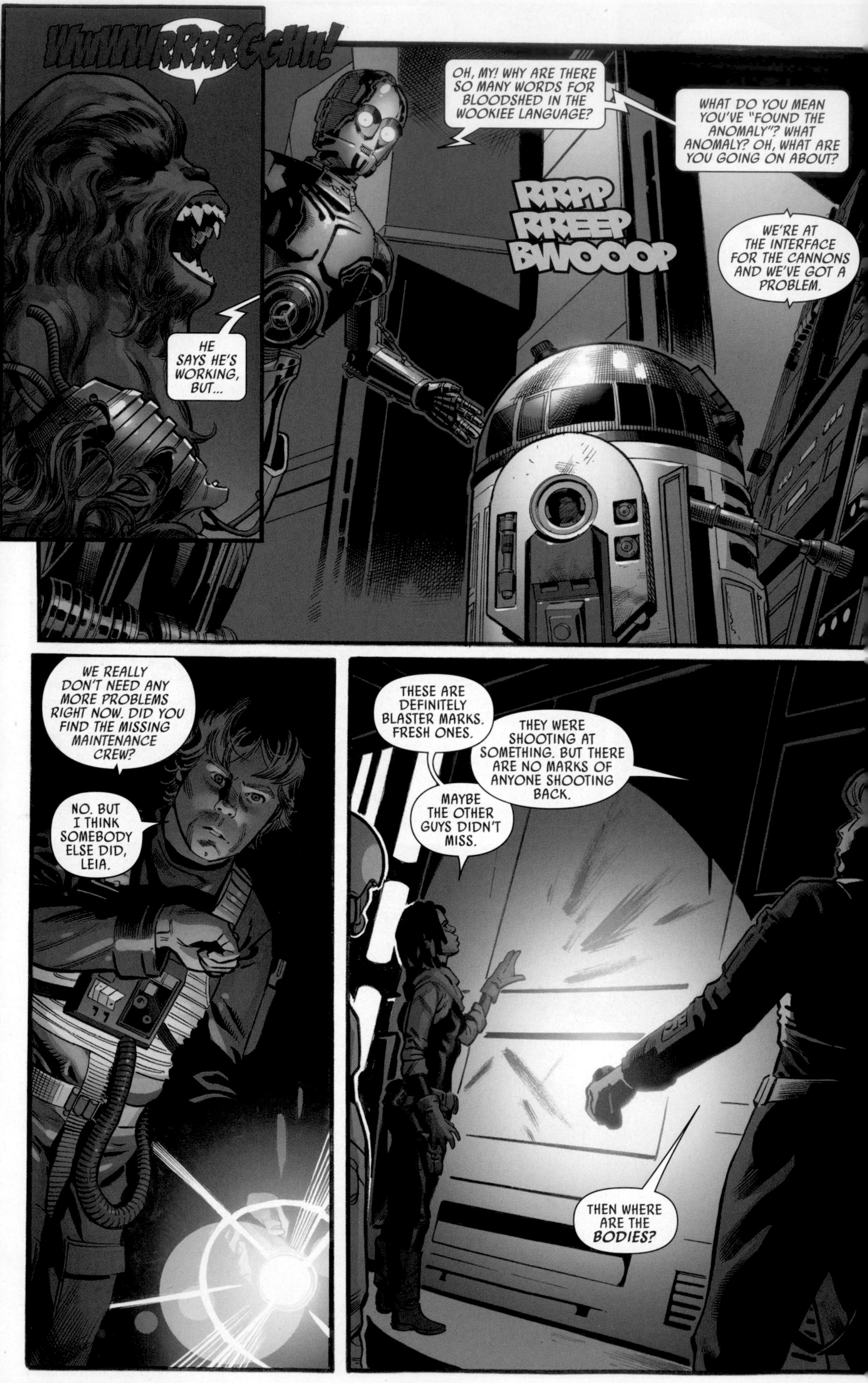
WWWWRRRRGGHH!
OH, MY! WHY ARE THERE SO MANY WORDS FOR BLOODSHED IN THE WOOKIEE LANGUAGE?
HE SAYS HE'S WORKING, BUT...
RRRPP RRREEP BWOOOP
WHAT DO YOU MEAN YOU'VE "FOUND THE ANOMALY"? WHAT ANOMALY? OH, WHAT ARE YOU GOING ON ABOUT?
WE'RE AT THE INTERFACE FOR THE CANNONS AND WE'VE GOT A PROBLEM.
WE REALLY DON'T NEED ANY MORE PROBLEMS RIGHT NOW. DID YOU FIND THE MISSING MAINTENANCE CREW?
NO. BUT I THINK SOMEBODY ELSE DID, LEIA.
THESE ARE DEFINITELY BLASTER MARKS. FRESH ONES.
THEY WERE SHOOTING AT SOMETHING. BUT THERE ARE NO MARKS OF ANYONE SHOOTING BACK.
MAYBE THE OTHER GUYS DIDN'T MISS.
THEN WHERE ARE THE BODIES?

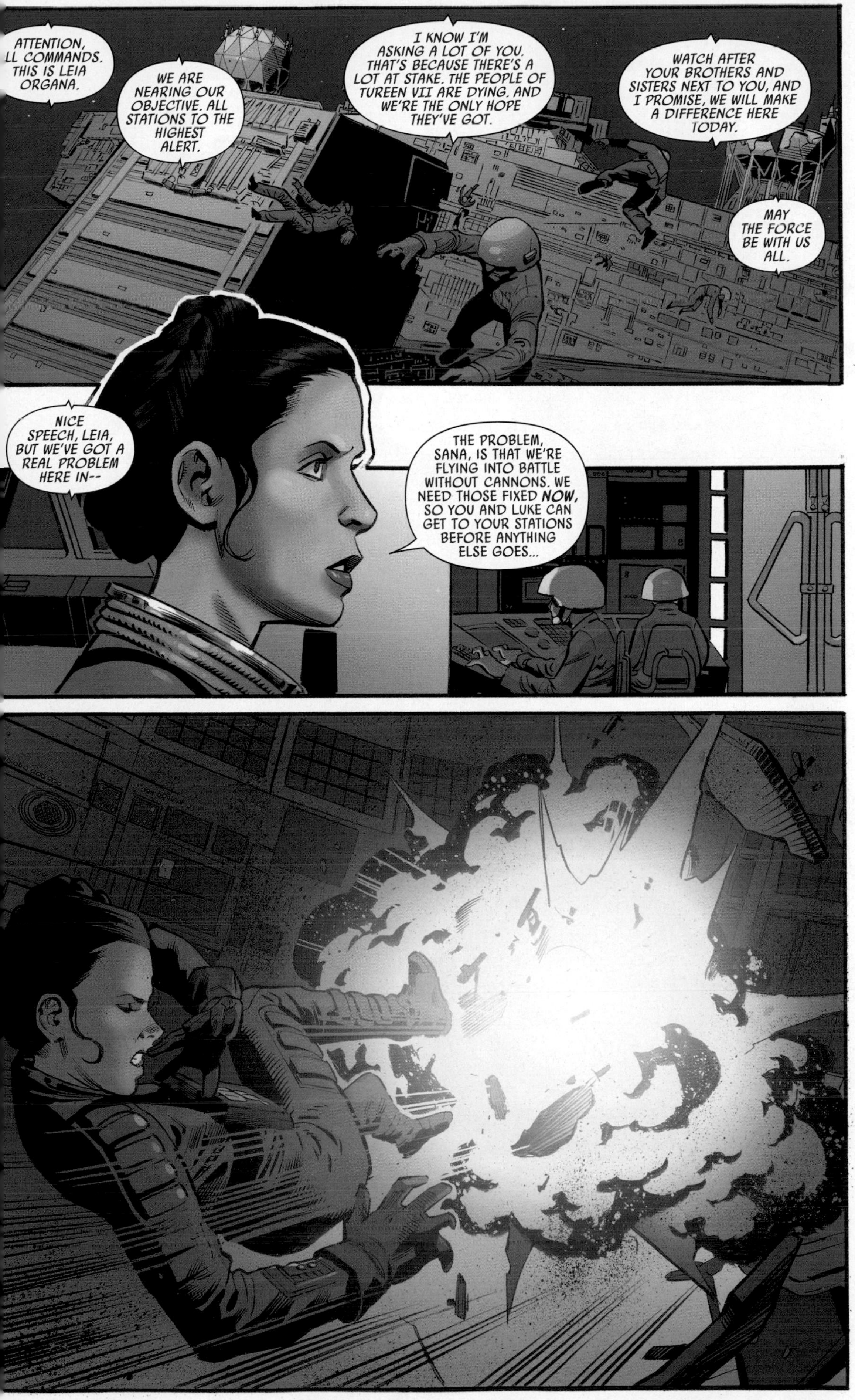

ATTENTION, ALL COMMANDS. THIS IS LEIA ORGANA.
WE ARE NEARING OUR OBJECTIVE. ALL STATIONS TO THE HIGHEST ALERT.
I KNOW I'M ASKING A LOT OF YOU. THAT'S BECAUSE THERE'S A LOT AT STAKE. THE PEOPLE OF TUREEN VII ARE DYING. AND WE'RE THE ONLY HOPE THEY'VE GOT.
WATCH AFTER YOUR BROTHERS AND SISTERS NEXT TO YOU, AND I PROMISE, WE WILL MAKE A DIFFERENCE HERE TODAY.
MAY THE FORCE BE WITH US ALL.
NICE SPEECH, LEIA, BUT WE'VE GOT A REAL PROBLEM HERE IN--
THE PROBLEM, SANA, IS THAT WE'RE FLYING INTO BATTLE WITHOUT CANNONS. WE NEED THOSE FIXED **NOW**, SO YOU AND LUKE CAN GET TO YOUR STATIONS BEFORE ANYTHING ELSE GOES...

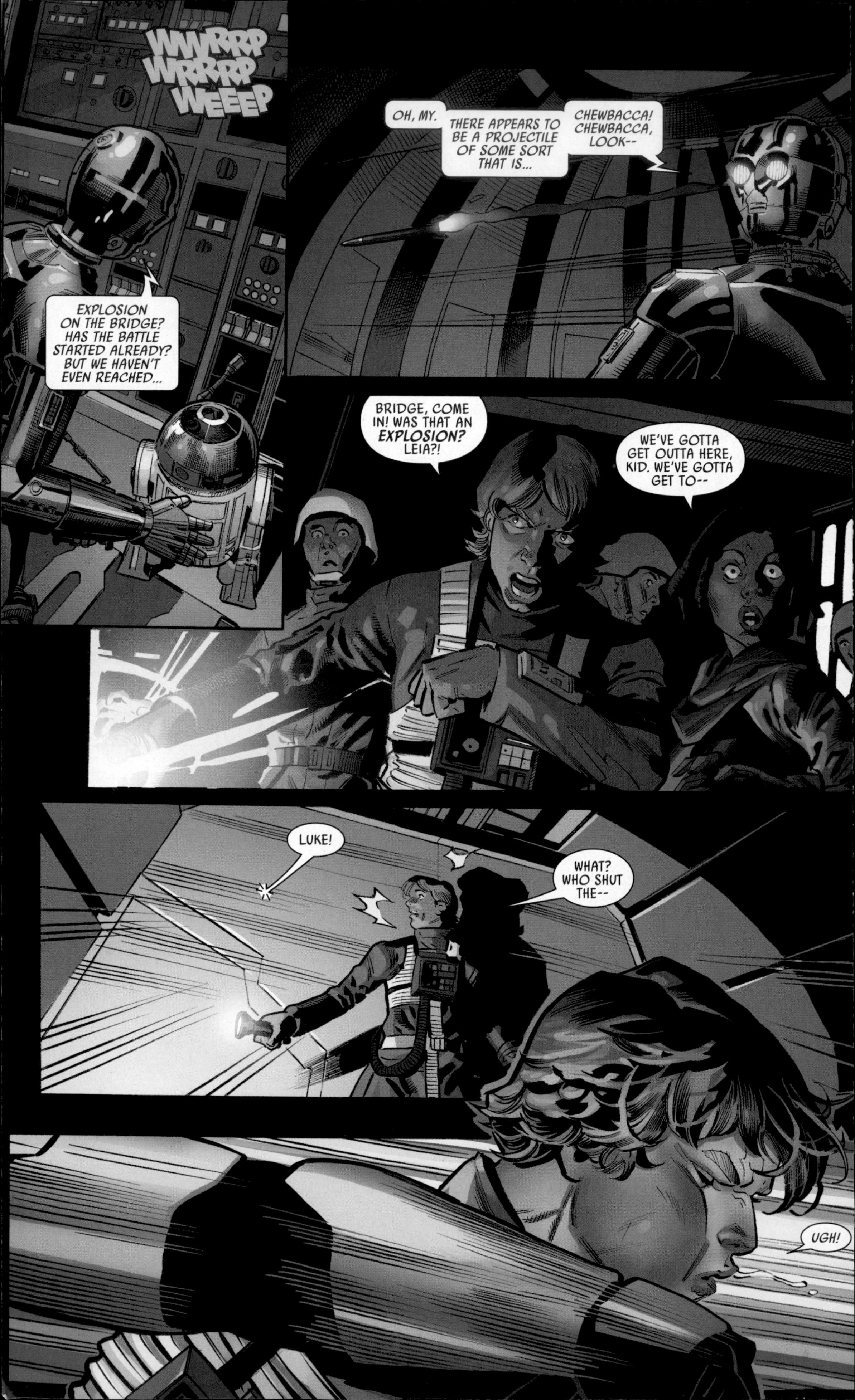
WWRRP WRRRP WEEEP
EXPLOSION ON THE BRIDGE? HAS THE BATTLE STARTED ALREADY? BUT WE HAVEN'T EVEN REACHED...
OH, MY.
THERE APPEARS TO BE A PROJECTILE OF SOME SORT THAT IS...
CHEWBACCA! CHEWBACCA, LOOK--
BRIDGE, COME IN! WAS THAT AN EXPLOSION? LEIA?!
WE'VE GOTTA GET OUTTA HERE, KID. WE'VE GOTTA GET TO--
LUKE!
WHAT? WHO SHUT THE--
UGH!

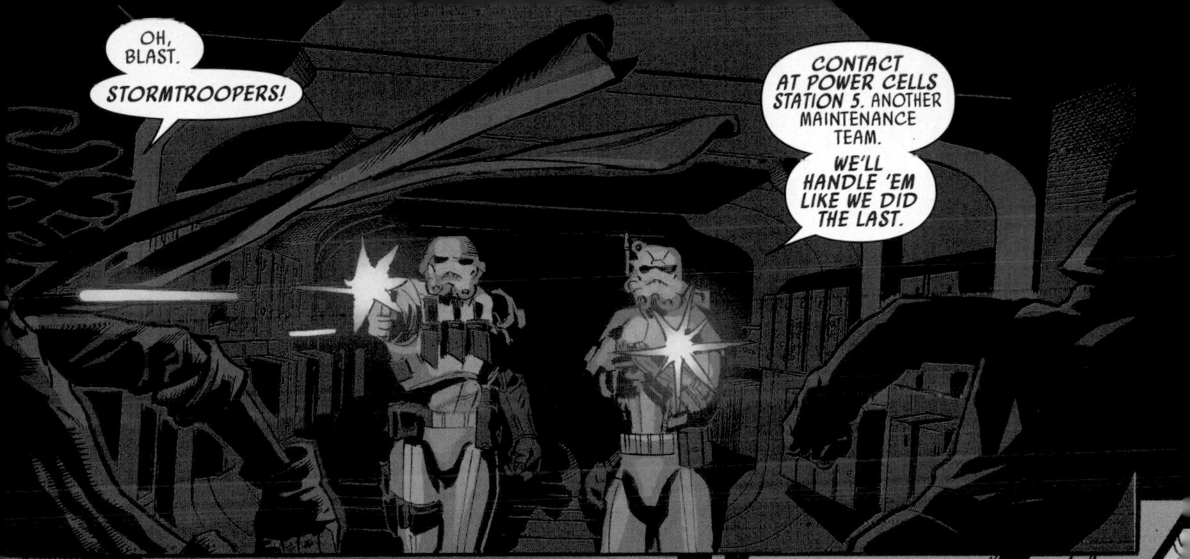
OH, BLAST.
STORMTROOPERS!
CONTACT AT POWER CELLS STATION 5. ANOTHER MAINTENANCE TEAM.
WE'LL HANDLE 'EM LIKE WE DID THE LAST.

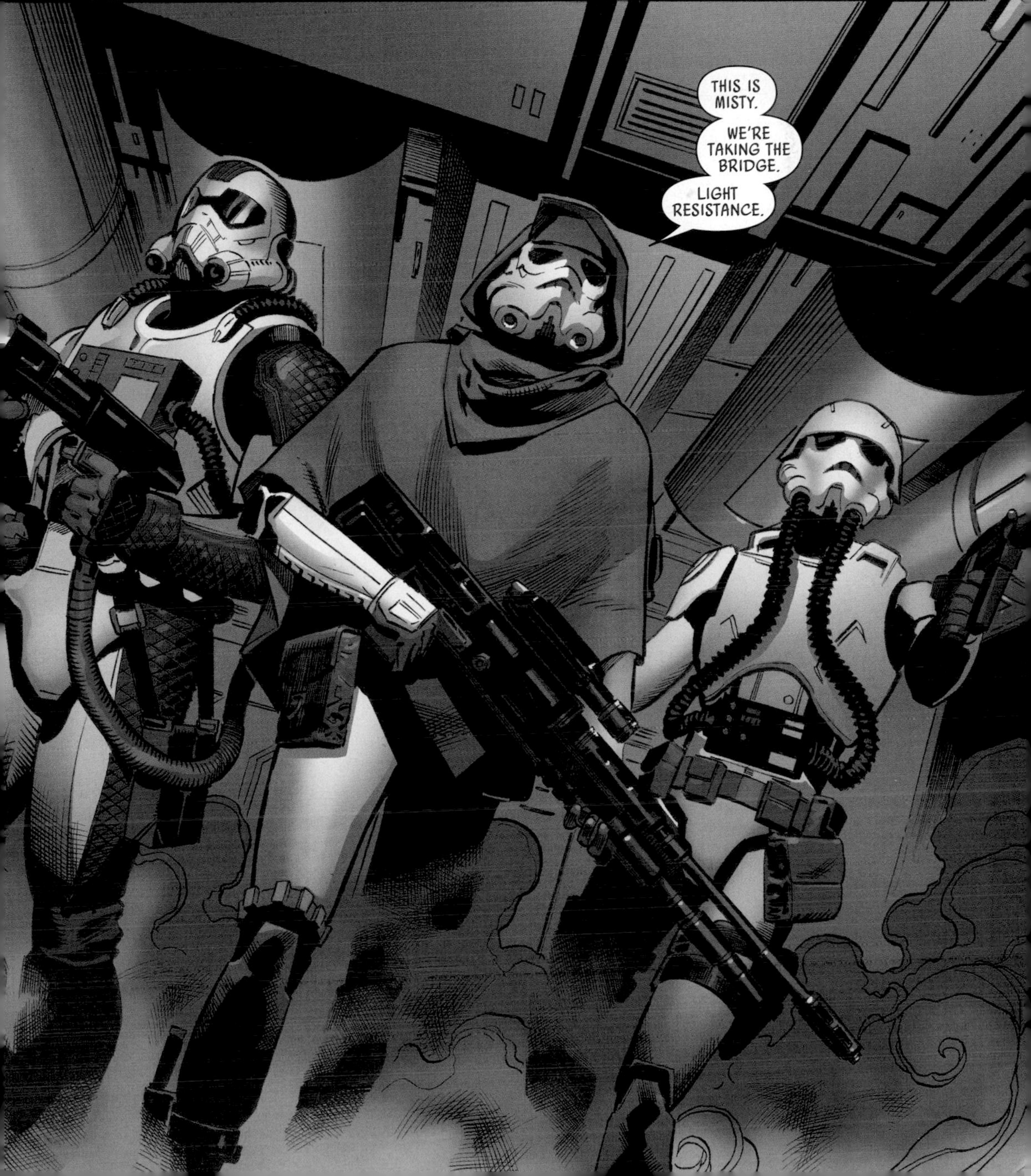
THIS IS MISTY.
WE'RE TAKING THE BRIDGE.
LIGHT RESISTANCE.

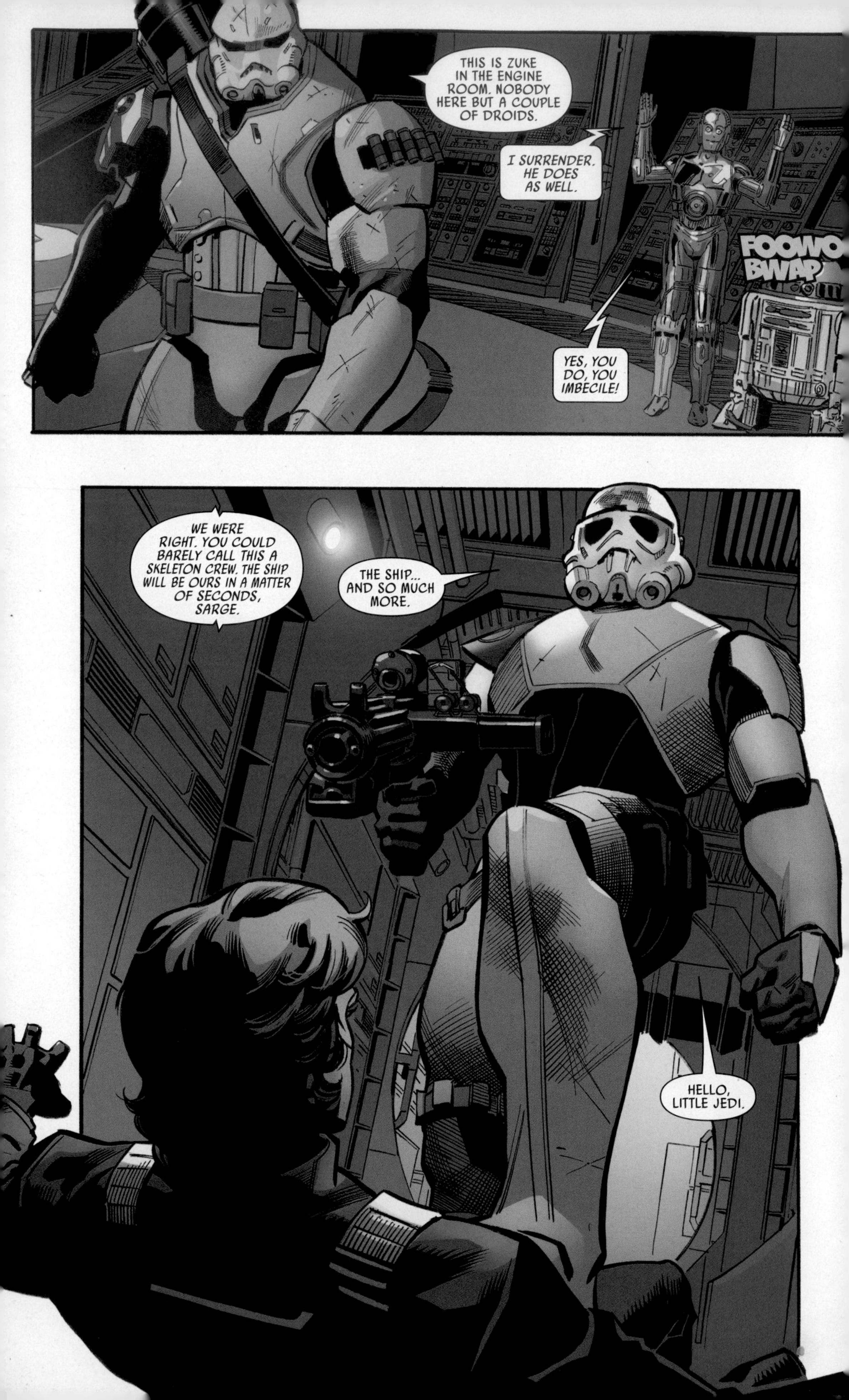
THIS IS ZUKE IN THE ENGINE ROOM. NOBODY HERE BUT A COUPLE OF DROIDS.
I SURRENDER. HE DOES AS WELL.
FOOWO BWAP
YES, YOU DO, YOU IMBECILE!
WE WERE RIGHT. YOU COULD BARELY CALL THIS A SKELETON CREW. THE SHIP WILL BE OURS IN A MATTER OF SECONDS, SARGE.
THE SHIP... AND SO MUCH MORE.
HELLO, LITTLE JEDI.

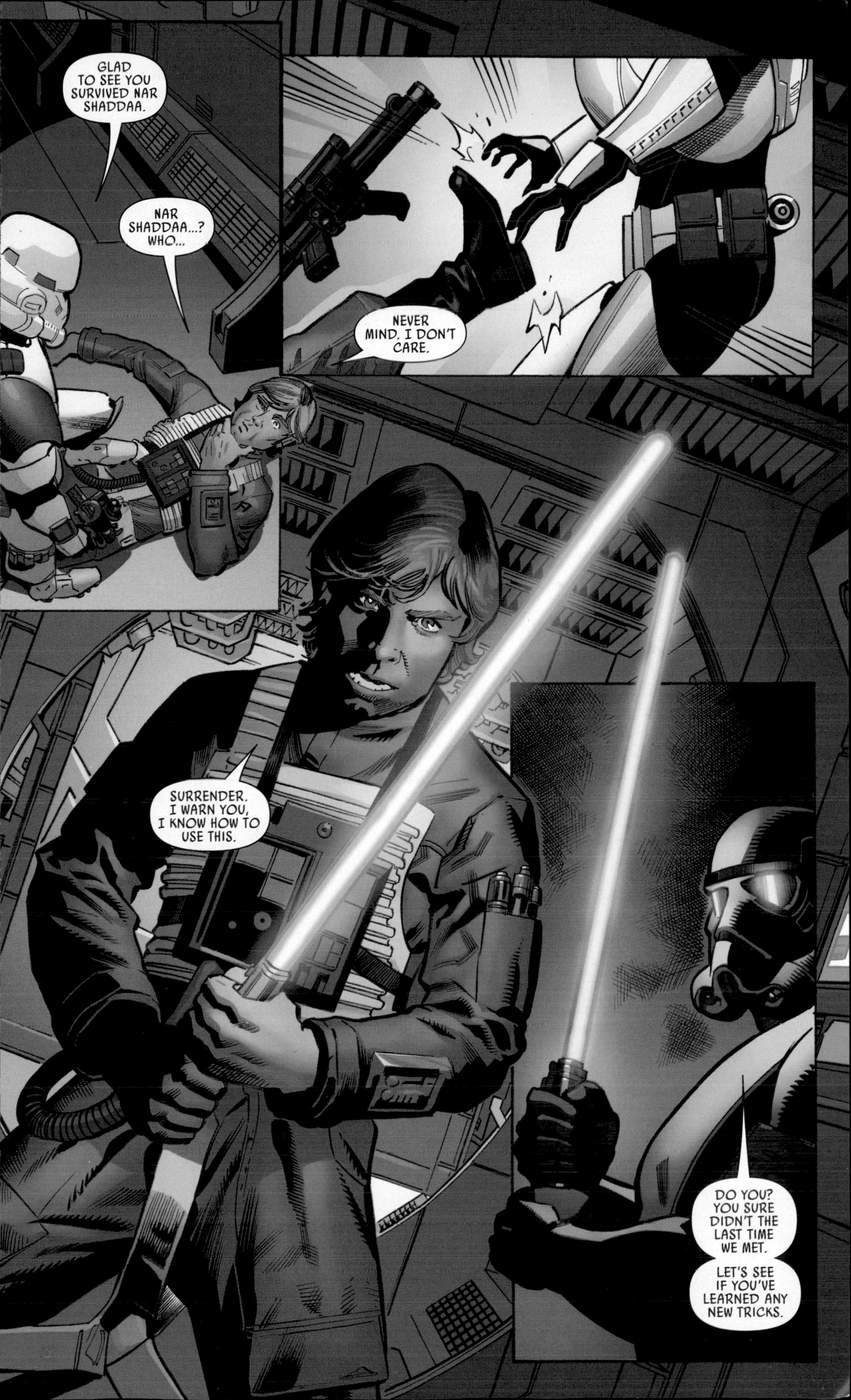

GLAD TO SEE YOU SURVIVED NAR SHADDAA.
NAR SHADDAA...? WHO...
NEVER MIND. I DON'T CARE.
SURRENDER. I WARN YOU, I KNOW HOW TO USE THIS.
DO YOU? YOU SURE DIDN'T THE LAST TIME WE MET.
LET'S SEE IF YOU'VE LEARNED ANY NEW TRICKS.

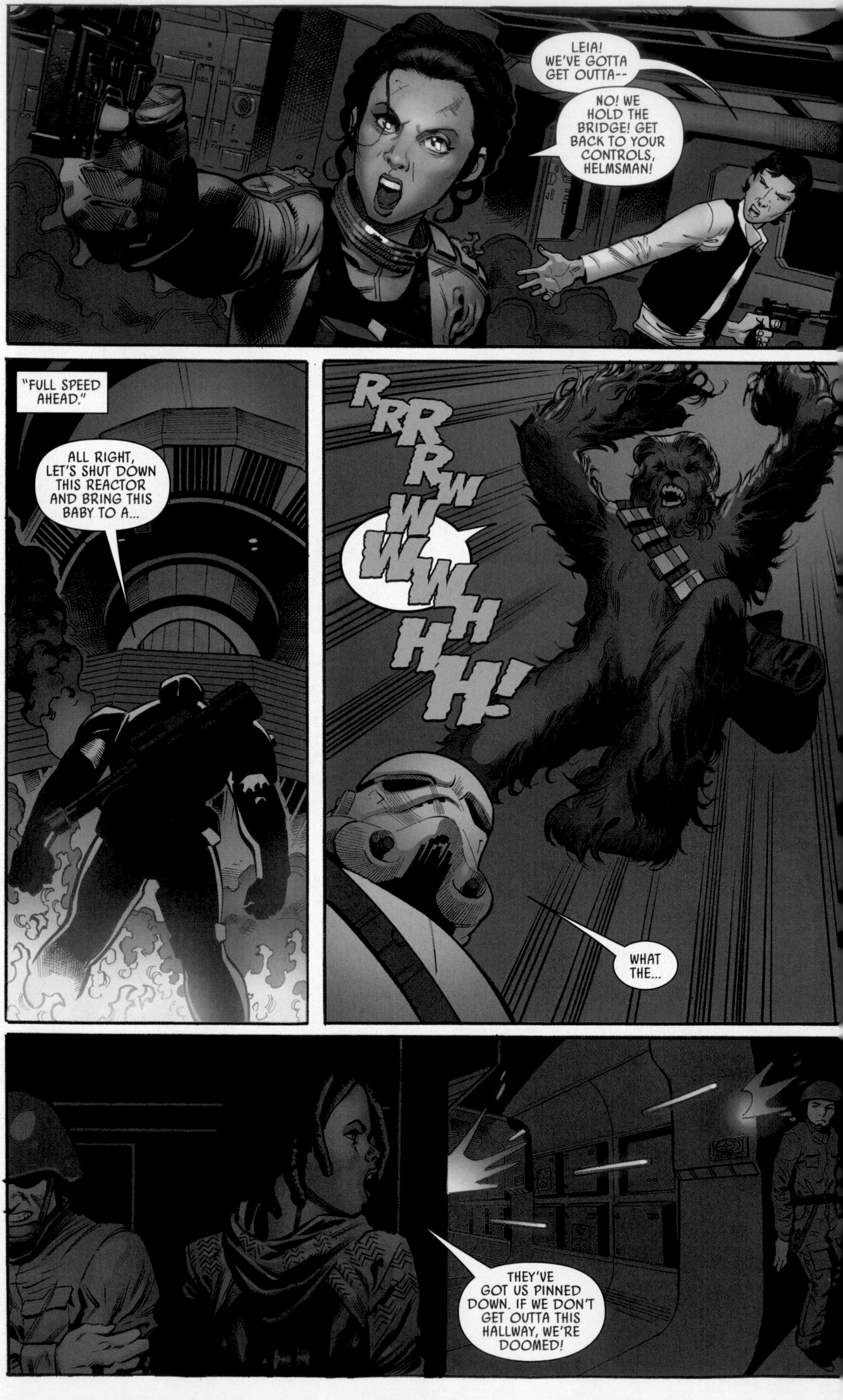
LEIA! WE'VE GOTTA GET OUTTA--
NO! WE HOLD THE BRIDGE! GET BACK TO YOUR CONTROLS, HELMSMAN!
"FULL SPEED AHEAD."
ALL RIGHT, LET'S SHUT DOWN THIS REACTOR AND BRING THIS BABY TO A...
RRRRWWWWWHHHH!
WHAT THE...
THEY'VE GOT US PINNED DOWN. IF WE DON'T GET OUTTA THIS HALLWAY, WE'RE DOOMED!

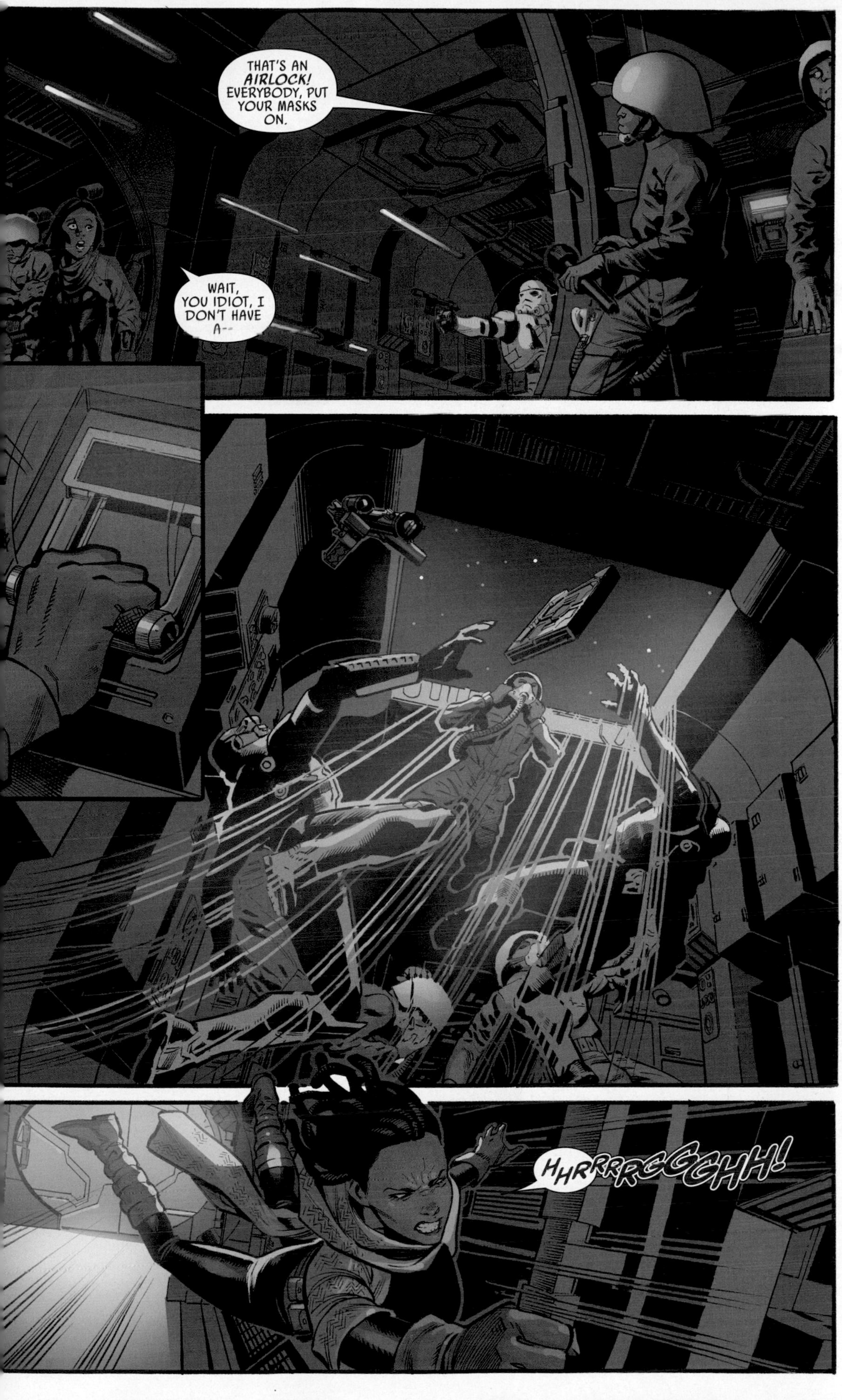
THAT'S AN AIRLOCK! EVERYBODY, PUT YOUR MASKS ON.
WAIT, YOU IDIOT, I DON'T HAVE A--
HHRRRRGGGHH!

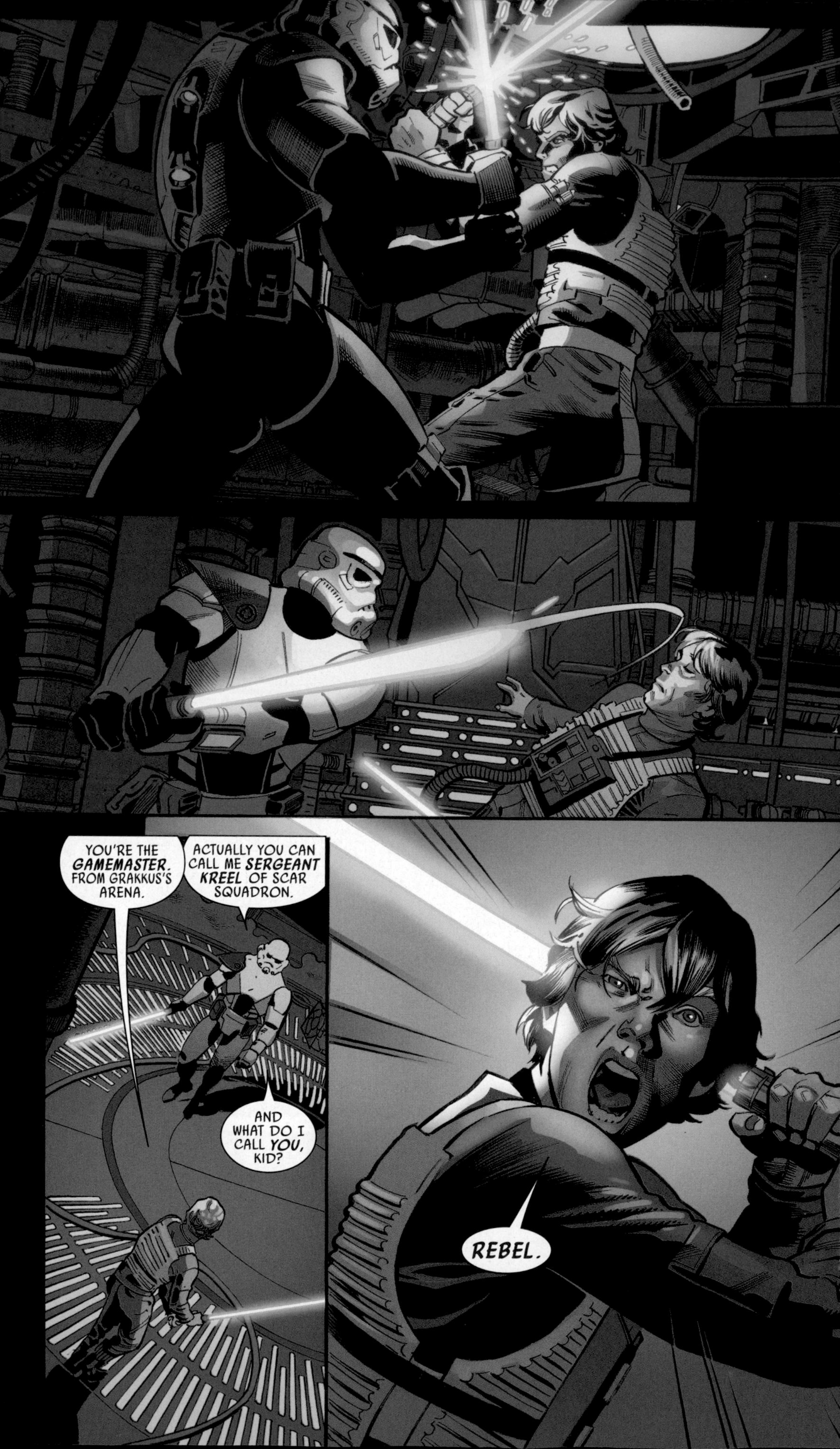

YOU'RE THE GAMEMASTER. FROM GRAKKUS'S ARENA.
ACTUALLY YOU CAN CALL ME SERGEANT KREEL OF SCAR SQUADRON.
AND WHAT DO I CALL YOU, KID?
REBEL.

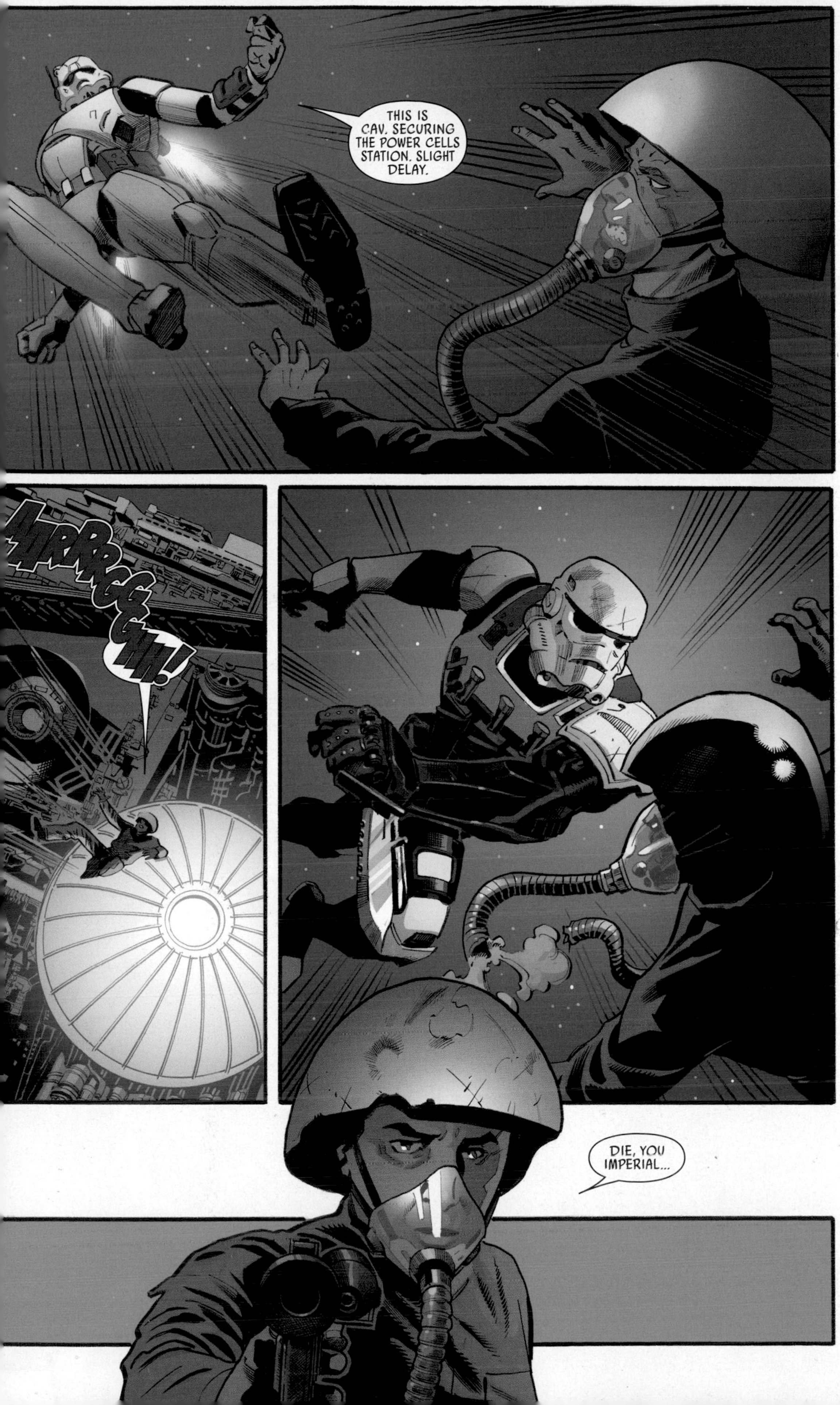
THIS IS CAV. SECURING THE POWER CELLS STATION. SLIGHT DELAY.
AHRRRGGGHH!
DIE, YOU IMPERIAL...

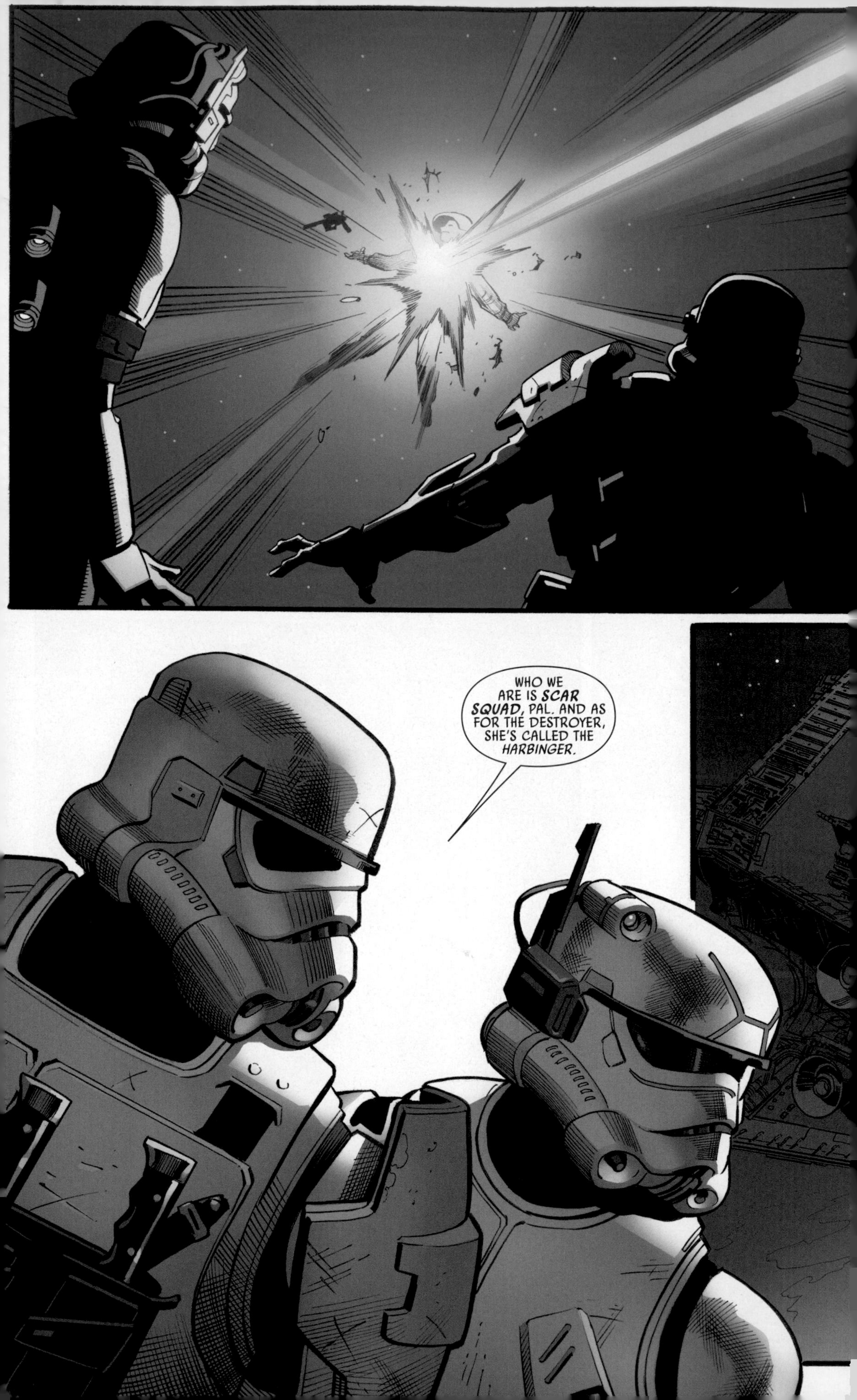
WHO WE ARE IS SCAR SQUAD, PAL. AND AS FOR THE DESTROYER, SHE'S CALLED THE HARBINGER.

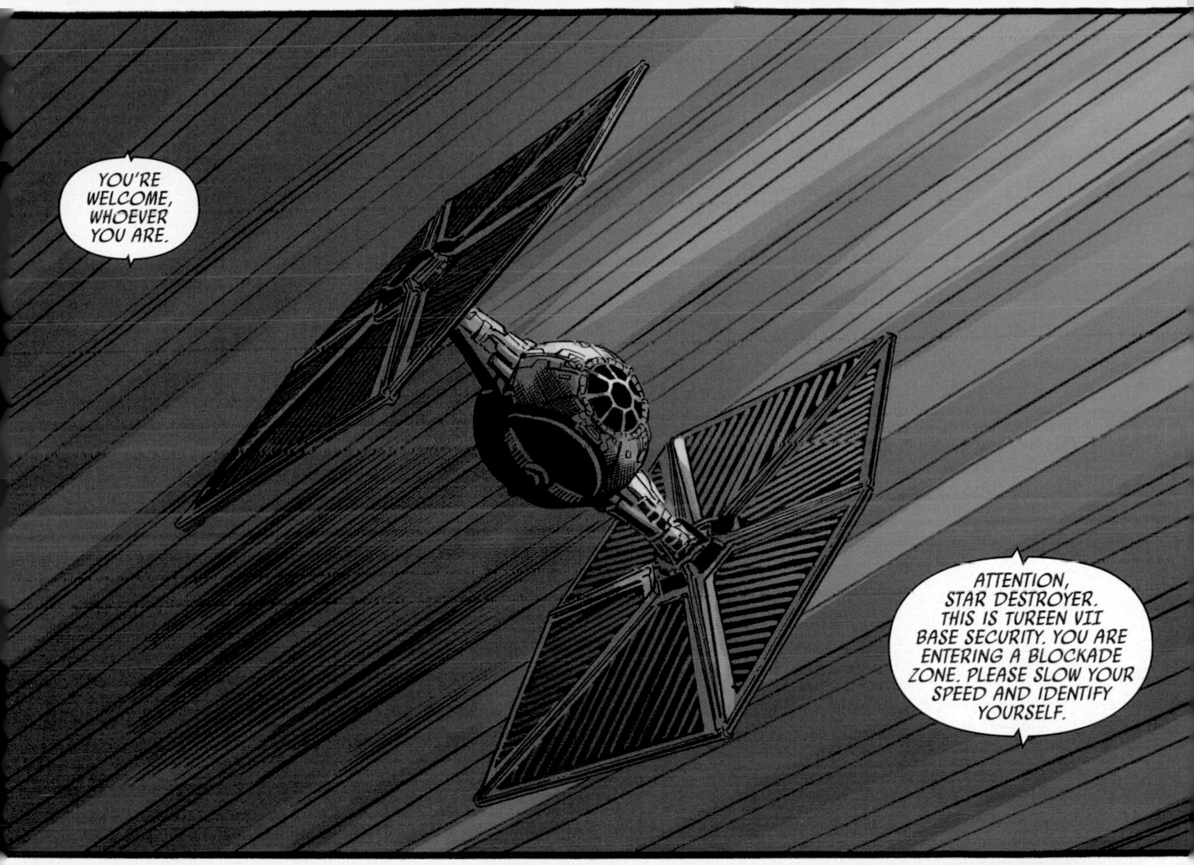
YOU'RE WELCOME, WHOEVER YOU ARE.
ATTENTION, STAR DESTROYER. THIS IS TUREEN VII BASE SECURITY. YOU ARE ENTERING A BLOCKADE ZONE. PLEASE SLOW YOUR SPEED AND IDENTIFY YOURSELF.

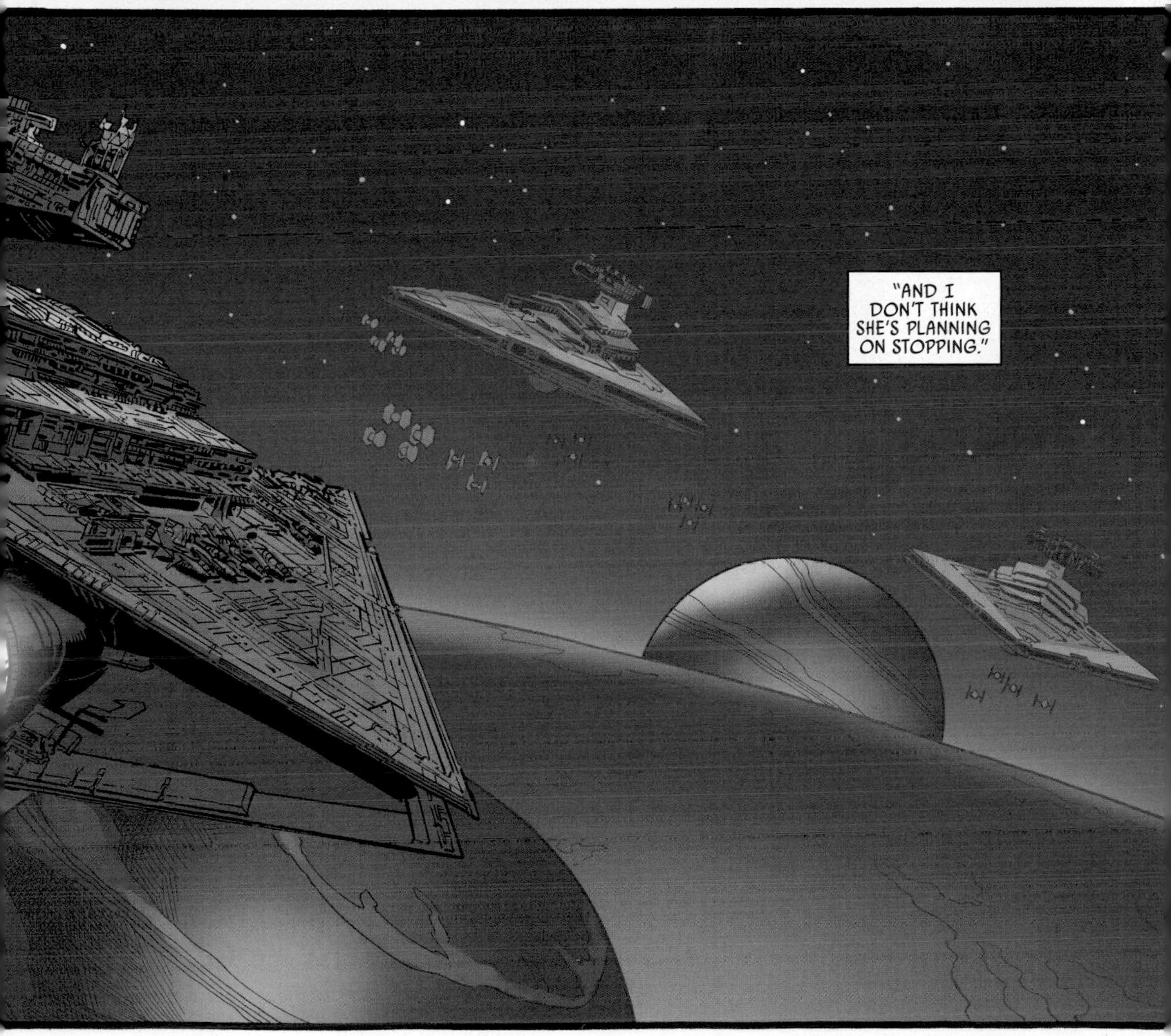
"AND I DON'T THINK SHE'S PLANNING ON STOPPING."

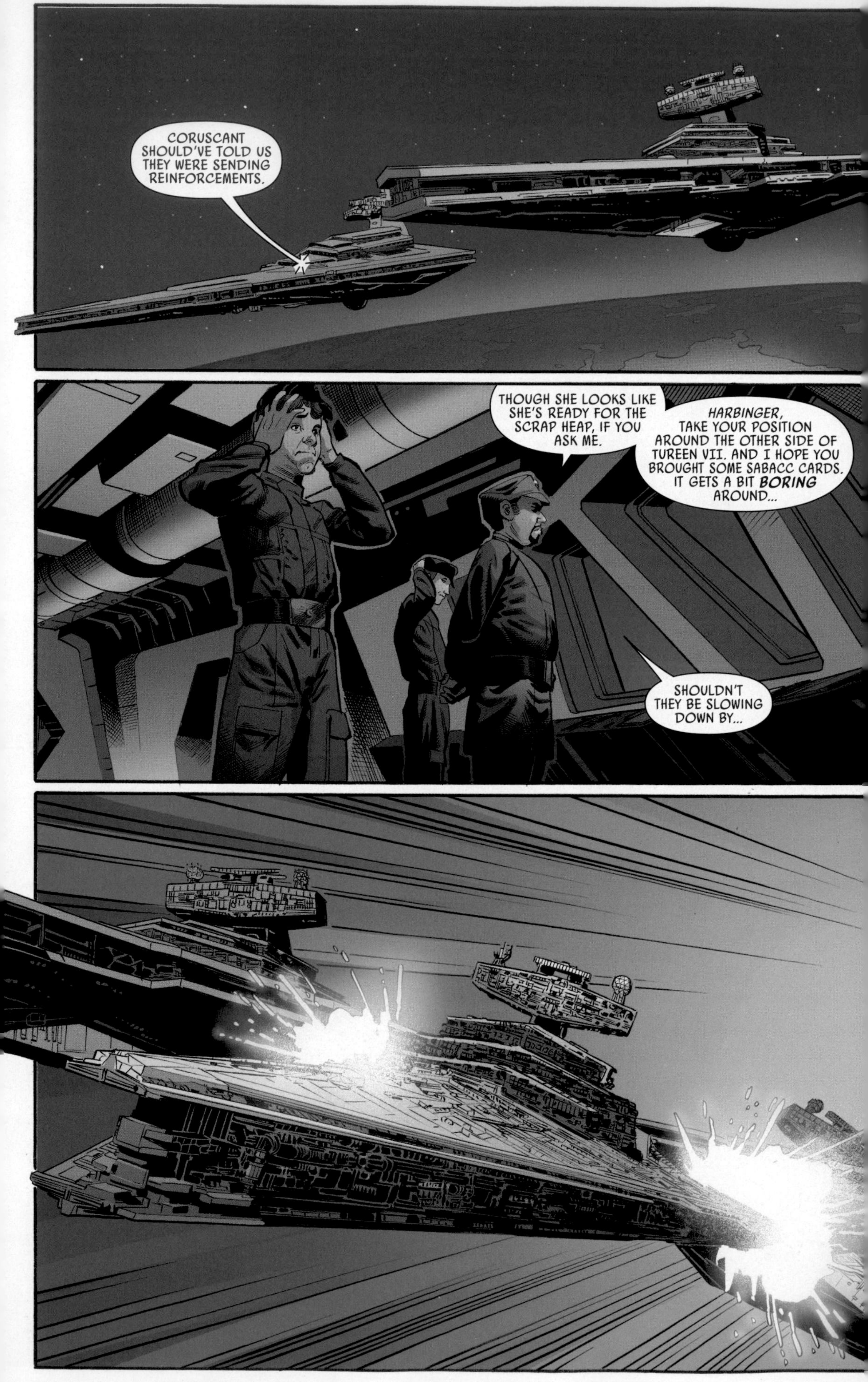
CORUSCANT SHOULD'VE TOLD US THEY WERE SENDING REINFORCEMENTS.
THOUGH SHE LOOKS LIKE SHE'S READY FOR THE SCRAP HEAP, IF YOU ASK ME.
HARBINGER, TAKE YOUR POSITION AROUND THE OTHER SIDE OF TUREEN VII. AND I HOPE YOU BROUGHT SOME SABACC CARDS. IT GETS A BIT ***BORING*** AROUND...
SHOULDN'T THEY BE SLOWING DOWN BY...

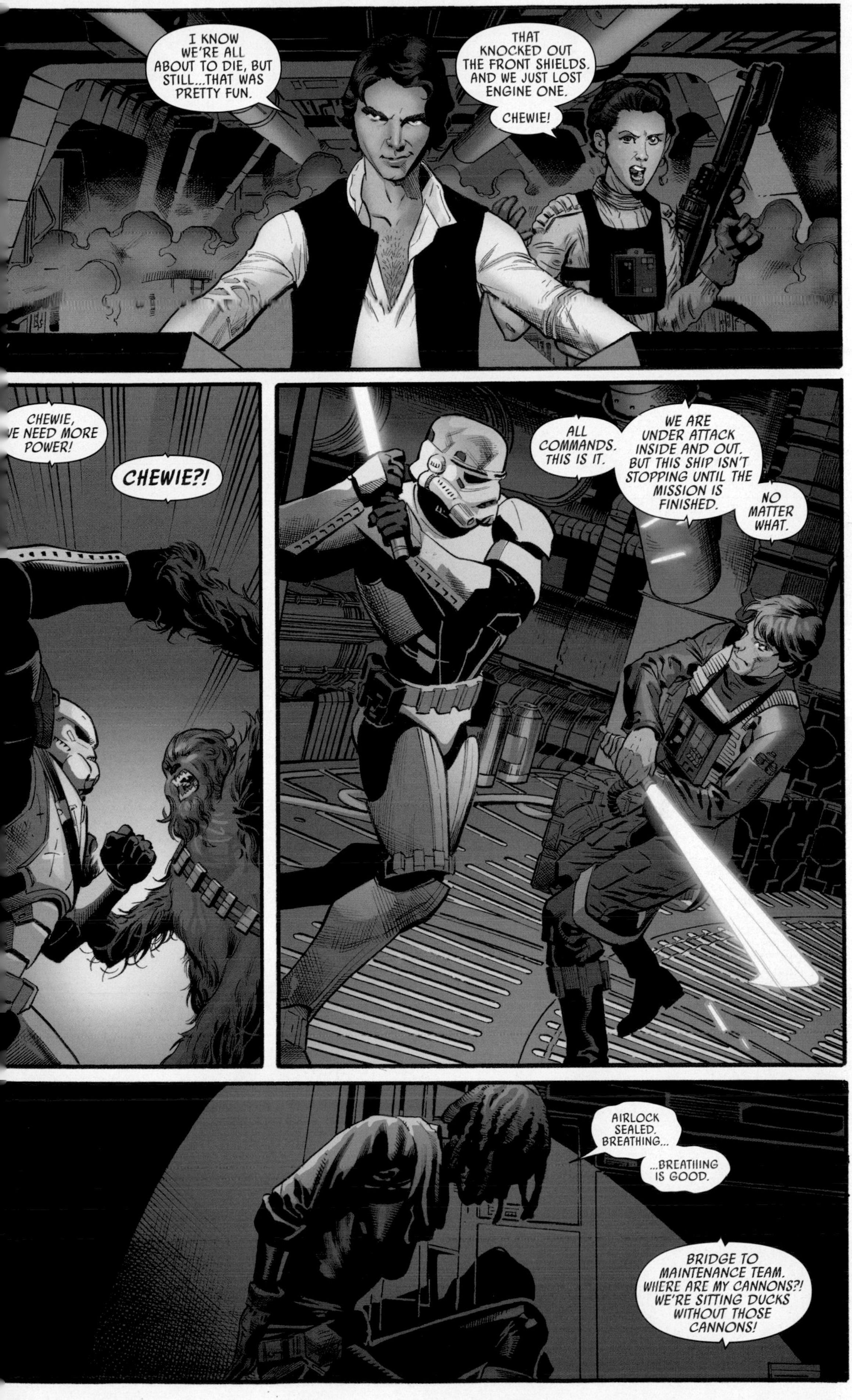

I KNOW WE'RE ALL ABOUT TO DIE, BUT STILL...THAT WAS PRETTY FUN.
THAT KNOCKED OUT THE FRONT SHIELDS. AND WE JUST LOST ENGINE ONE.
CHEWIE!
CHEWIE, WE NEED MORE POWER!
CHEWIE?!
ALL COMMANDS. THIS IS IT.
WE ARE UNDER ATTACK INSIDE AND OUT. BUT THIS SHIP ISN'T STOPPING UNTIL THE MISSION IS FINISHED.
NO MATTER WHAT.
AIRLOCK SEALED. BREATHING...
...BREATHING IS GOOD.
BRIDGE TO MAINTENANCE TEAM. WHERE ARE MY CANNONS?! WE'RE SITTING DUCKS WITHOUT THOSE CANNONS!

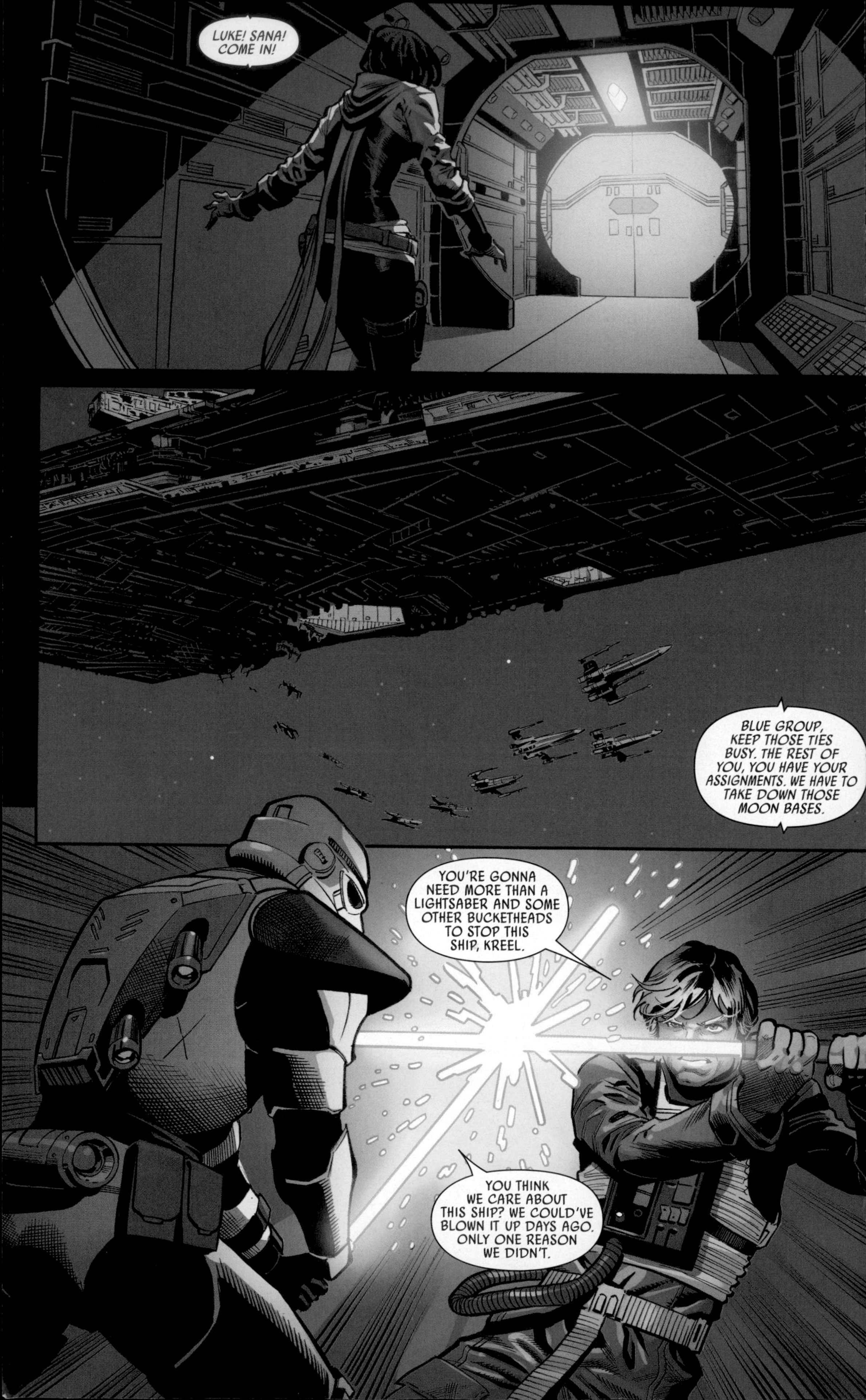
LUKE! SANA! COME IN!
BLUE GROUP, KEEP THOSE TIES BUSY. THE REST OF YOU, YOU HAVE YOUR ASSIGNMENTS. WE HAVE TO TAKE DOWN THOSE MOON BASES.
YOU'RE GONNA NEED MORE THAN A LIGHTSABER AND SOME OTHER BUCKETHEADS TO STOP THIS SHIP, KREEL.
YOU THINK WE CARE ABOUT THIS SHIP? WE COULD'VE BLOWN IT UP DAYS AGO. ONLY ONE REASON WE DIDN'T.

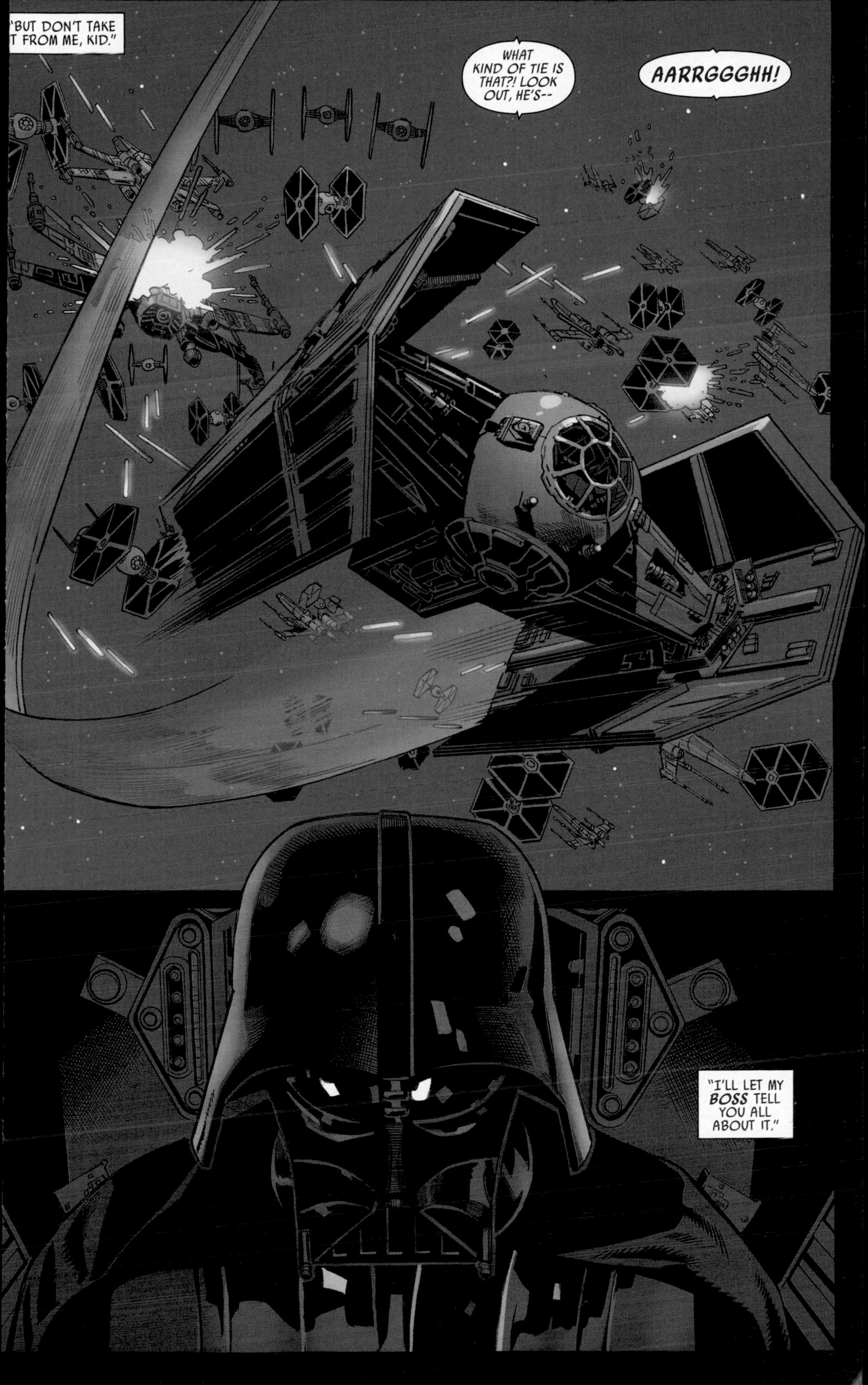
"BUT DON'T TAKE
T FROM ME, KID."
WHAT KIND OF TIE IS THAT?! LOOK OUT, HE'S--
AARRGGGHH!
"I'LL LET MY BOSS TELL YOU ALL ABOUT IT."

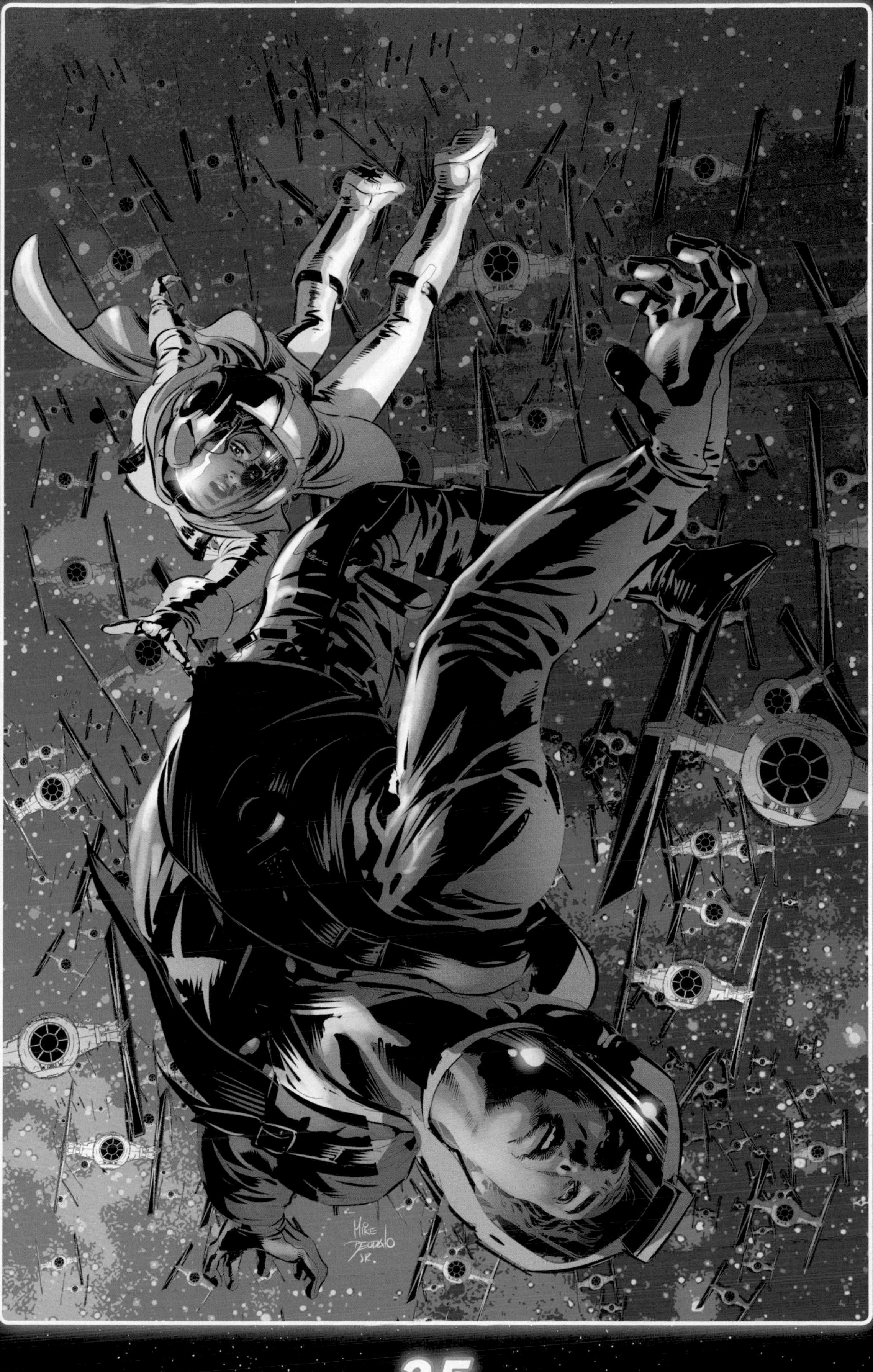

25

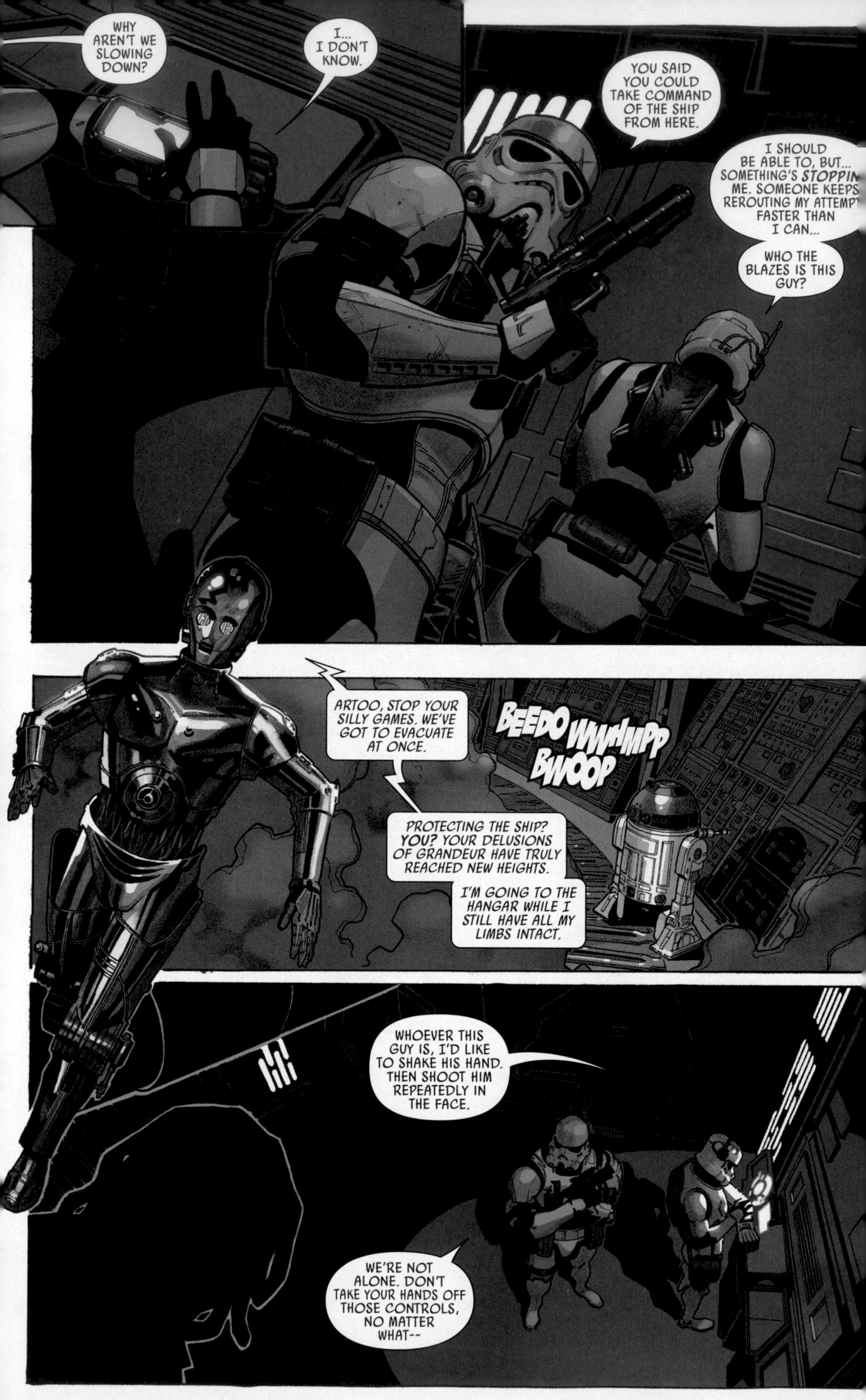
WHY AREN'T WE SLOWING DOWN?
I... I DON'T KNOW.
YOU SAID YOU COULD TAKE COMMAND OF THE SHIP FROM HERE.
I SHOULD BE ABLE TO, BUT... SOMETHING'S *STOPPIN* ME. SOMEONE KEEPS REROUTING MY ATTEMPT FASTER THAN I CAN...
WHO THE BLAZES IS THIS GUY?
ARTOO, STOP YOUR SILLY GAMES. WE'VE GOT TO EVACUATE AT ONCE.
BEEDO WWHMPP BWOOP
PROTECTING THE SHIP? **YOU?** YOUR DELUSIONS OF GRANDEUR HAVE TRULY REACHED NEW HEIGHTS.
I'M GOING TO THE HANGAR WHILE I STILL HAVE ALL MY LIMBS INTACT.
WHOEVER THIS GUY IS, I'D LIKE TO SHAKE HIS HAND. THEN SHOOT HIM REPEATEDLY IN THE FACE.
WE'RE NOT ALONE. DON'T TAKE YOUR HANDS OFF THOSE CONTROLS, NO MATTER WHAT--

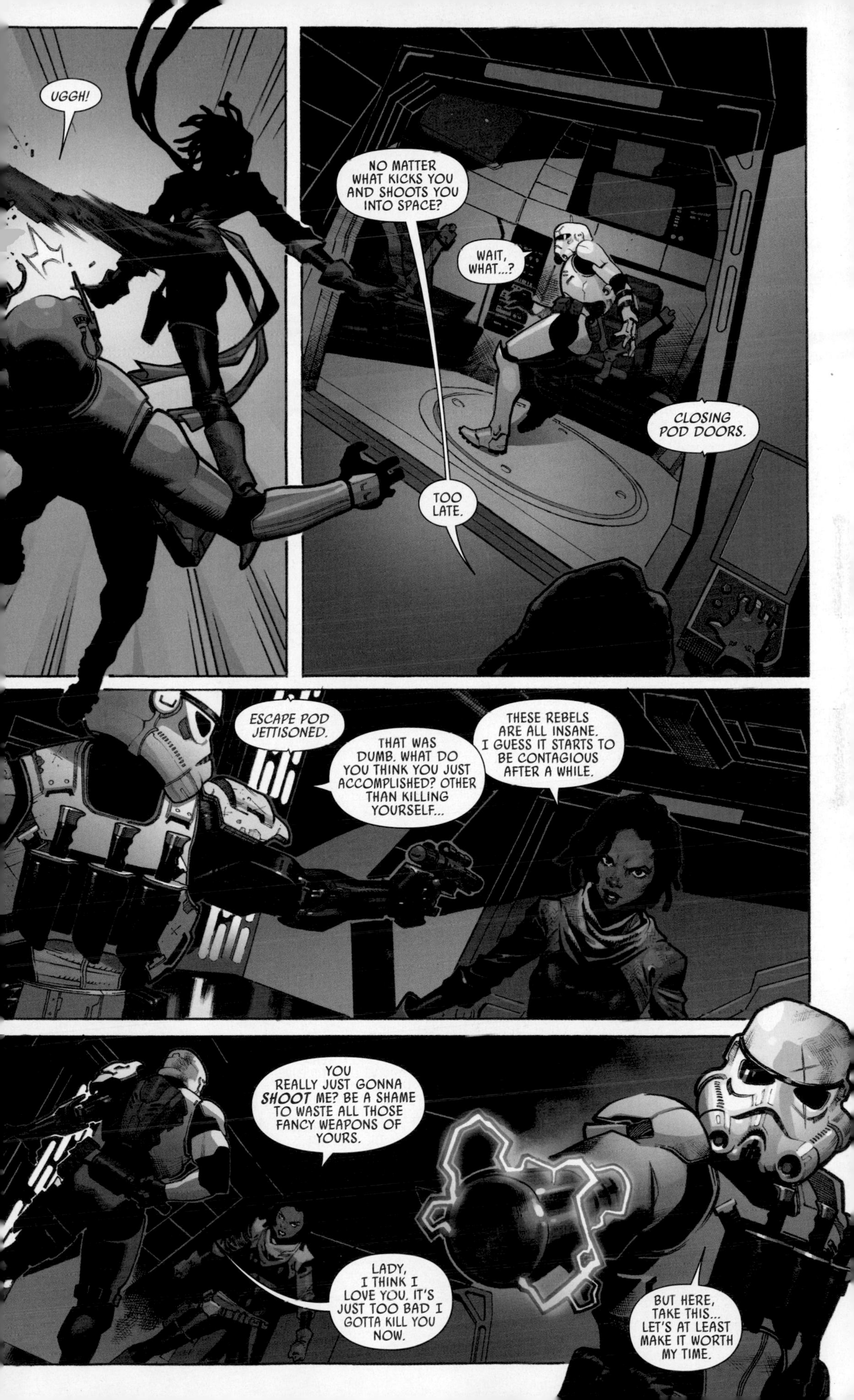
UGGH!
NO MATTER WHAT KICKS YOU AND SHOOTS YOU INTO SPACE?
WAIT, WHAT...?
CLOSING POD DOORS.
TOO LATE.
ESCAPE POD JETTISONED.
THAT WAS DUMB. WHAT DO YOU THINK YOU JUST ACCOMPLISHED? OTHER THAN KILLING YOURSELF...
THESE REBELS ARE ALL INSANE. I GUESS IT STARTS TO BE CONTAGIOUS AFTER A WHILE.
YOU REALLY JUST GONNA SHOOT ME? BE A SHAME TO WASTE ALL THOSE FANCY WEAPONS OF YOURS.
LADY, I THINK I LOVE YOU. IT'S JUST TOO BAD I GOTTA KILL YOU NOW.
BUT HERE, TAKE THIS... LET'S AT LEAST MAKE IT WORTH MY TIME.

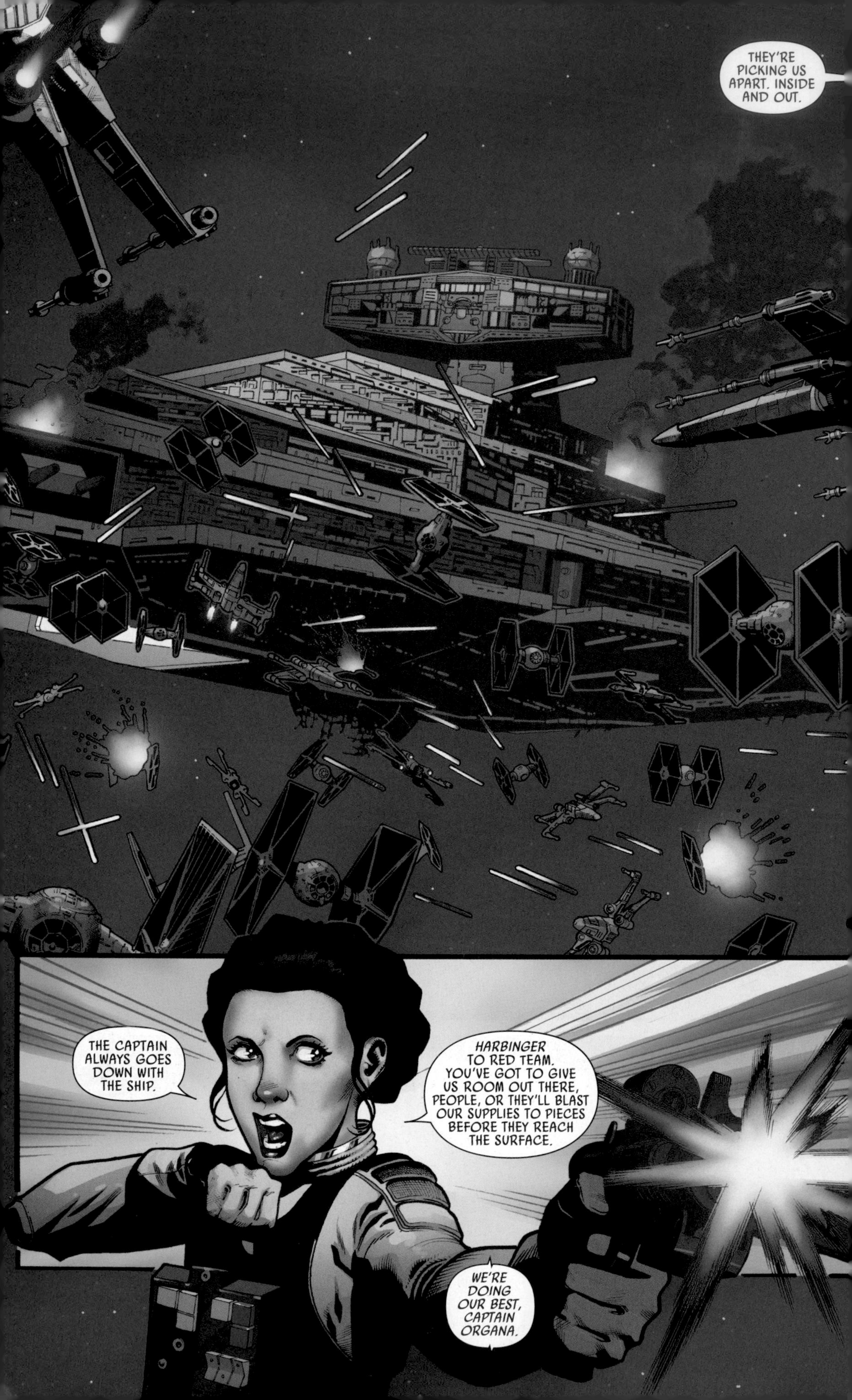
THEY'RE PICKING US APART. INSIDE AND OUT.
THE CAPTAIN ALWAYS GOES DOWN WITH THE SHIP.
HARBINGER TO RED TEAM. YOU'VE GOT TO GIVE US ROOM OUT THERE, PEOPLE, OR THEY'LL BLAST OUR SUPPLIES TO PIECES BEFORE THEY REACH THE SURFACE.
WE'RE DOING OUR BEST, CAPTAIN ORGANA.

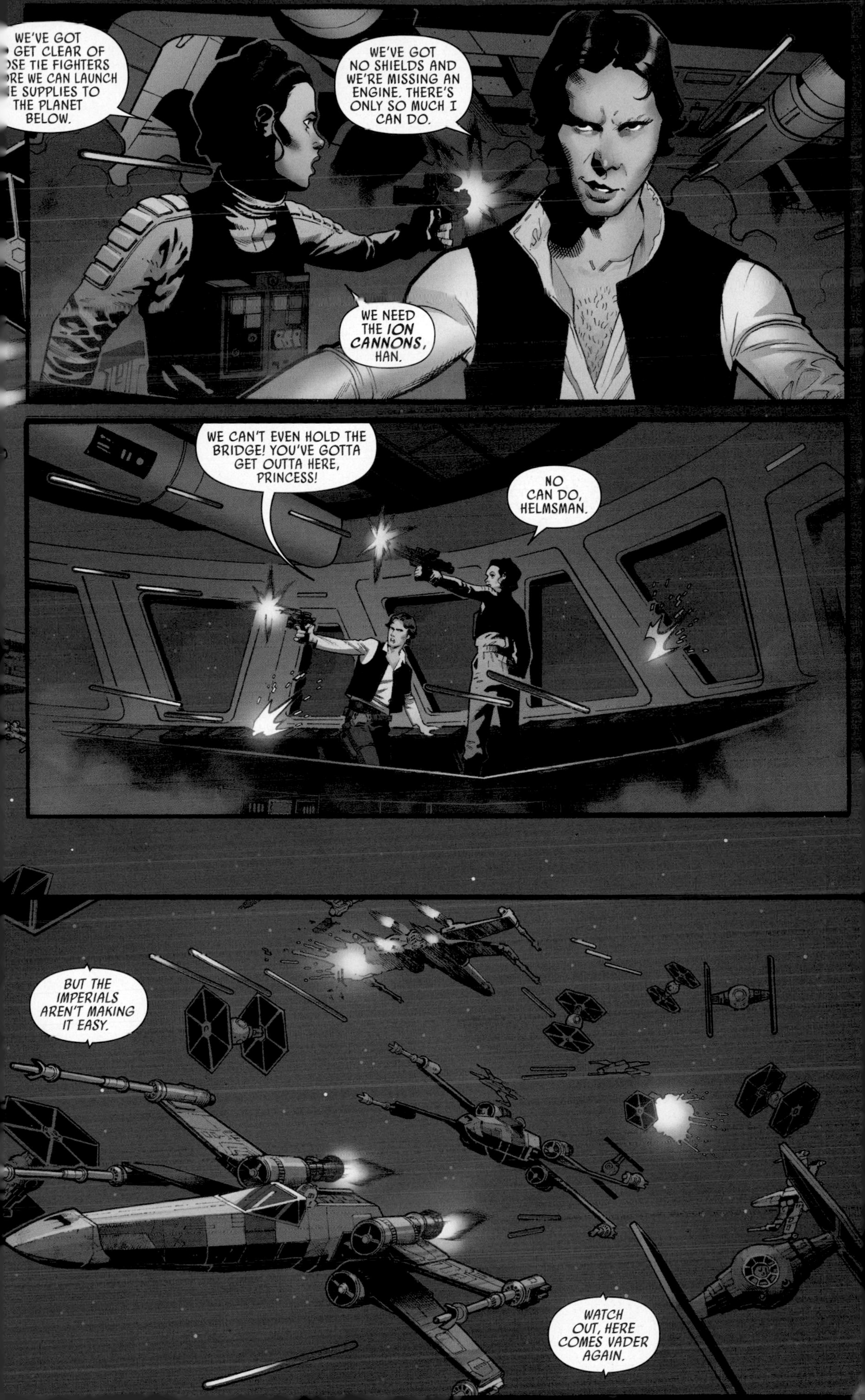
WE'VE GOT O GET CLEAR OF OSE TIE FIGHTERS ORE WE CAN LAUNCH E SUPPLIES TO THE PLANET BELOW.
WE'VE GOT NO SHIELDS AND WE'RE MISSING AN ENGINE. THERE'S ONLY SO MUCH I CAN DO.
WE NEED THE ION CANNONS, HAN.
WE CAN'T EVEN HOLD THE BRIDGE! YOU'VE GOTTA GET OUTTA HERE, PRINCESS!
NO CAN DO, HELMSMAN.
BUT THE IMPERIALS AREN'T MAKING IT EASY.
WATCH OUT, HERE COMES VADER AGAIN.

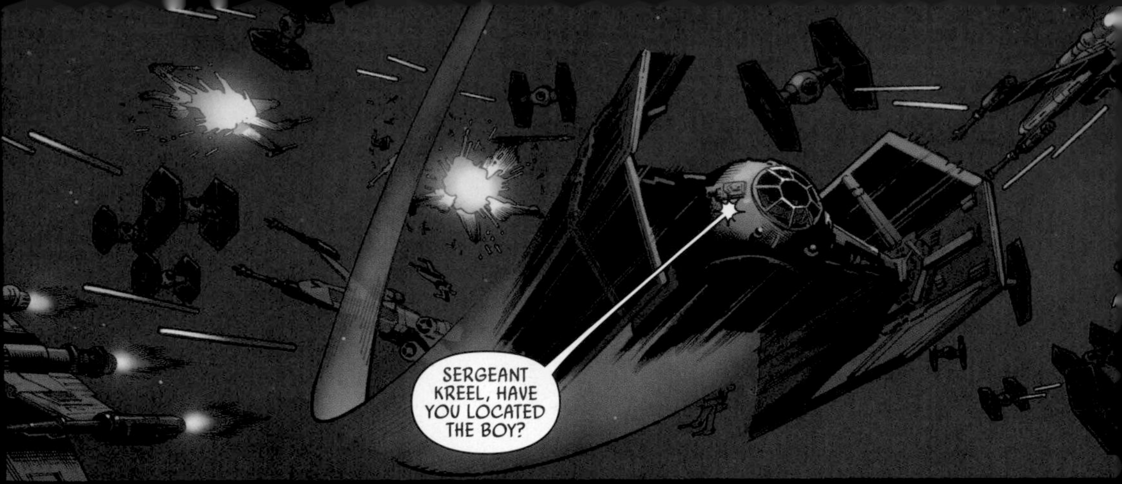
SERGEANT KREEL, HAVE YOU LOCATED THE BOY?

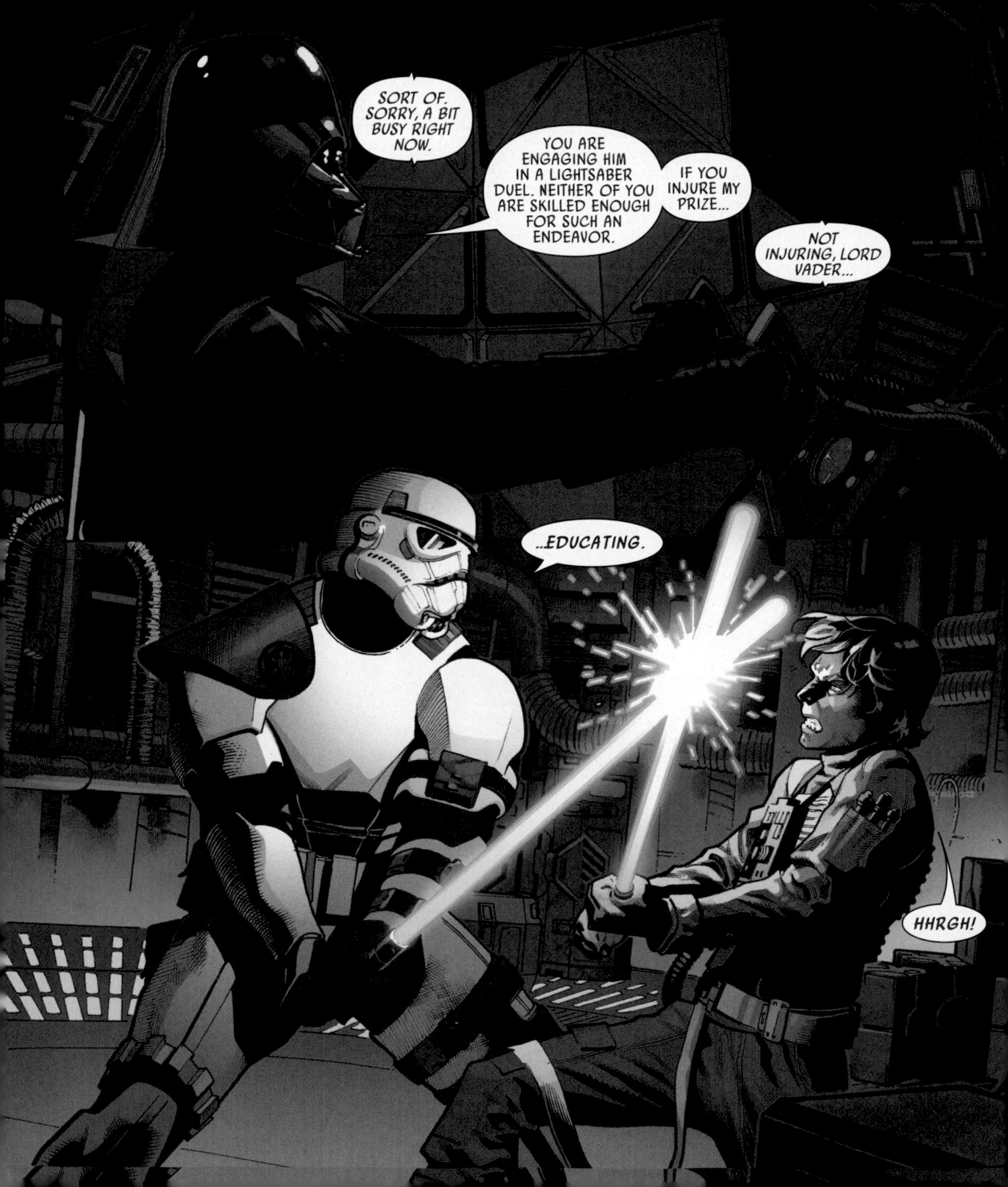
SORT OF. SORRY, A BIT BUSY RIGHT NOW.
YOU ARE ENGAGING HIM IN A LIGHTSABER DUEL. NEITHER OF YOU ARE SKILLED ENOUGH FOR SUCH AN ENDEAVOR.
IF YOU INJURE MY PRIZE...
NOT INJURING, LORD VADER...
...EDUCATING.
HHRGH!

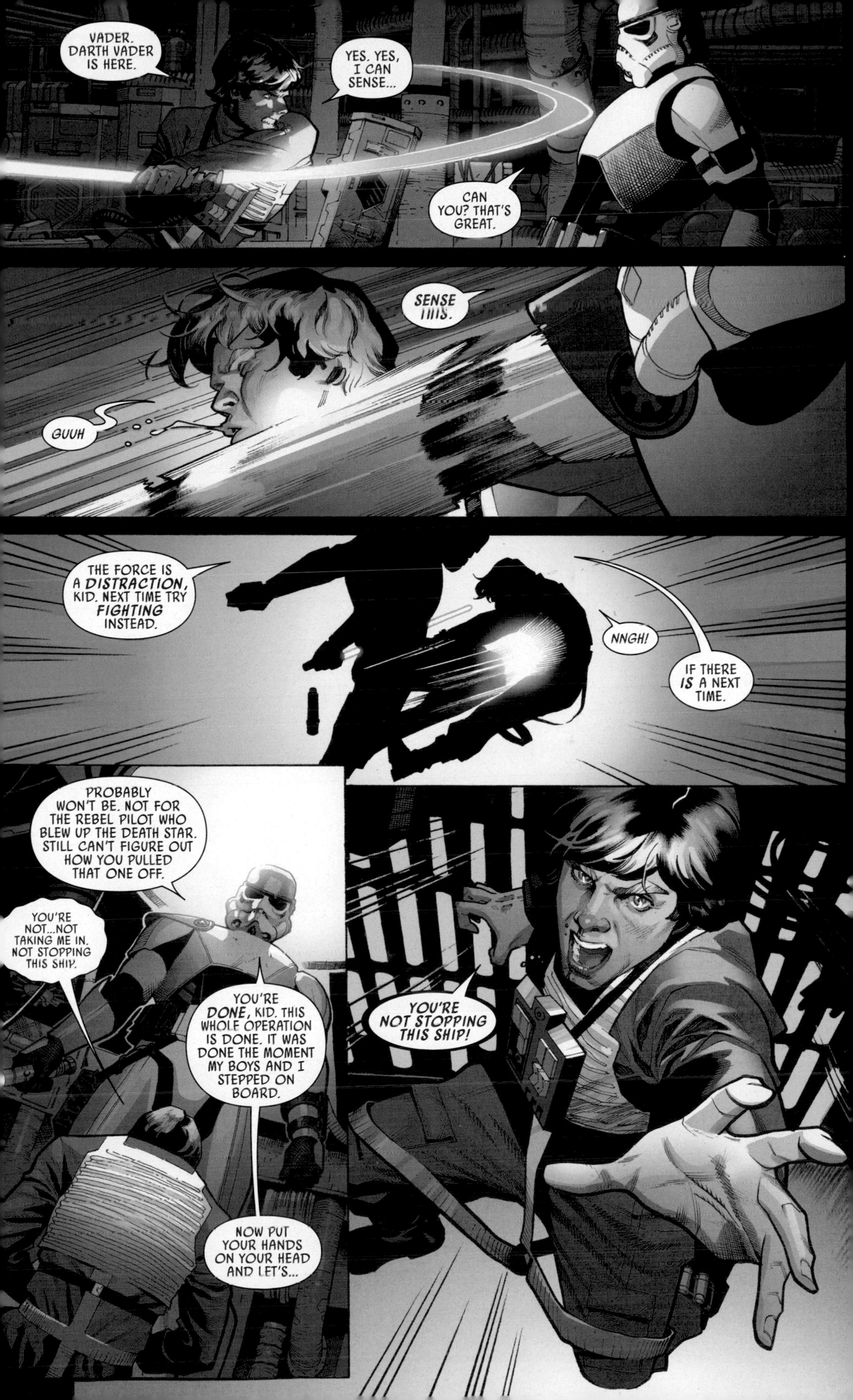

VADER. DARTH VADER IS HERE.
YES. YES, I CAN SENSE...
CAN YOU? THAT'S GREAT.
SENSE THIS.
GUUH
THE FORCE IS A DISTRACTION, KID. NEXT TIME TRY FIGHTING INSTEAD.
NNGH!
IF THERE IS A NEXT TIME.
PROBABLY WON'T BE. NOT FOR THE REBEL PILOT WHO BLEW UP THE DEATH STAR. STILL CAN'T FIGURE OUT HOW YOU PULLED THAT ONE OFF.
YOU'RE NOT...NOT TAKING ME IN. NOT STOPPING THIS SHIP.
YOU'RE DONE, KID. THIS WHOLE OPERATION IS DONE. IT WAS DONE THE MOMENT MY BOYS AND I STEPPED ON BOARD.
NOW PUT YOUR HANDS ON YOUR HEAD AND LET'S...
YOU'RE NOT STOPPING THIS SHIP!

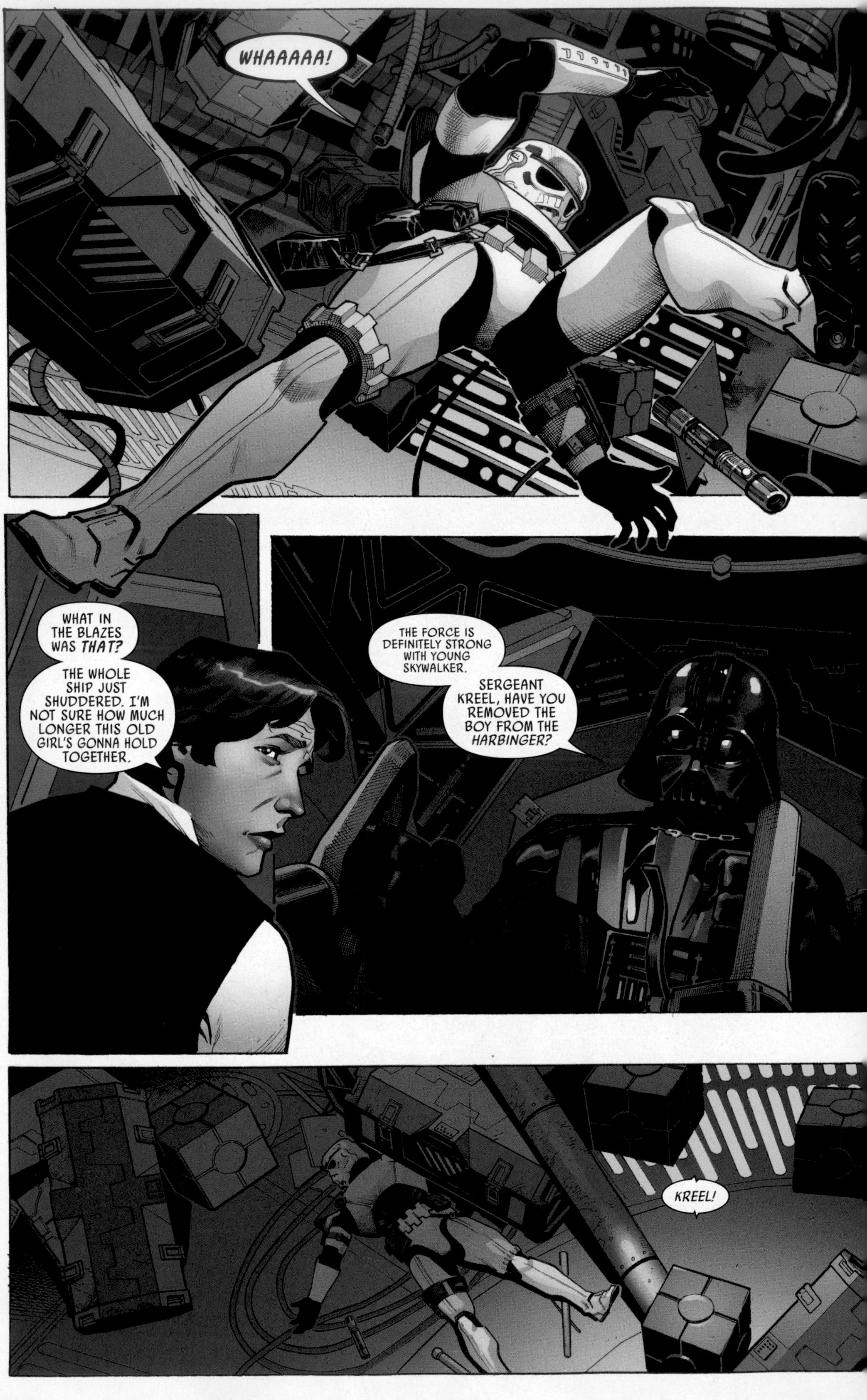

WHAAAAA!
WHAT IN THE BLAZES WAS *THAT?*
THE WHOLE SHIP JUST SHUDDERED. I'M NOT SURE HOW MUCH LONGER THIS OLD GIRL'S GONNA HOLD TOGETHER.
THE FORCE IS DEFINITELY STRONG WITH YOUNG SKYWALKER.
SERGEANT KREEL, HAVE YOU REMOVED THE BOY FROM THE *HARBINGER?*
KREEL!

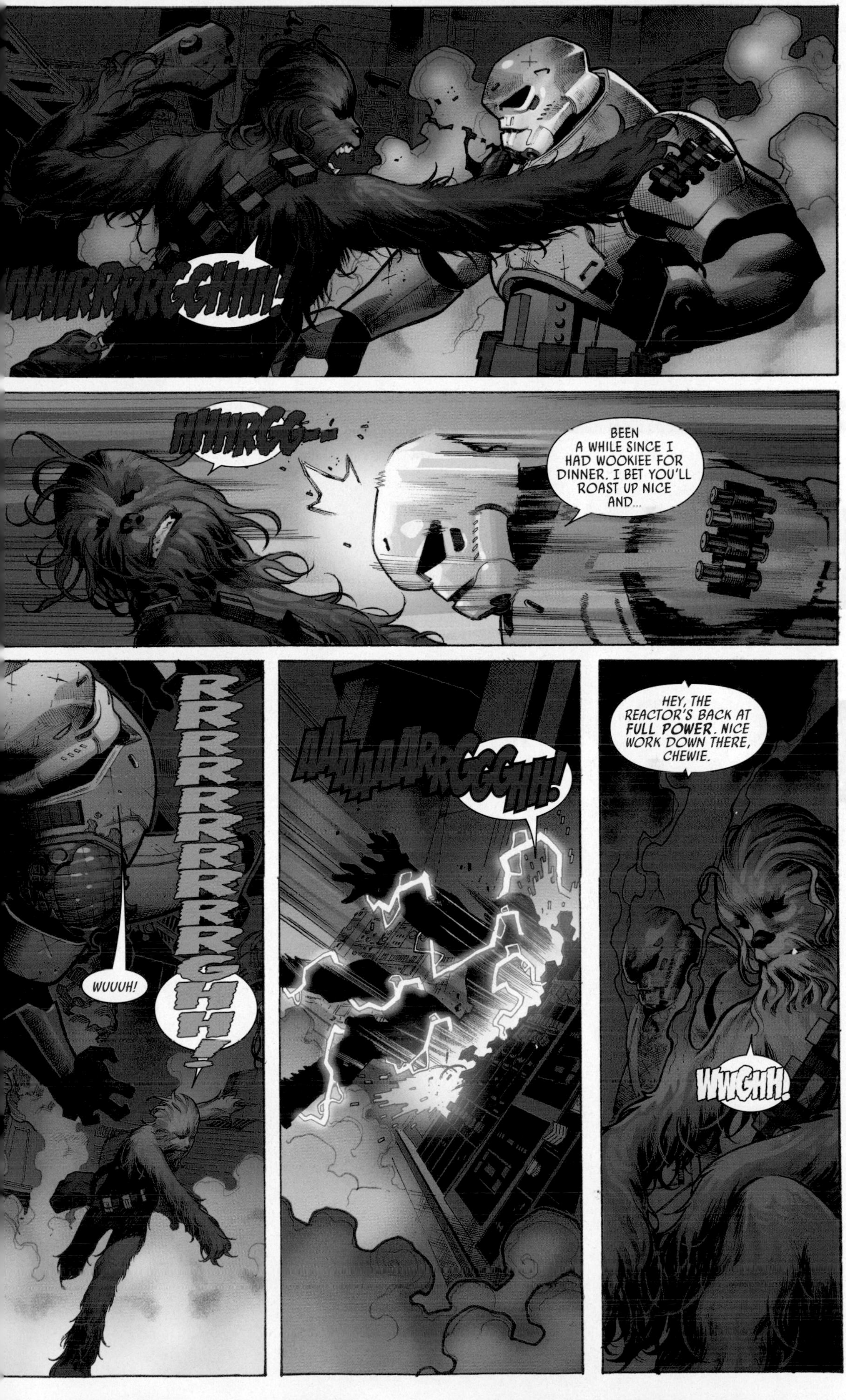
WWURRRRGGHHH!
HHHRGG...
BEEN A WHILE SINCE I HAD WOOKIEE FOR DINNER. I BET YOU'LL ROAST UP NICE AND...
WUUUH!
RRRRRRRRRGHH!
AAAAAARRGGGHH!
HEY, THE REACTOR'S BACK AT **FULL POWER**. NICE WORK DOWN THERE, CHEWIE.
WWGHH!

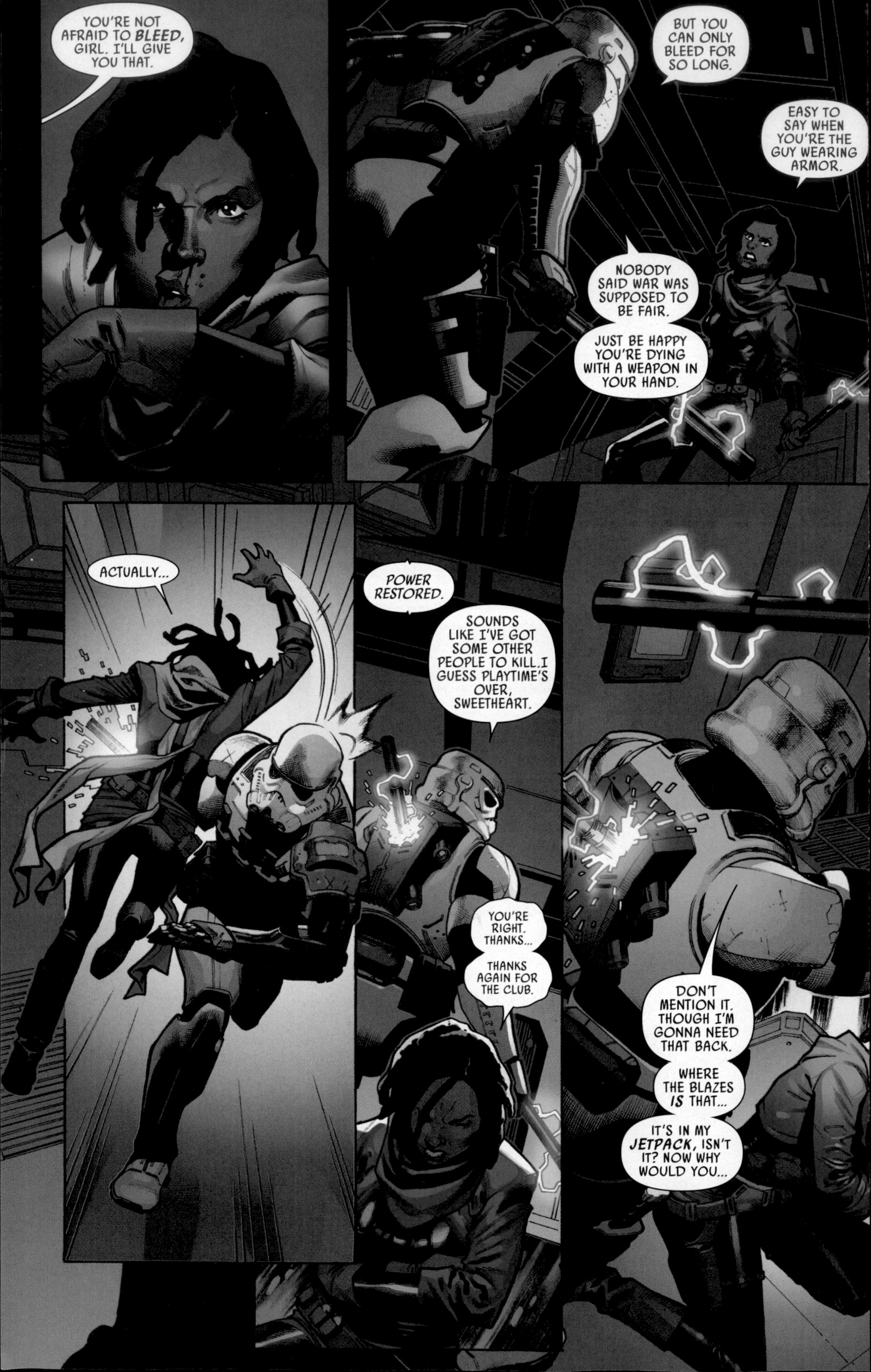
YOU'RE NOT AFRAID TO BLEED, GIRL. I'LL GIVE YOU THAT.
BUT YOU CAN ONLY BLEED FOR SO LONG.
EASY TO SAY WHEN YOU'RE THE GUY WEARING ARMOR.
NOBODY SAID WAR WAS SUPPOSED TO BE FAIR.
JUST BE HAPPY YOU'RE DYING WITH A WEAPON IN YOUR HAND.
ACTUALLY...
POWER RESTORED.
SOUNDS LIKE I'VE GOT SOME OTHER PEOPLE TO KILL. I GUESS PLAYTIME'S OVER, SWEETHEART.
YOU'RE RIGHT. THANKS...
THANKS AGAIN FOR THE CLUB.
DON'T MENTION IT. THOUGH I'M GONNA NEED THAT BACK.
WHERE THE BLAZES IS THAT...
IT'S IN MY JETPACK, ISN'T IT? NOW WHY WOULD YOU...

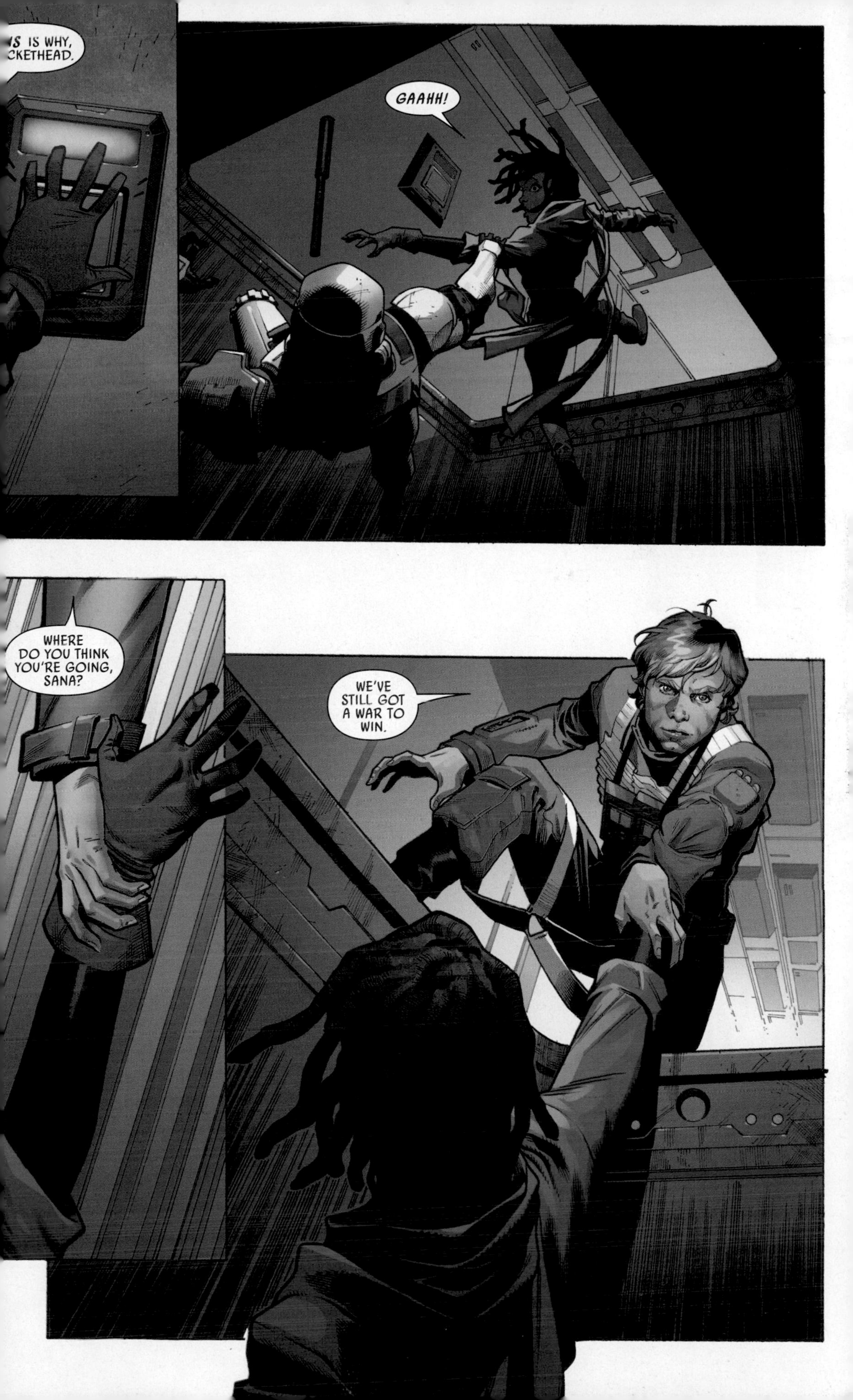
IS IS WHY, CKETHEAD.
GAAHH!
WHERE DO YOU THINK YOU'RE GOING, SANA?
WE'VE STILL GOT A WAR TO WIN.

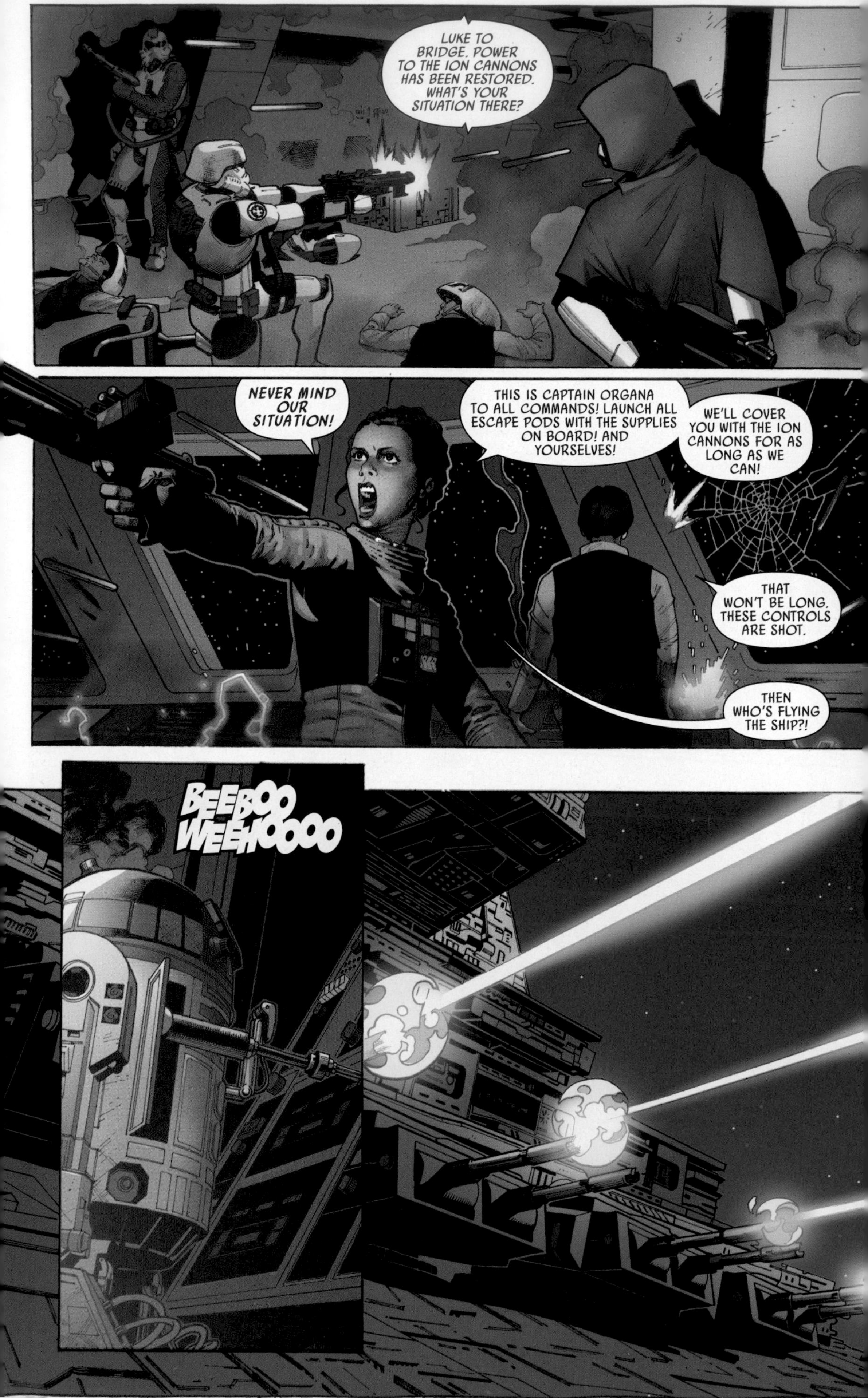
LUKE TO BRIDGE. POWER TO THE ION CANNONS HAS BEEN RESTORED. WHAT'S YOUR SITUATION THERE?
NEVER MIND OUR SITUATION!
THIS IS CAPTAIN ORGANA TO ALL COMMANDS! LAUNCH ALL ESCAPE PODS WITH THE SUPPLIES ON BOARD! AND YOURSELVES!
WE'LL COVER YOU WITH THE ION CANNONS FOR AS LONG AS WE CAN!
THAT WON'T BE LONG. THESE CONTROLS ARE SHOT.
THEN WHO'S FLYING THE SHIP?!
BEEBOO WEEHOOOO

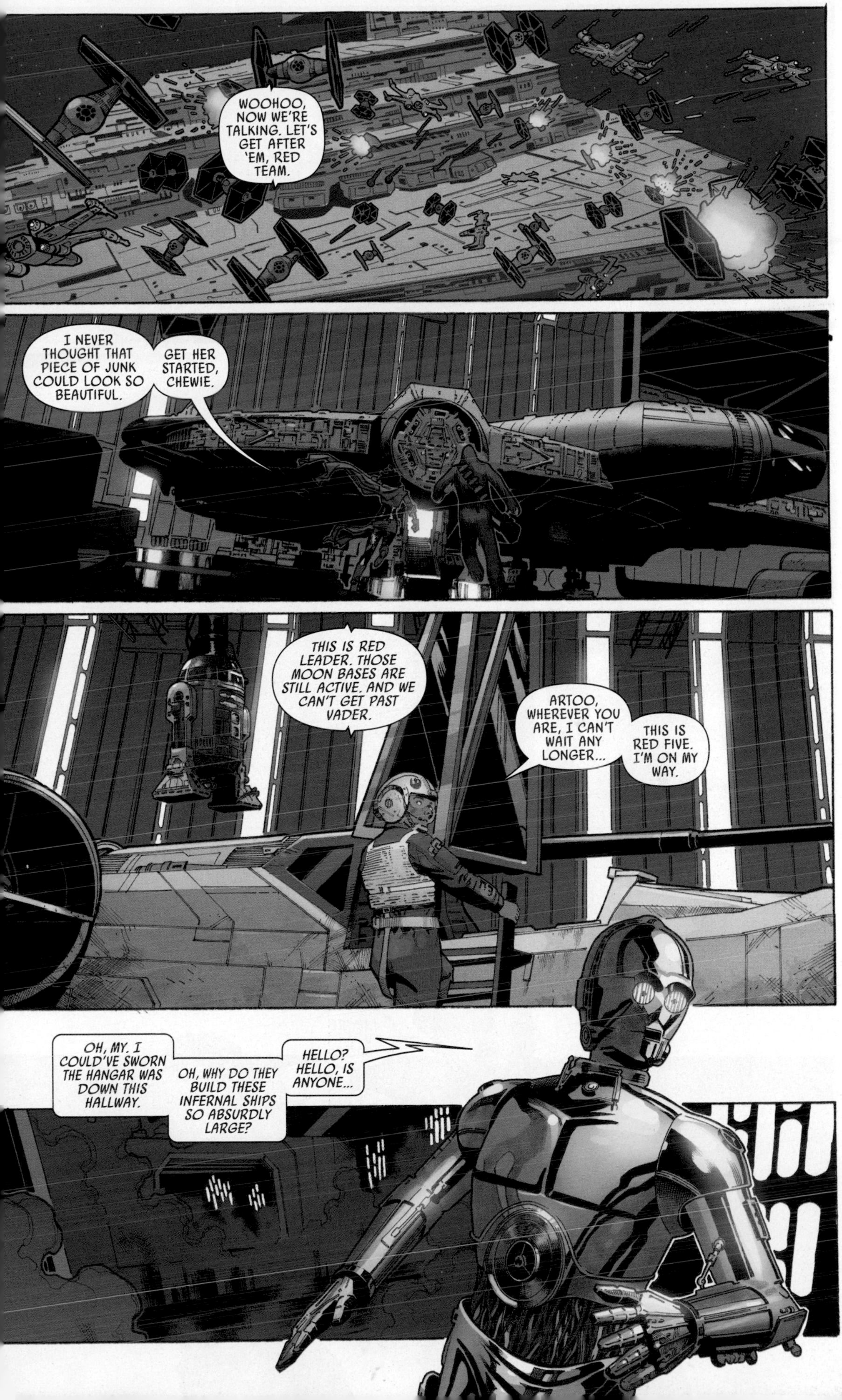
WOOHOO, NOW WE'RE TALKING. LET'S GET AFTER 'EM, RED TEAM.
I NEVER THOUGHT THAT PIECE OF JUNK COULD LOOK SO BEAUTIFUL.
GET HER STARTED, CHEWIE.
THIS IS RED LEADER. THOSE MOON BASES ARE STILL ACTIVE. AND WE CAN'T GET PAST VADER.
ARTOO, WHEREVER YOU ARE, I CAN'T WAIT ANY LONGER...
THIS IS RED FIVE. I'M ON MY WAY.
OH, MY. I COULD'VE SWORN THE HANGAR WAS DOWN THIS HALLWAY.
OH, WHY DO THEY BUILD THESE INFERNAL SHIPS SO ABSURDLY LARGE?
HELLO? HELLO, IS ANYONE...

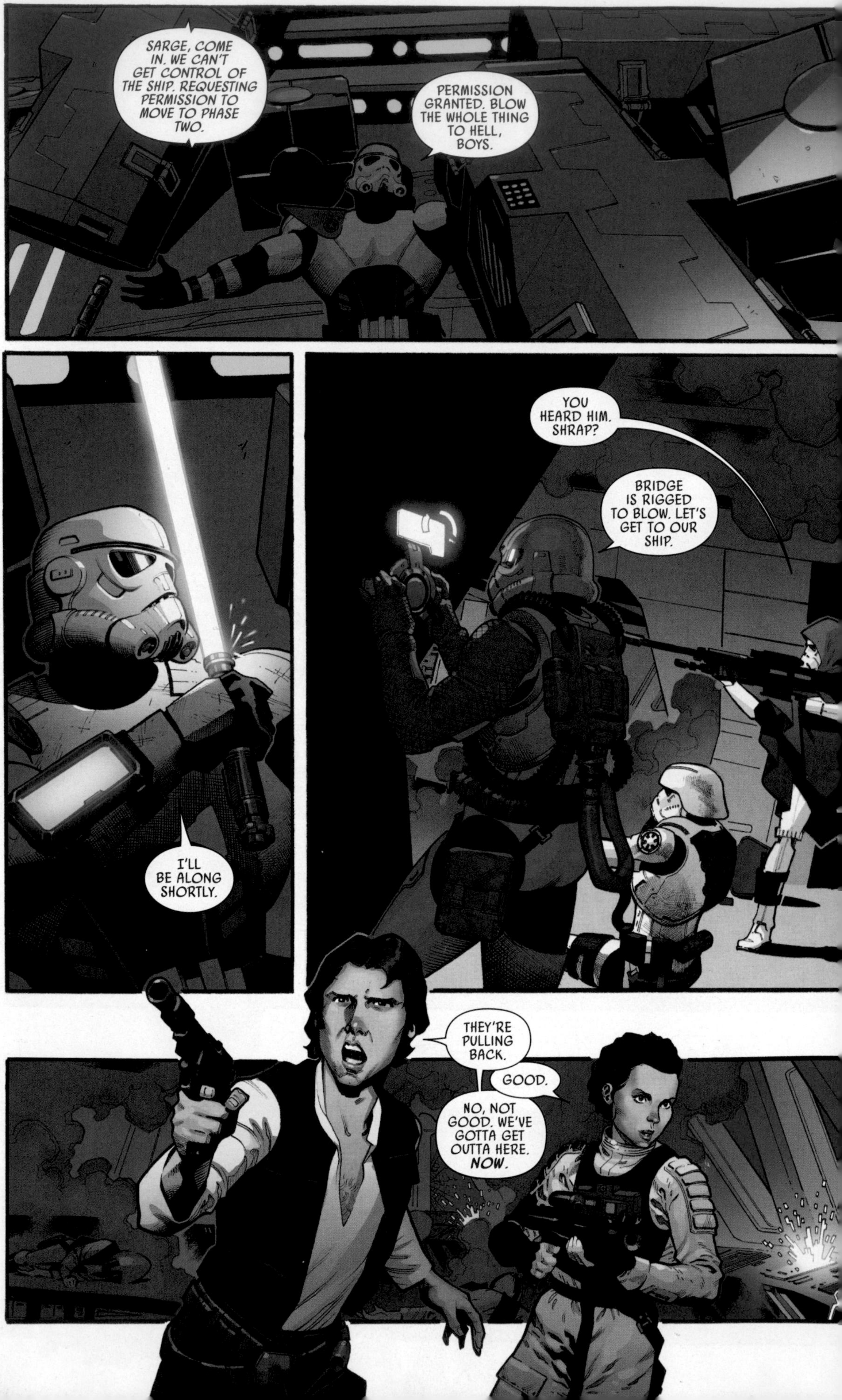
SARGE, COME IN. WE CAN'T GET CONTROL OF THE SHIP. REQUESTING PERMISSION TO MOVE TO PHASE TWO.
PERMISSION GRANTED. BLOW THE WHOLE THING TO HELL, BOYS.
YOU HEARD HIM. SHRAP?
BRIDGE IS RIGGED TO BLOW. LET'S GET TO OUR SHIP.
I'LL BE ALONG SHORTLY.
THEY'RE PULLING BACK.
GOOD.
NO, NOT GOOD. WE'VE GOTTA GET OUTTA HERE. NOW.

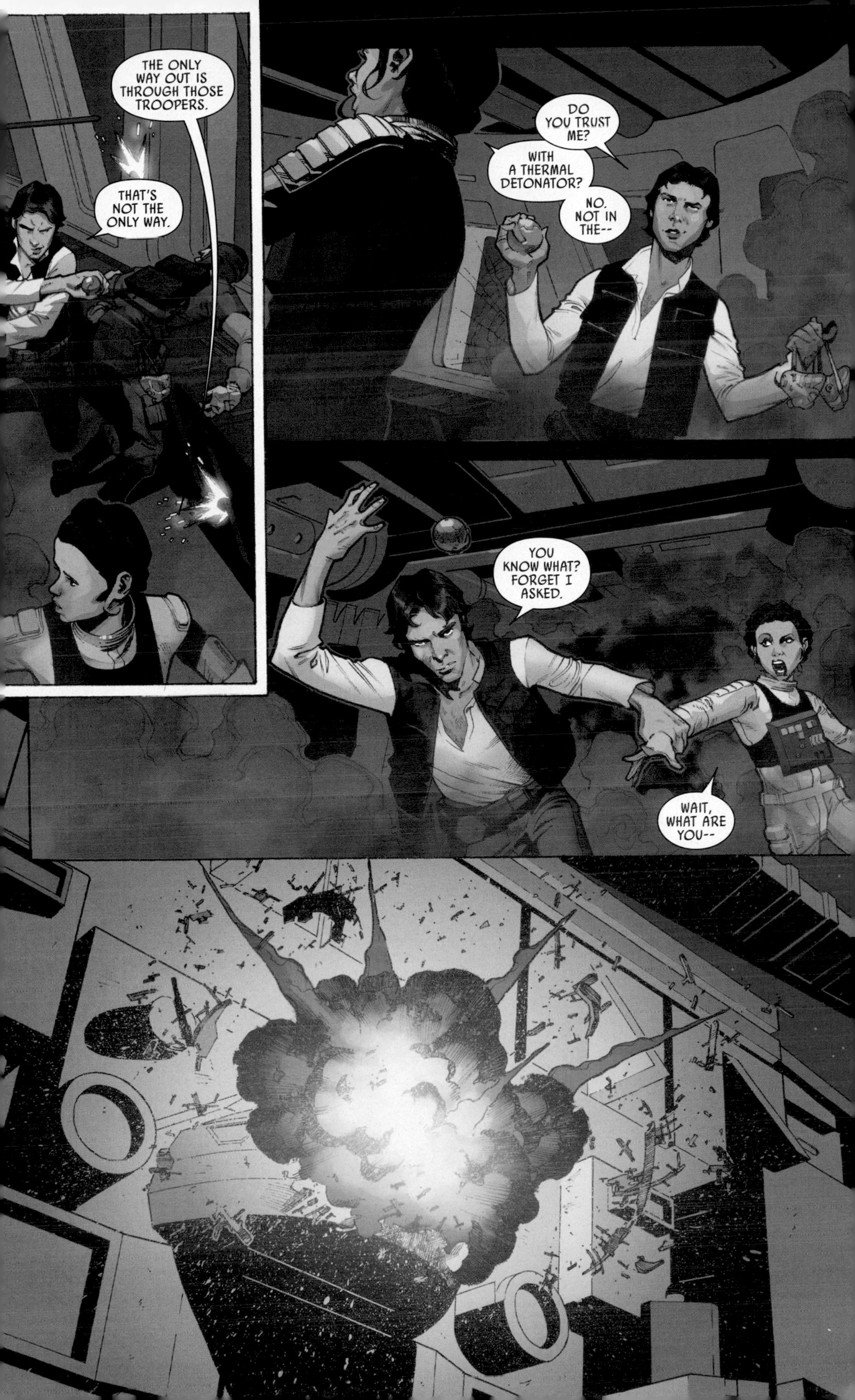
THE ONLY WAY OUT IS THROUGH THOSE TROOPERS.
THAT'S NOT THE ONLY WAY.
DO YOU TRUST ME?
WITH A THERMAL DETONATOR?
NO. NOT IN THE--
YOU KNOW WHAT? FORGET I ASKED.
WAIT, WHAT ARE YOU--

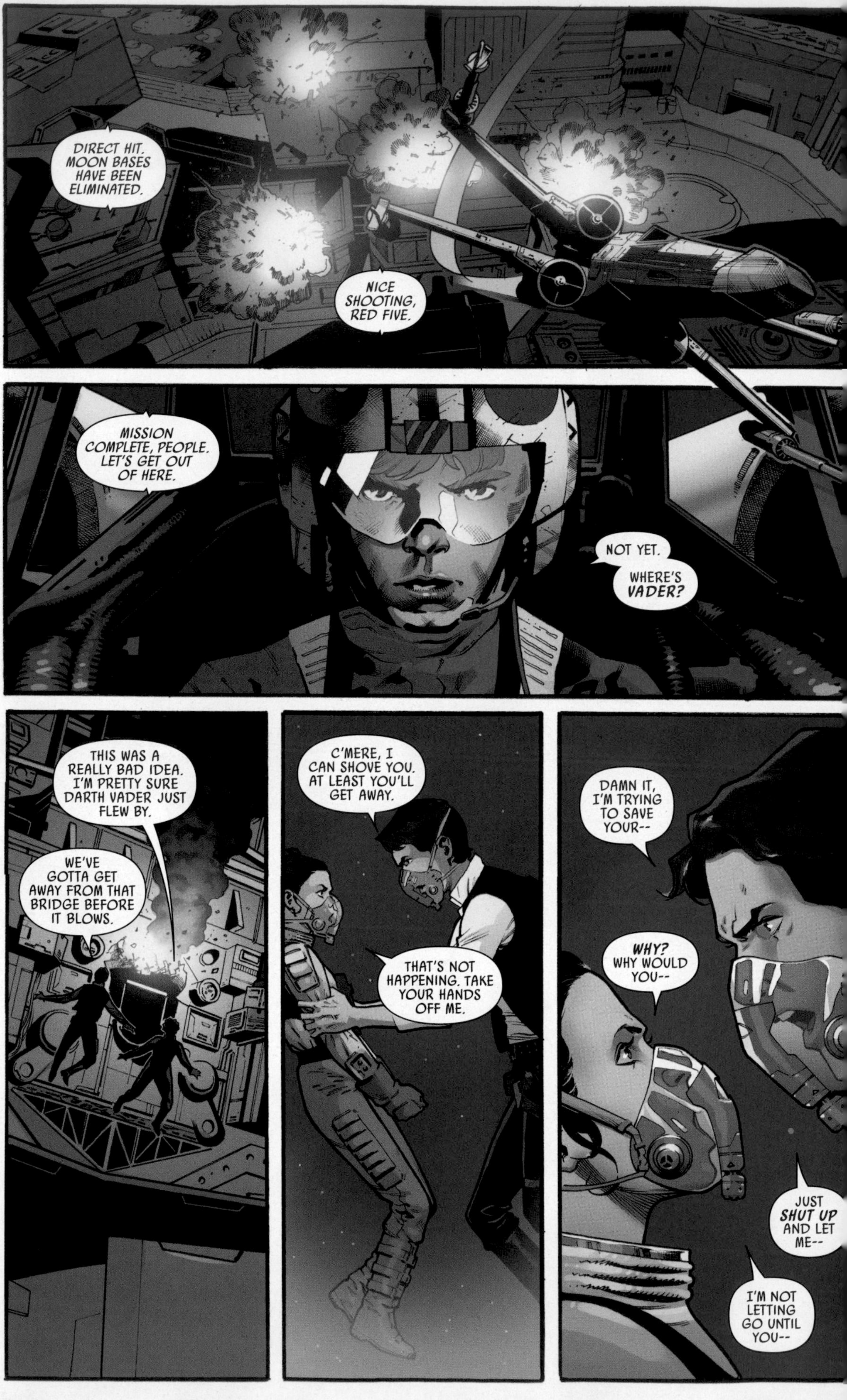
DIRECT HIT. MOON BASES HAVE BEEN ELIMINATED.
NICE SHOOTING, RED FIVE.
MISSION COMPLETE, PEOPLE. LET'S GET OUT OF HERE.
NOT YET.
WHERE'S VADER?
THIS WAS A REALLY BAD IDEA. I'M PRETTY SURE DARTH VADER JUST FLEW BY.
WE'VE GOTTA GET AWAY FROM THAT BRIDGE BEFORE IT BLOWS.
C'MERE, I CAN SHOVE YOU. AT LEAST YOU'LL GET AWAY.
THAT'S NOT HAPPENING. TAKE YOUR HANDS OFF ME.
DAMN IT, I'M TRYING TO SAVE YOUR--
WHY? WHY WOULD YOU--
JUST SHUT UP AND LET ME--
I'M NOT LETTING GO UNTIL YOU--

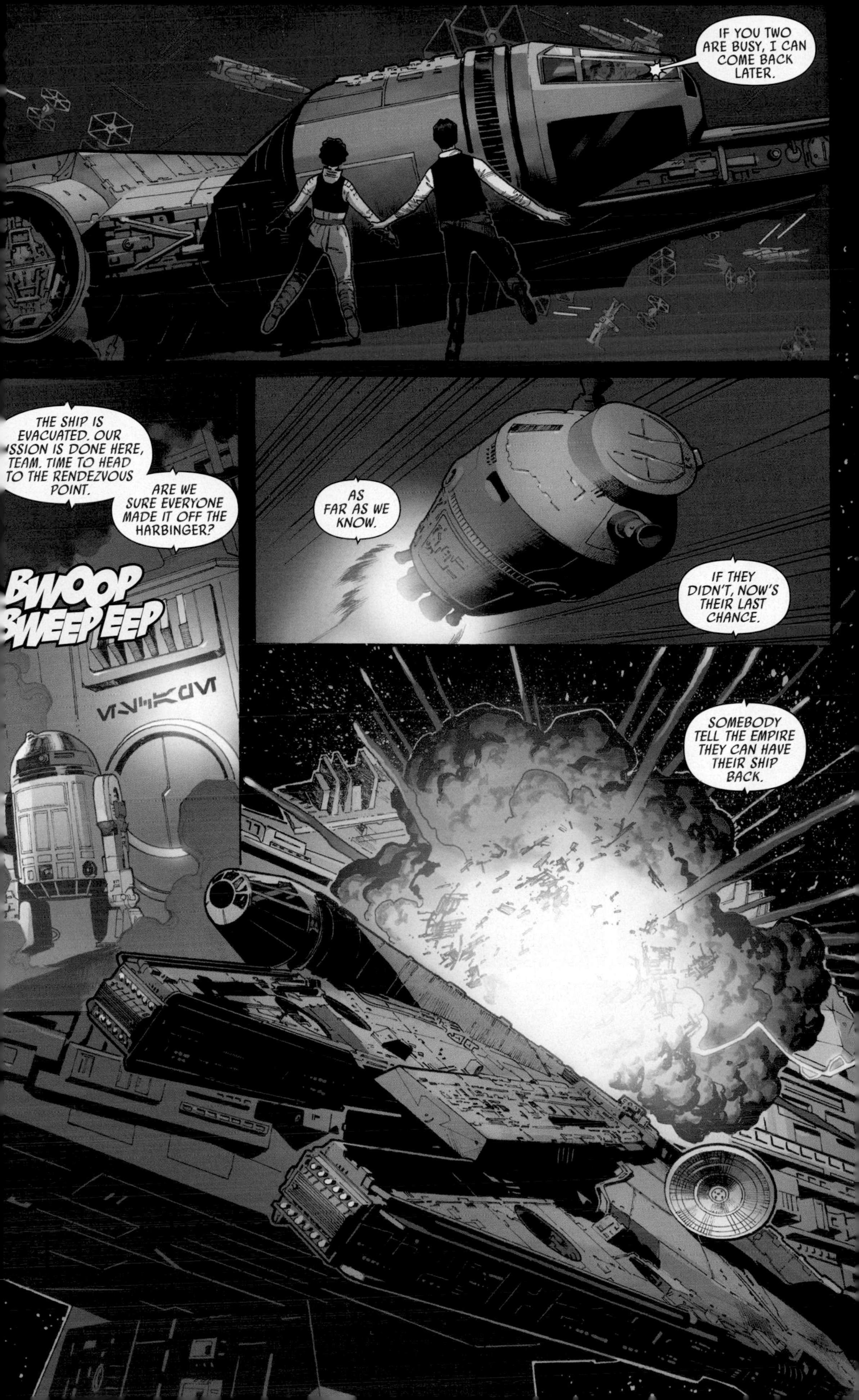
IF YOU TWO ARE BUSY, I CAN COME BACK LATER.
THE SHIP IS EVACUATED. OUR ISSION IS DONE HERE, TEAM. TIME TO HEAD TO THE RENDEZVOUS POINT.
ARE WE SURE EVERYONE MADE IT OFF THE HARBINGER?
AS FAR AS WE KNOW.
BWOOP BWEEP EEP
IF THEY DIDN'T, NOW'S THEIR LAST CHANCE.
SOMEBODY TELL THE EMPIRE THEY CAN HAVE THEIR SHIP BACK.

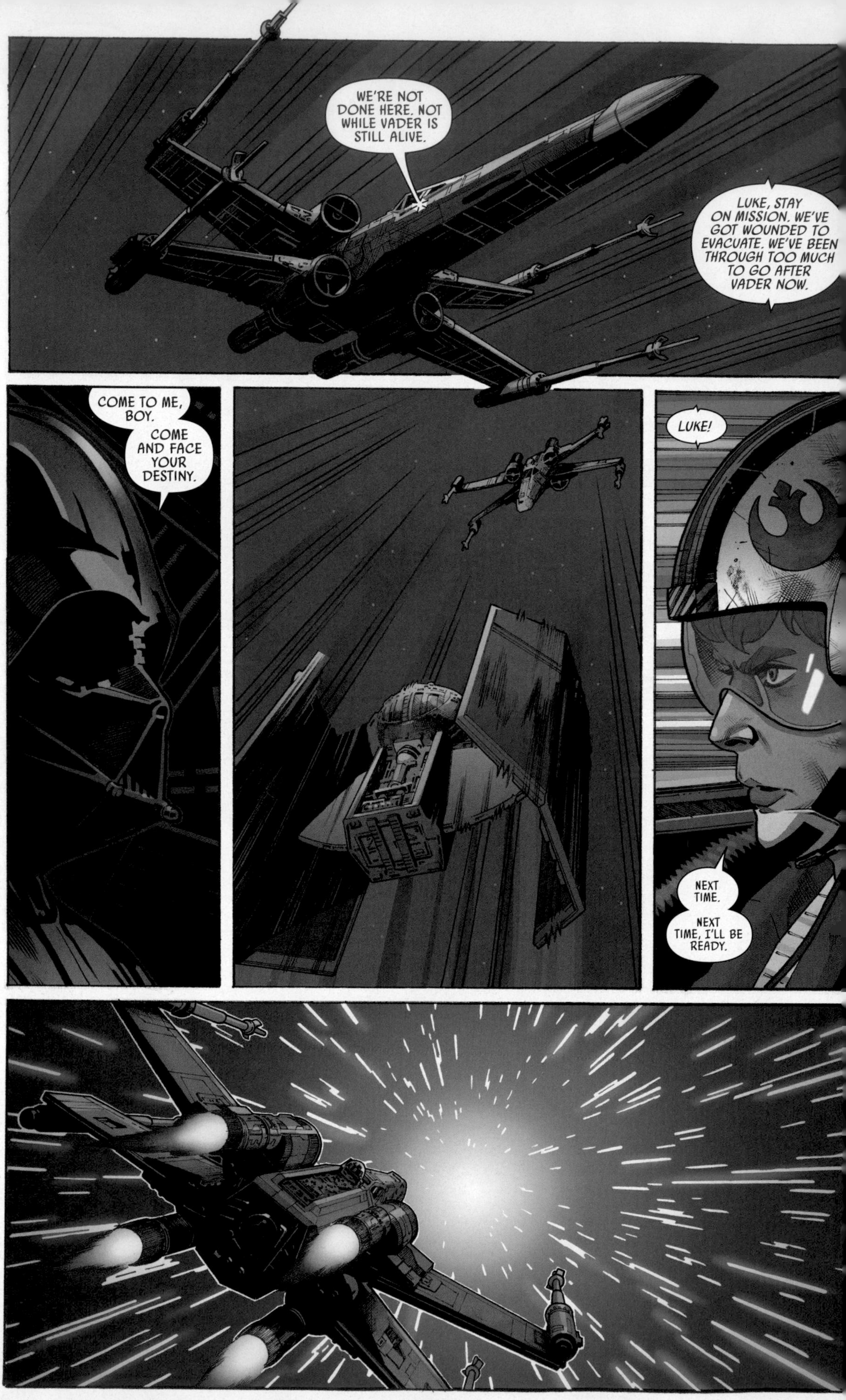
WE'RE NOT DONE HERE. NOT WHILE VADER IS STILL ALIVE.
LUKE, STAY ON MISSION. WE'VE GOT WOUNDED TO EVACUATE. WE'VE BEEN THROUGH TOO MUCH TO GO AFTER VADER NOW.
COME TO ME, BOY.
COME AND FACE YOUR DESTINY.
LUKE!
NEXT TIME.
NEXT TIME, I'LL BE READY.

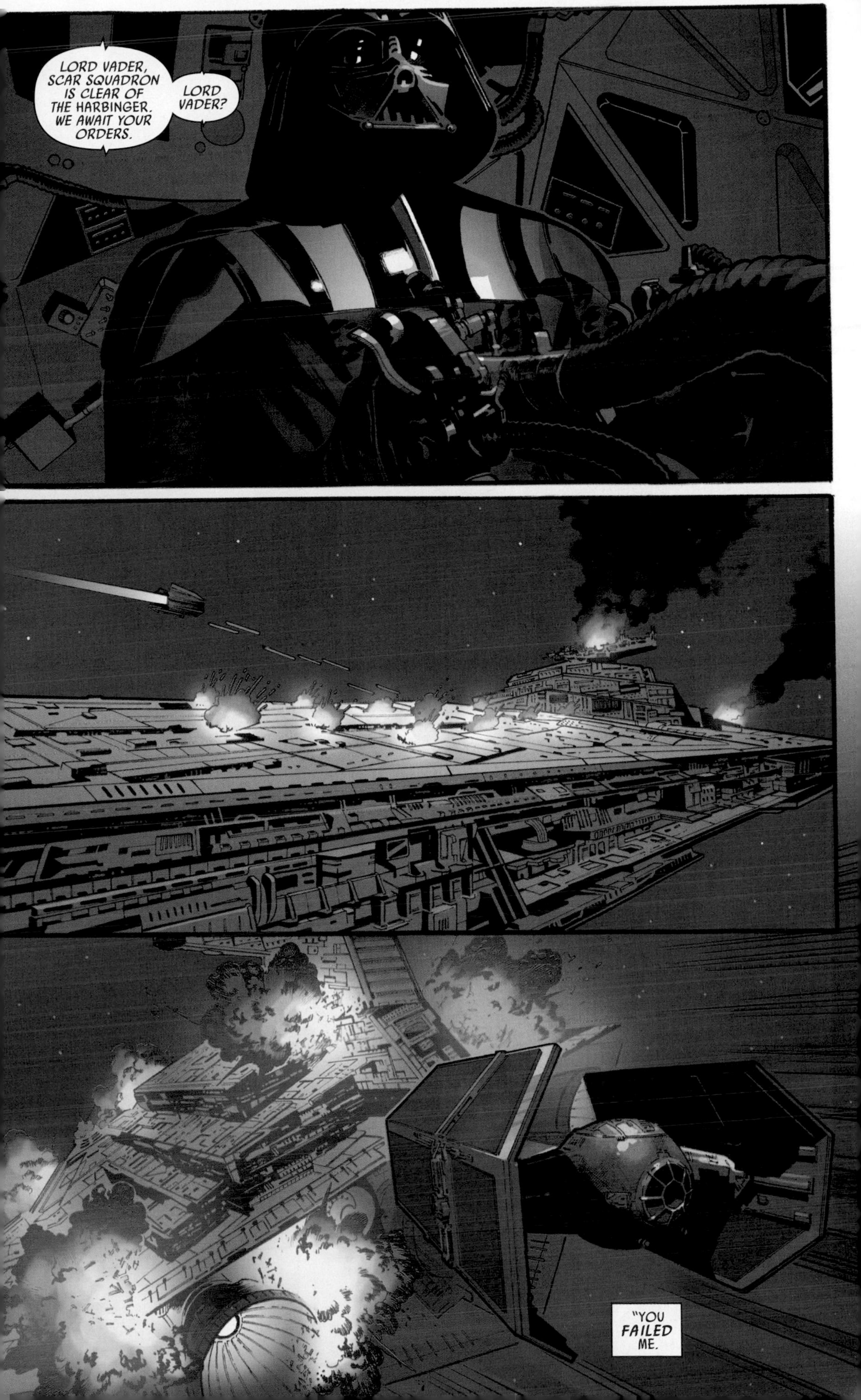
LORD VADER, SCAR SQUADRON IS CLEAR OF THE HARBINGER. WE AWAIT YOUR ORDERS.
LORD VADER?
"YOU FAILED ME.

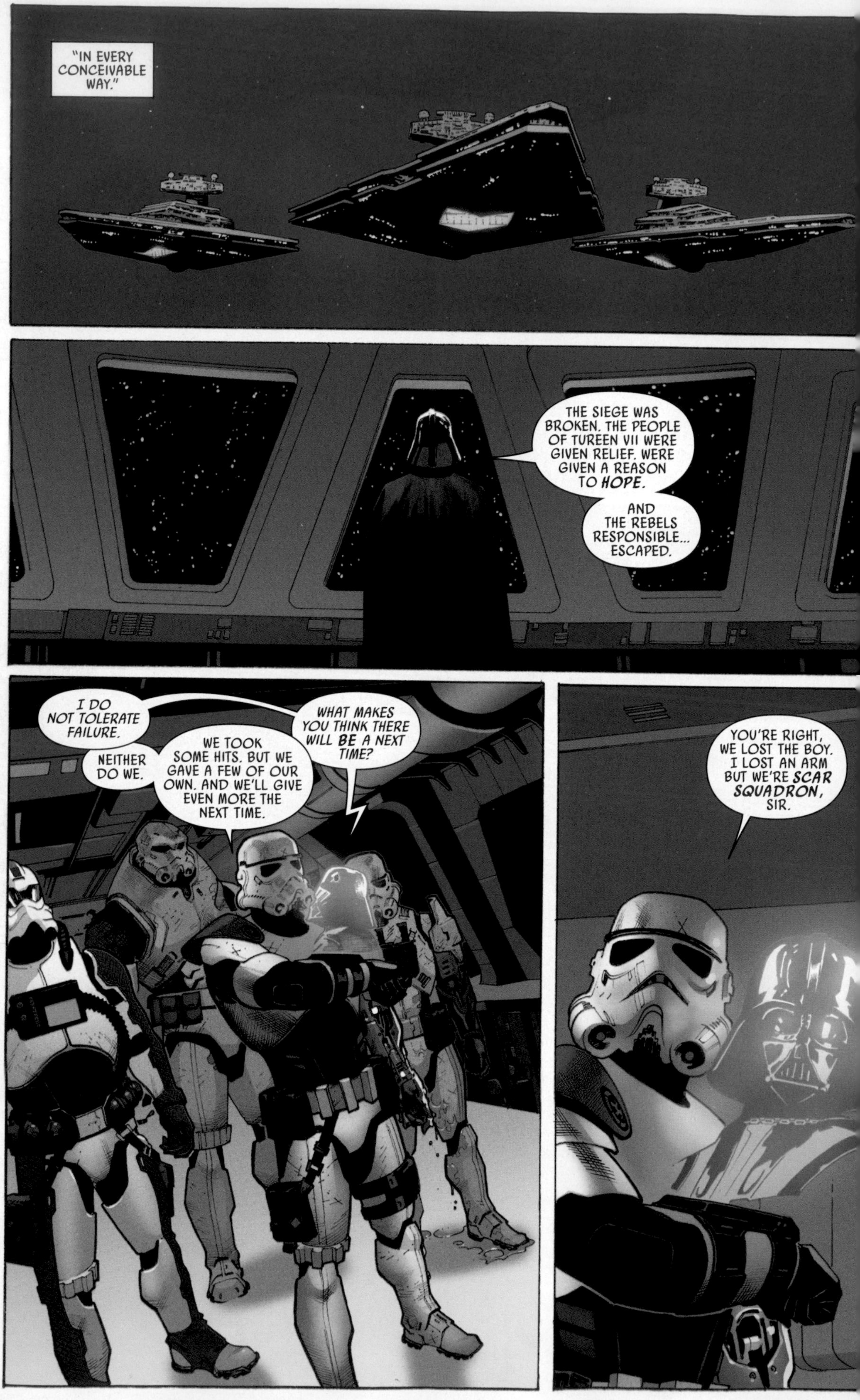
"IN EVERY CONCEIVABLE WAY."
THE SIEGE WAS BROKEN. THE PEOPLE OF TUREEN VII WERE GIVEN RELIEF. WERE GIVEN A REASON TO HOPE.
AND THE REBELS RESPONSIBLE... ESCAPED.
I DO NOT TOLERATE FAILURE.
NEITHER DO WE.
WE TOOK SOME HITS. BUT WE GAVE A FEW OF OUR OWN. AND WE'LL GIVE EVEN MORE THE NEXT TIME.
WHAT MAKES YOU THINK THERE WILL BE A NEXT TIME?
YOU'RE RIGHT, WE LOST THE BOY. I LOST AN ARM BUT WE'RE SCAR SQUADRON, SIR.

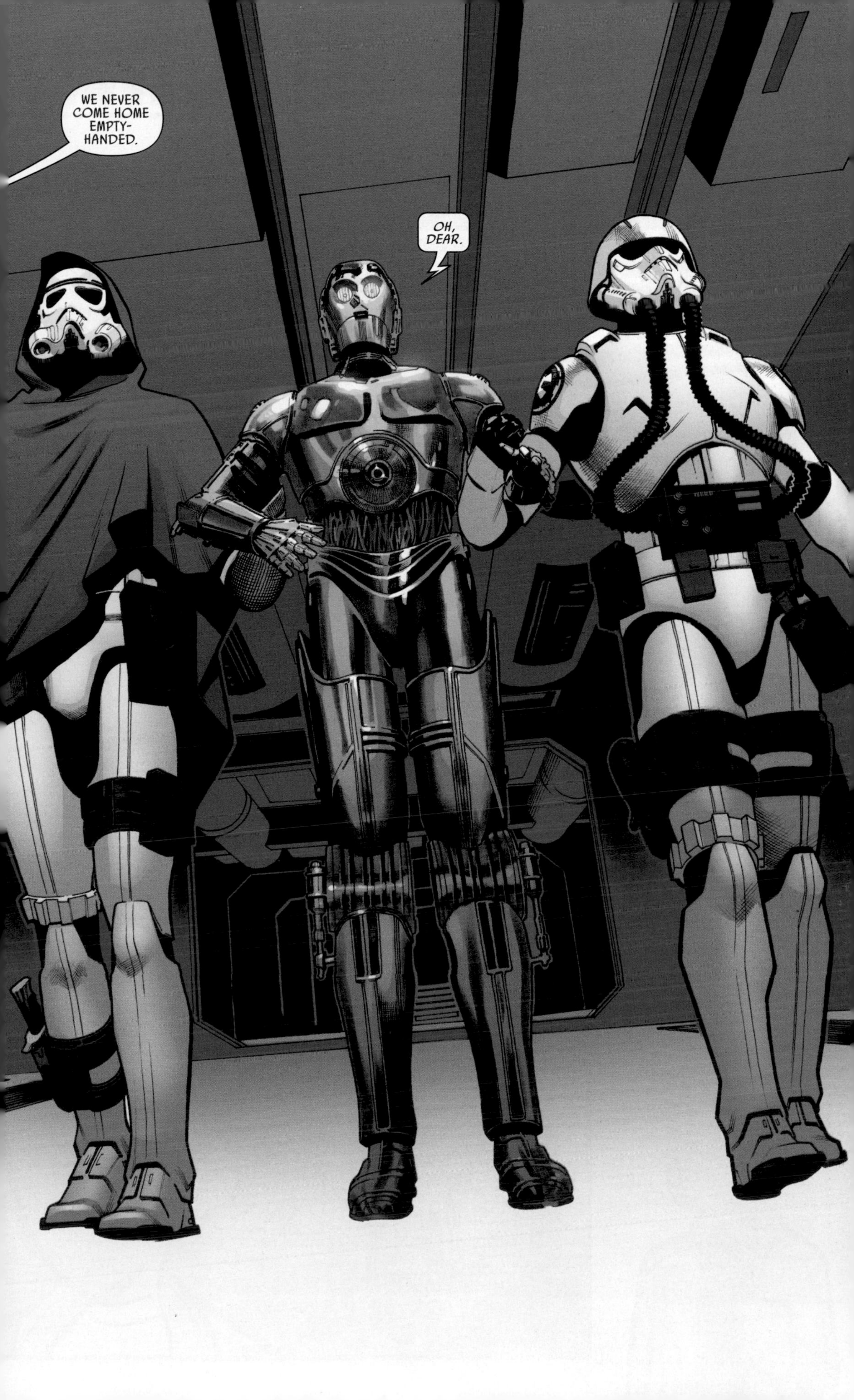
WE NEVER COME HOME EMPTY-HANDED.
OH, DEAR.

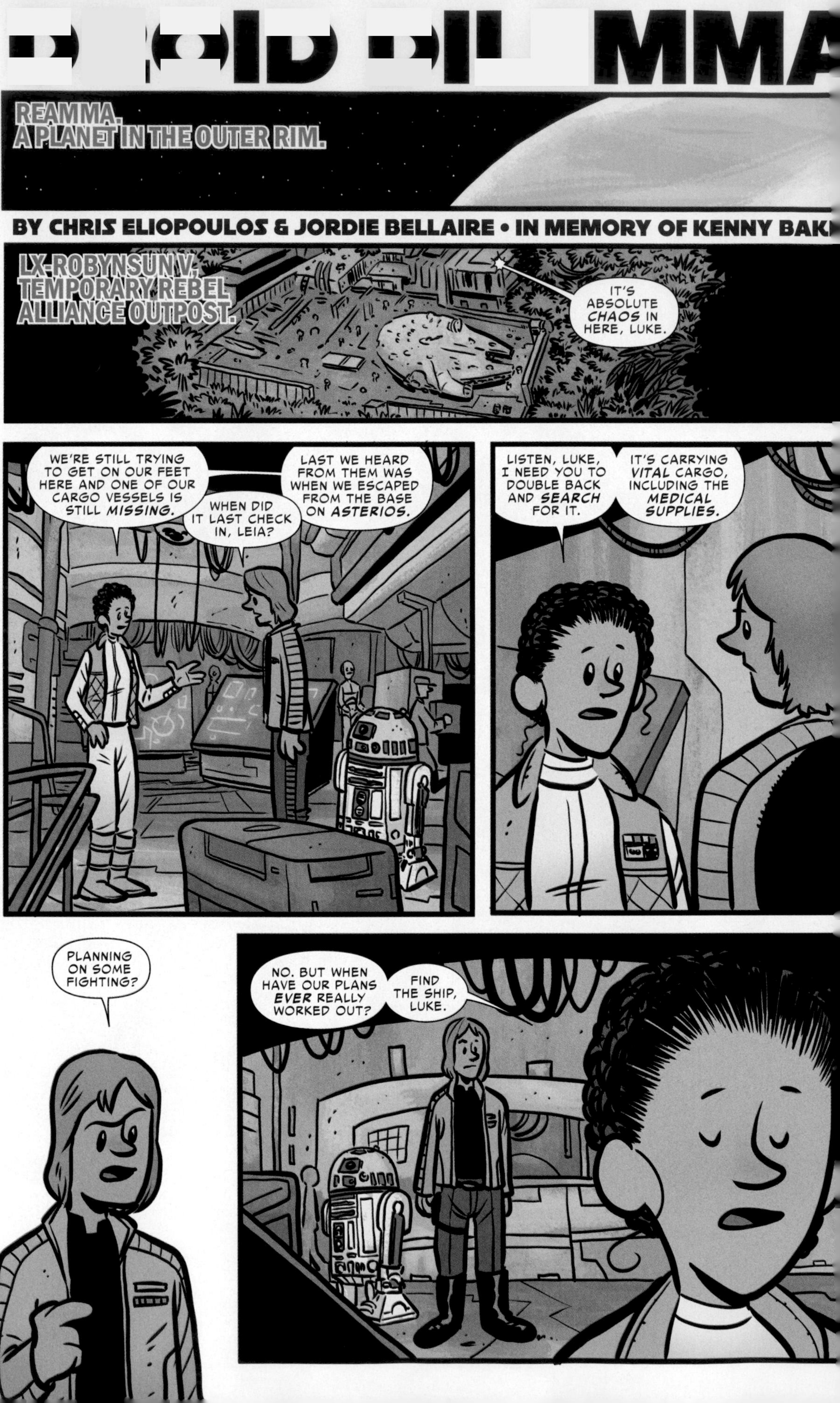
REAMMA.
A PLANET IN THE OUTER RIM.
BY CHRIS ELIOPOULOS & JORDIE BELLAIRE • IN MEMORY OF KENNY BAK
LX-ROBYNSUN V. TEMPORARY REBEL ALLIANCE OUTPOST.
IT'S ABSOLUTE CHAOS IN HERE, LUKE.
WE'RE STILL TRYING TO GET ON OUR FEET HERE AND ONE OF OUR CARGO VESSELS IS STILL MISSING.
WHEN DID IT LAST CHECK IN, LEIA?
LAST WE HEARD FROM THEM WAS WHEN WE ESCAPED FROM THE BASE ON ASTERIOS.
LISTEN, LUKE, I NEED YOU TO DOUBLE BACK AND SEARCH FOR IT.
IT'S CARRYING VITAL CARGO, INCLUDING THE MEDICAL SUPPLIES.
PLANNING ON SOME FIGHTING?
NO. BUT WHEN HAVE OUR PLANS EVER REALLY WORKED OUT?
FIND THE SHIP, LUKE.

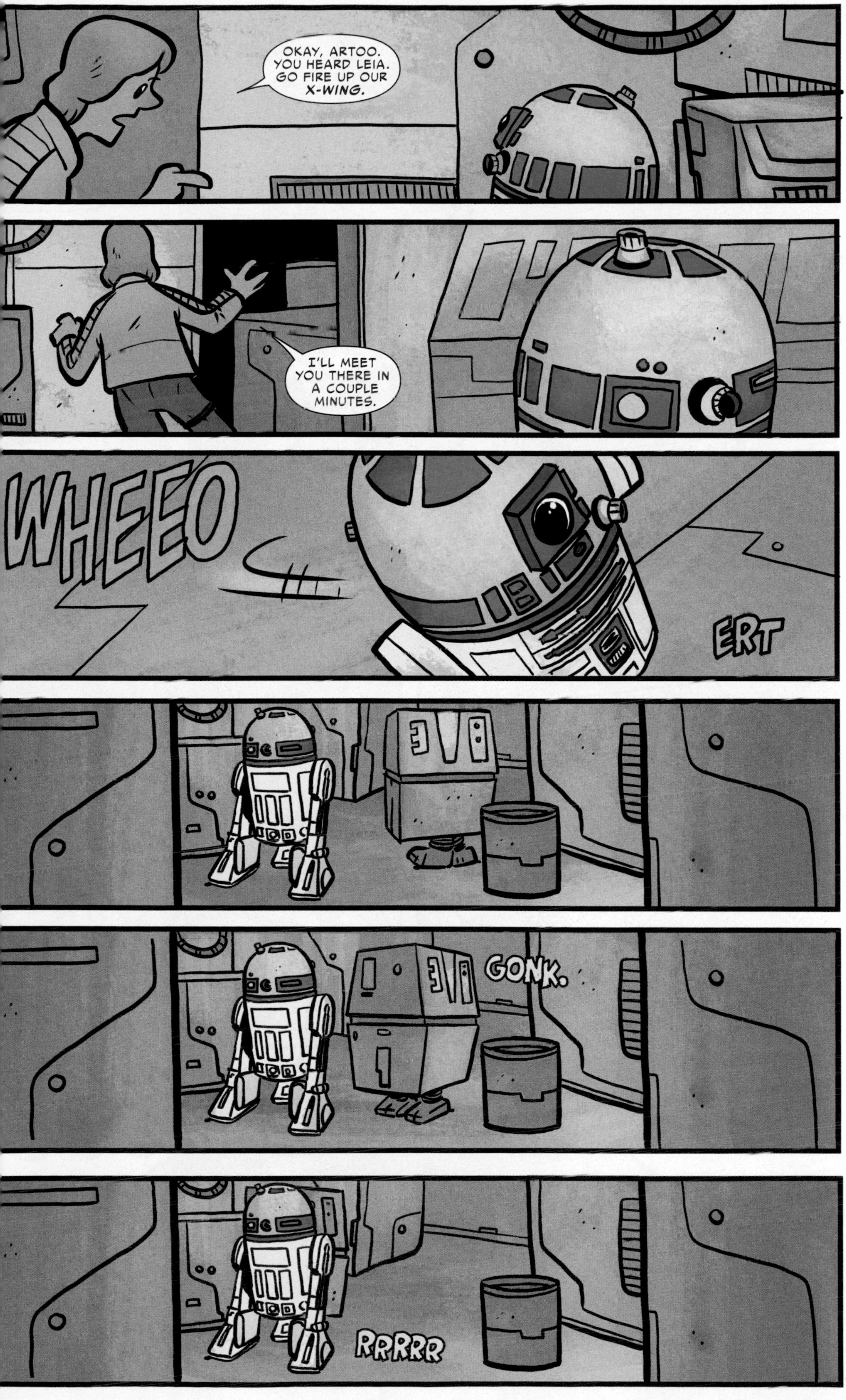
OKAY, ARTOO. YOU HEARD LEIA. GO FIRE UP OUR X-WING.
I'LL MEET YOU THERE IN A COUPLE MINUTES.
WHEEO
ERT
GONK.
RRRRR

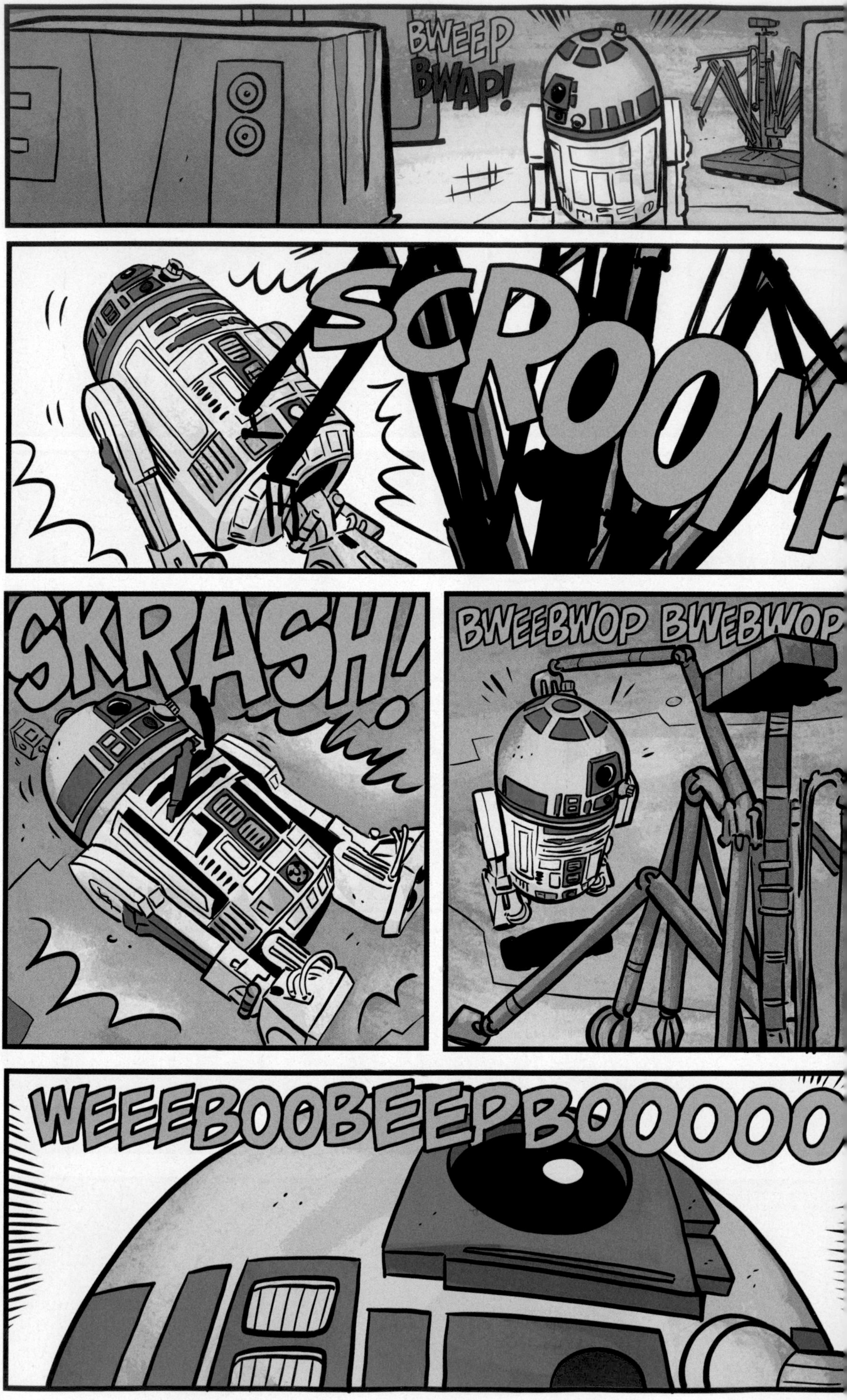
BWEEP
BWAP!
SCROOM
SKRASH!
BWEEBWOP BWEBWOP
WEEEBOOBEEPBOOOOO

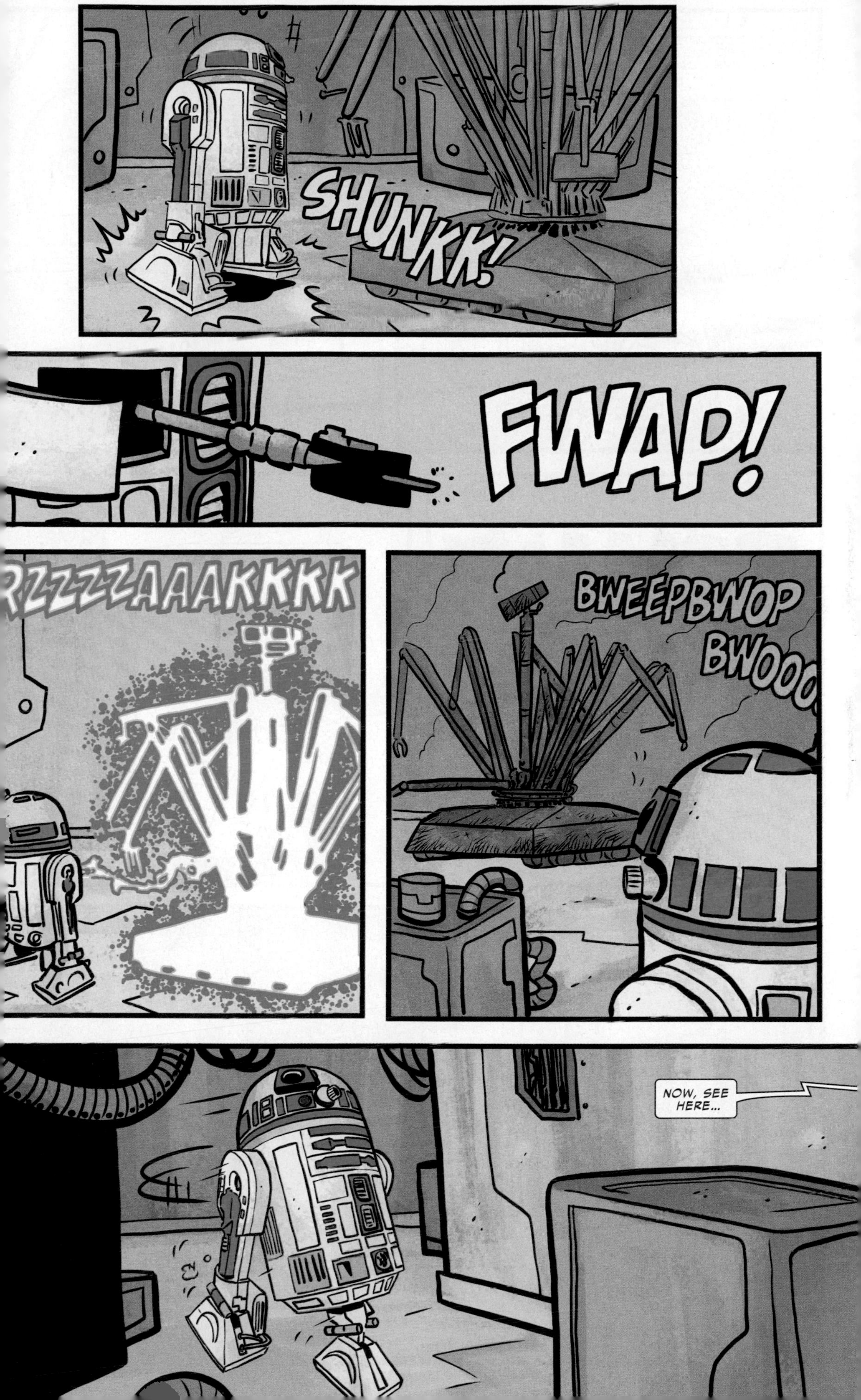
SHUNKK!
FWAP!
RZZZZZAAAKKKK
BWEEPBWOP
BWOOO
NOW, SEE HERE...

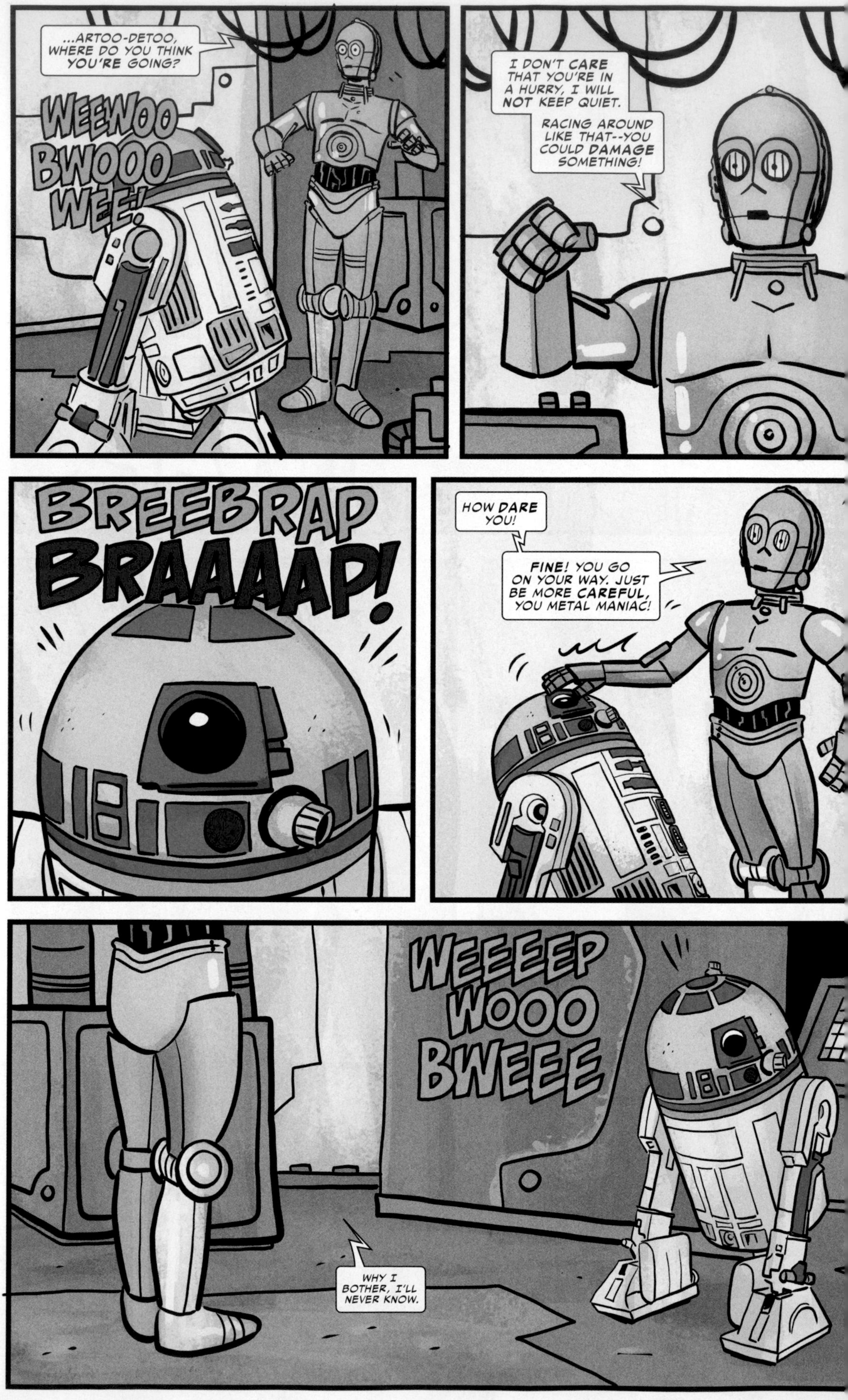
...ARTOO-DETOO, WHERE DO YOU THINK YOU'RE GOING?
WEENOO BWOOO WEE!
I DON'T CARE THAT YOU'RE IN A HURRY, I WILL NOT KEEP QUIET.
RACING AROUND LIKE THAT--YOU COULD DAMAGE SOMETHING!
BREEBRAP BRAAAAP!
HOW DARE YOU!
FINE! YOU GO ON YOUR WAY. JUST BE MORE CAREFUL, YOU METAL MANIAC!
WEEEEP WOOO BWEEE
WHY I BOTHER, I'LL NEVER KNOW.

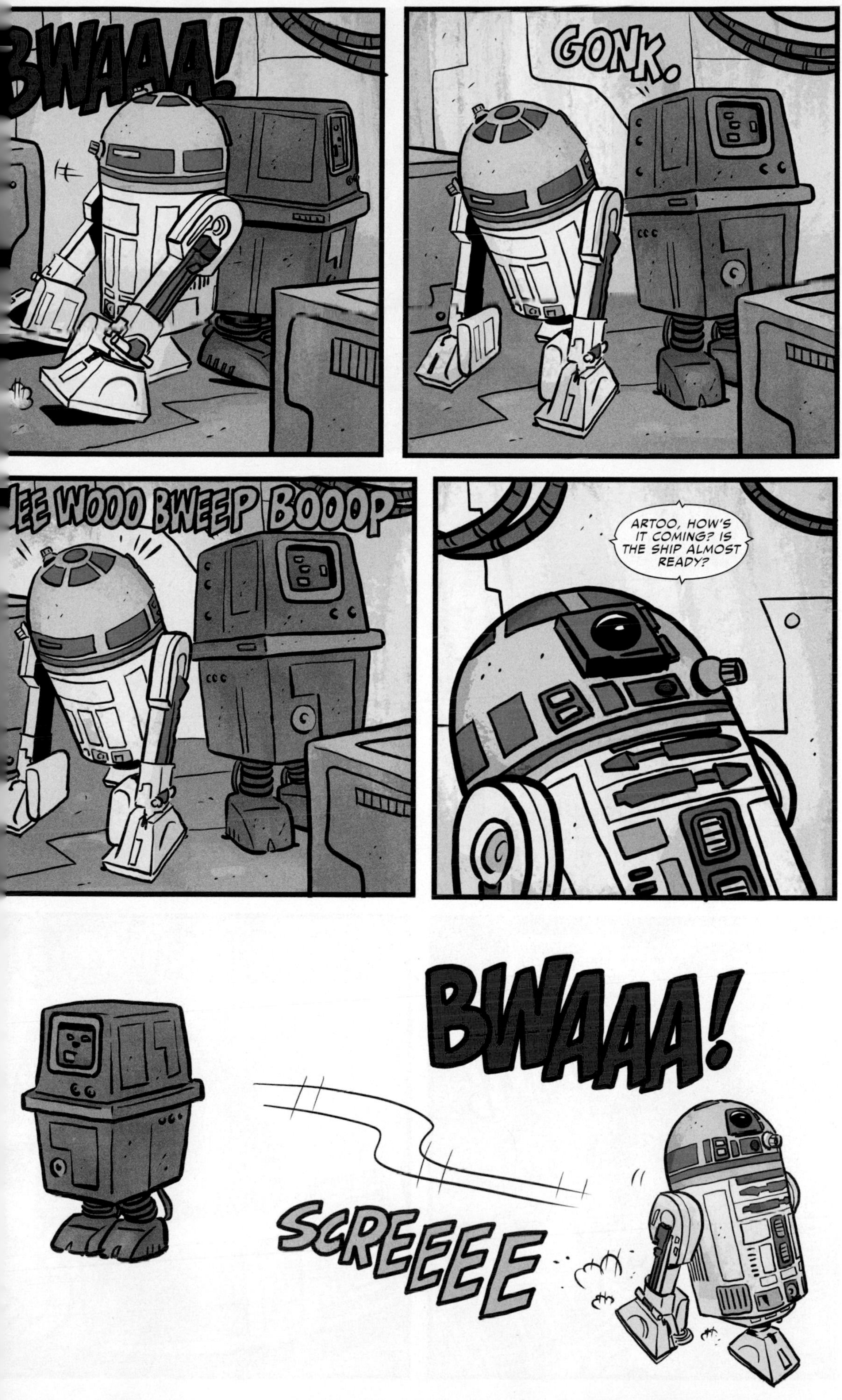
BWAAA!
GONK.
EE WOOO BWEEP BOOOP
ARTOO, HOW'S IT COMING? IS THE SHIP ALMOST READY?
BWAAA!
SCREEEEE

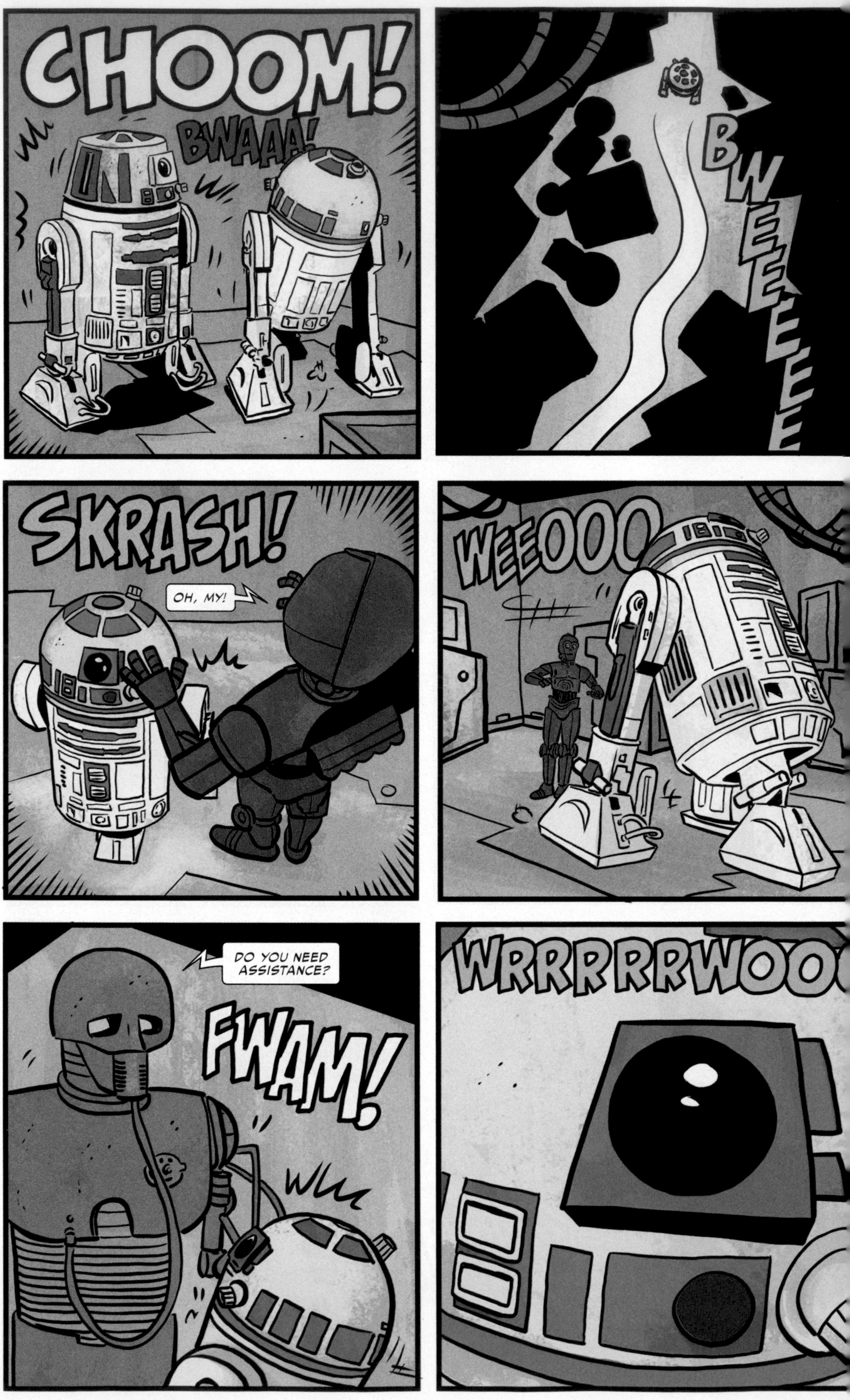
CHOOM!
BWAAA!
BWEEEEEE
SKRASH!
OH, MY!
WEEOOO
DO YOU NEED ASSISTANCE?
FWAM!
WRRRRRWOO

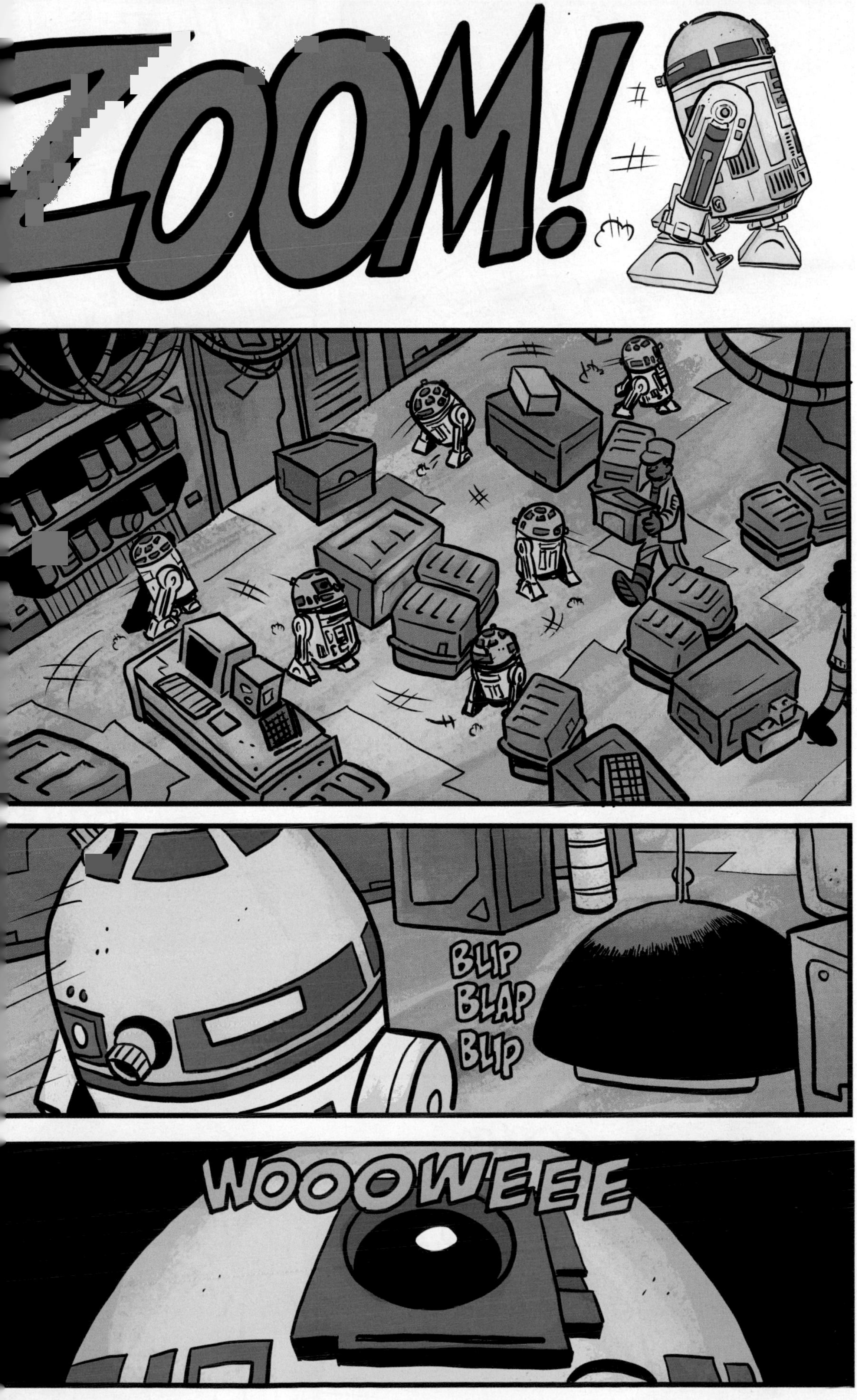
ZOOM!
BLIP
BLAP
BLIP
WOOOWEEE

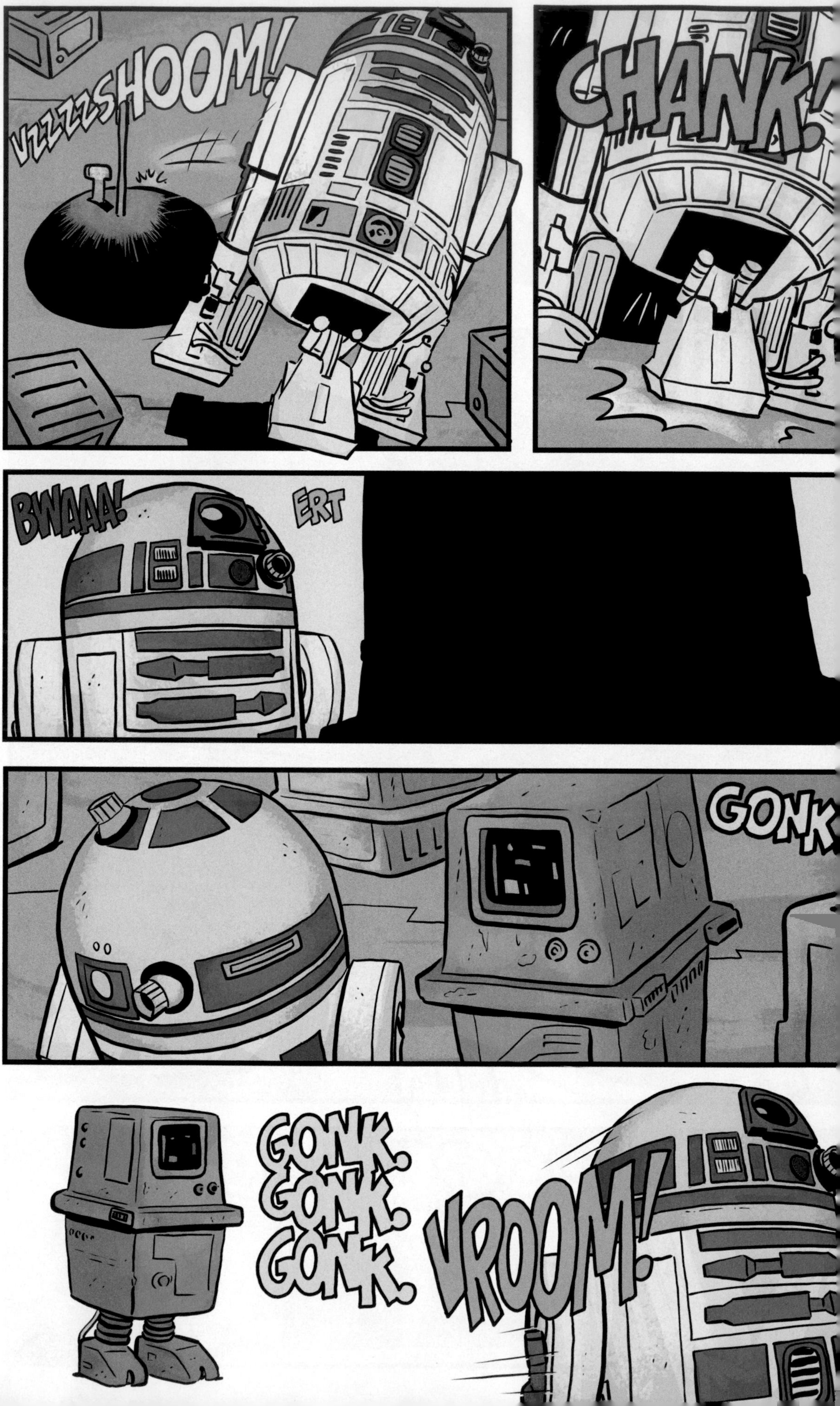
VZZZZSHOOM!
WUL
CHANK!
BWAAA!
ERT
GONK
GONK.
GONK.
GONK.
VROOM!

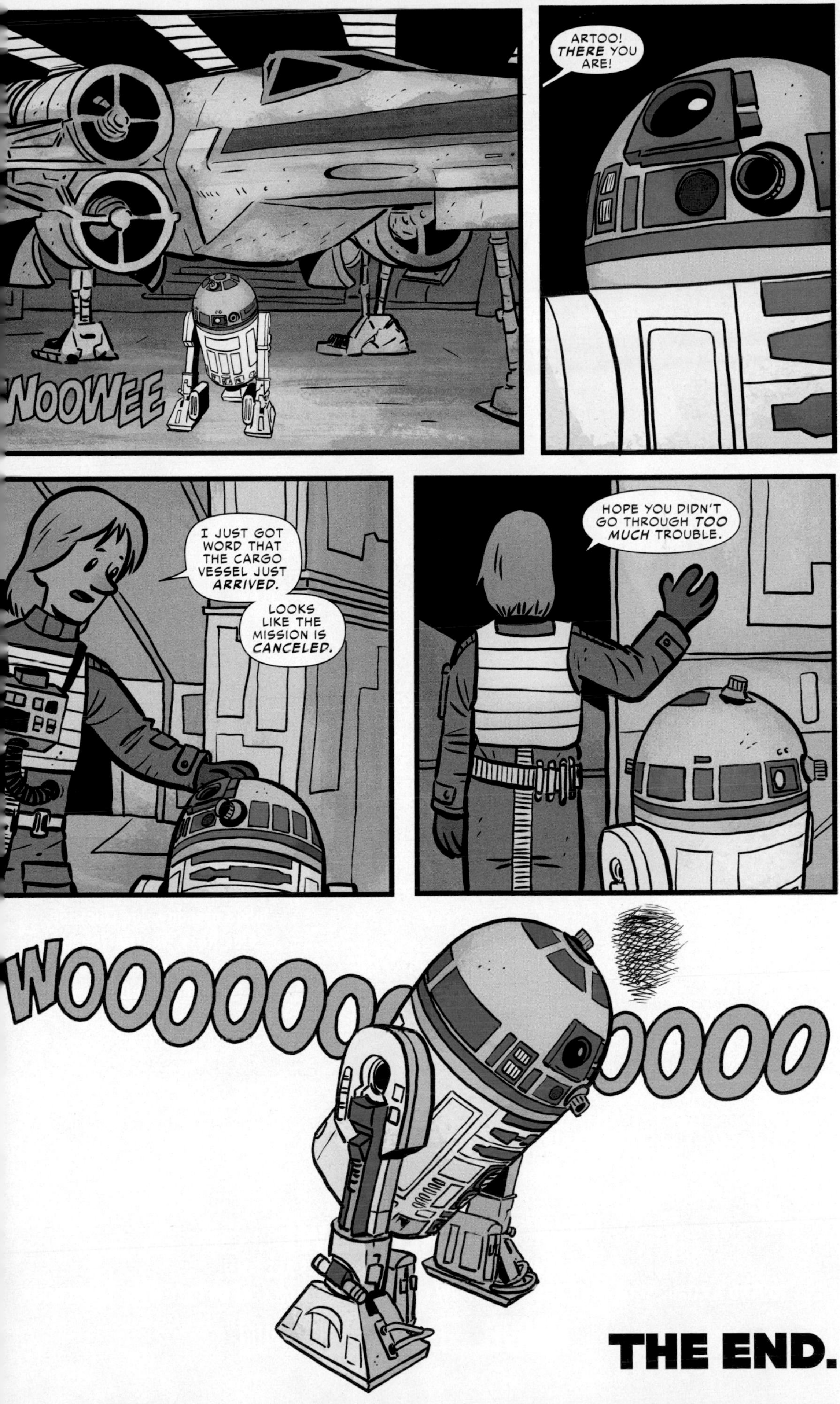
WOOWEE
ARTOO! *THERE* YOU ARE!
I JUST GOT WORD THAT THE CARGO VESSEL JUST *ARRIVED*.
LOOKS LIKE THE MISSION IS *CANCELED*.
HOPE YOU DIDN'T GO THROUGH *TOO MUCH* TROUBLE.
WOOOOOOOOOOOO
THE END.

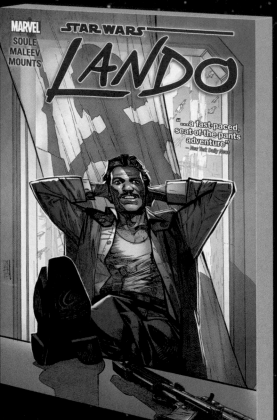

RETURN TO A GA[LAXY]
THE CLASSIC MARVEL ADAPTATIO[N]
NOW WITH REM[ASTERED]

Y FAR, FAR AWAY!

THE BIGGEST MOVIES IN HISTORY,
RED INTERIORS!

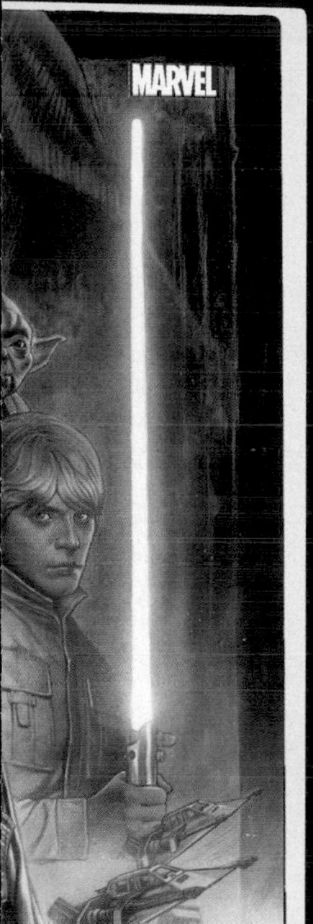
MARVEL
E
CK
LLIAMS

RE STRIKES BACK HC

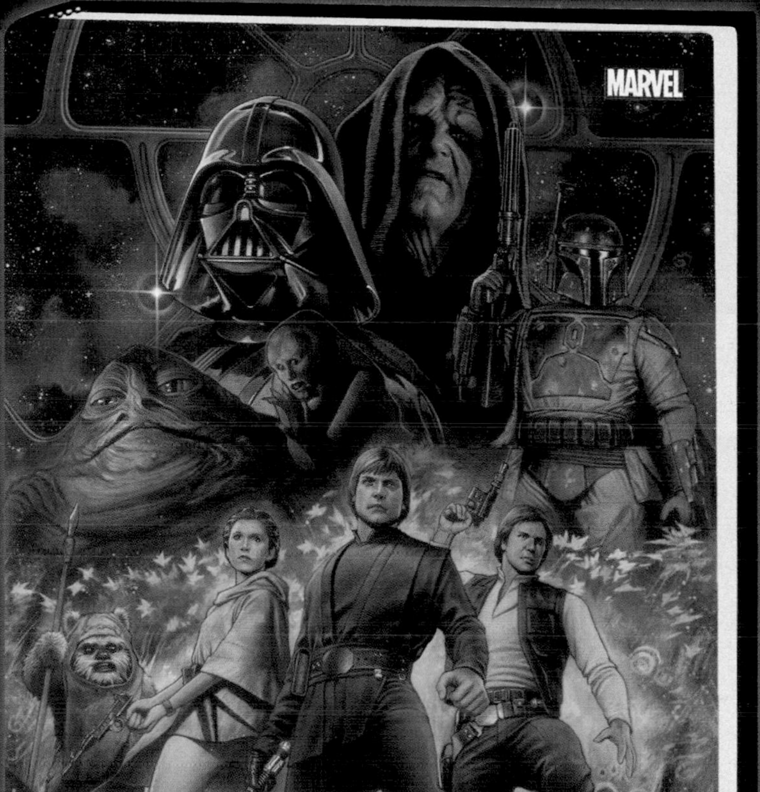
MARVEL
STAR WARS
RETURN OF THE
JEDI
EPISODE VI

STAR WARS: EPISODE VI – RETURN OF THE JEDI HC
978-0-7851-9369-2

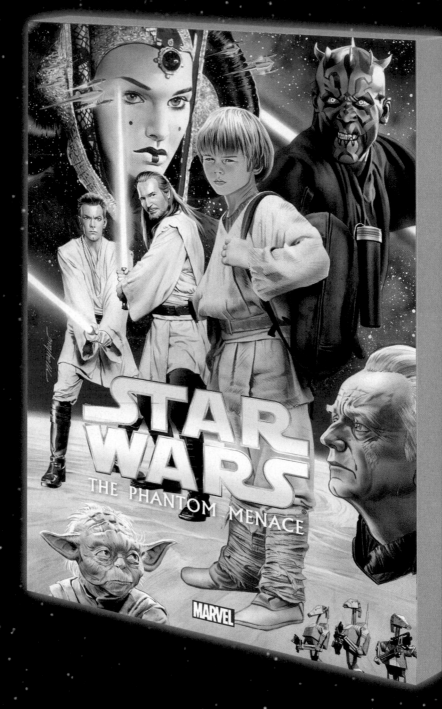

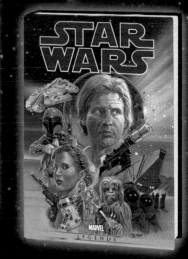

AN EPIC JOURNEY FROM THE BEGINNINGS O
THE OLD REPUBLIC TO THE RISE OF THE EMPIR
AND BEYOND!

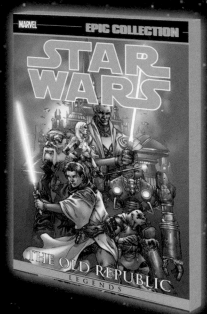

**STAR WARS LEGENDS EPIC COLLECTION:
THE OLD REPUBLIC VOL. 1 TPB
978-0-7851-9717-1**

**STAR WARS LEGENDS EPIC COLLECTION:
RISE OF THE SITH VOL. 1 TPB
978-0-7851-9722-5**

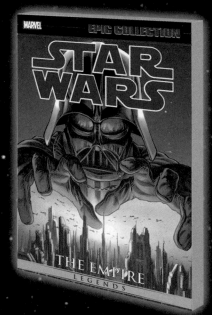

**STAR WARS LEGENDS EPIC COLLECTION:
THE EMPIRE VOL. 1 TPB
978-0-7851-9398-2**

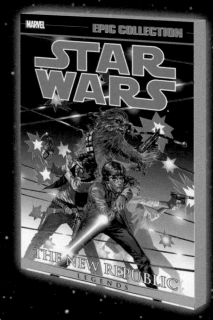

**STAR WARS LEGENDS EPIC COLLECTION:
THE NEW REPUBLIC VOL. 1 TPB
978-0-7851-9716-4**

AVAILABLE NOW WHEREVER BOOKS ARE SOLD